Praise for *The L_____ers*

"Explains all the myriad of legal issues facing a pub_____ ___ today's digital environment without overwhelming the reader with legalese."

—Nancy E. Wolff, partner, Cowan, DeBaets,
Abrahams & Sheppard LLP (from *Publishing Research Quarterly*)

"A treasure trove of relevant information for industry professionals, new publishers, and indie authors, covering a comprehensive range of topics from the fine points of freedom of speech, privacy and defamation, copyright, infringement, and fair use to agents, publishing contracts, piracy, taxes, and more."

—Kevin J. Anderson, international bestselling
author and publisher of WordFire Press

"The ideal legal resource for every upstart and seasoned publisher! From his extensive career as an expert IP attorney, Leonard DuBoff and his knowledgeable coauthor Amanda Bryan present an easy-to-understand, thorough yet concise, and extremely well-written treatment of the legal concerns publishers must know to operate with integrity and excellence. Highly recommended!"

—Bob Hawkins Jr., president, Harvest House Publishers

"Understanding copyright law is one of the greatest challenges every publisher faces. *The Law (in Plain English)*® *for Publishers* offers a practical roadmap for navigating the law, written—as its name implies—in language that even the most legally challenged among us can understand. Publishers large and small should keep a copy of this valuable resource within easy reach."

—John Limb, publisher emeritus of Oregon Catholic Press

"Leonard DuBoff's Law (in Plain English)® series has been a go-to resource for the media industry for decades, and this volume is a worthy addition to the collection. Whether one is publishing a lengthy annual list for the trade or a single highly specialized occasional title, *The Law (in Plain English)*® *for Publishers* offers up-to-date, trustworthy information, advice, and guidance. It's all here: copyrights, contracts, protections, pitfalls—all rendered in easily comprehensible language. The extensive section on electronic publishing is timely and forward-thinking."

—Linda Ligon, Thrums Books and Interweave Press

"This is an essential book for anyone who is working, or plans to work, in the book publishing field. Whether you're a junior editor, a senior executive, or an author, this book offers essential advice and information that will undoubtedly enhance your publishing expertise."

—Tony Lyons, author and publisher, Skyhorse Publishing

"A very informative book for new publishers looking to set up shop as well as a good review for the seasoned ones!"

—Jennifer Weltz, Jean V. Naggar Literary Agency

The **Law**

(in Plain English)®

for

Publishers

The Law

(in Plain English)®

for

Publishers

Leonard D. DuBoff *and* **Amanda Bryan**

Attorneys-at-Law

ALLWORTH PRESS
NEW YORK

Allworth Press books may be purchased in bulk at special discounts for sales
promotion, corporate gifts, fund-raising, or educational purposes. Special
editions can also be created to specifications. For details, contact the Special Sales
Department, Allworth Press, 307 West 36th Street, 11th Floor, New York, NY 10018
or info@skyhorsepublishing.com.

23 22 21 20 19   5 4 3 2 1

Published by Allworth Press, an imprint of Skyhorse Publishing, Inc. 307 West 36th
Street, 11th Floor, New York, NY 10018. Allworth Press® is a registered trademark of
Skyhorse Publishing, Inc.®, a Delaware corporation.

www.allworth.com

Cover design by Mary Belibasakis

Library of Congress Cataloging-in-Publication Data
Names: DuBoff, Leonard D., author. | Bryan, Amanda.
Title: The law (in plain English) for publishers / Leonard D. DuBoff and
    Amanda Bryan, Attorneys-at-Law.
Description: New York, New York: Allworth Press, An imprint of Skyhorse
    Publishing, Inc., 2019. | Includes index.
Identifiers: LCCN 2018025821 (print) | LCCN 2018026694 (ebook) | ISBN
    9781621537106 (eBook) | ISBN 9781621536765 (pbk.: alk. paper)
Subjects: LCSH: Law—United States. | Authors and publishers—United States.
    | Press law—United States. | Publishers and publishing—United
    States—Handbooks, manuals, etc.
Classification: LCC KF390.A96 (ebook) | LCC KF390.A96 D828 2019 (print) | DDC
    349.7302/40705—dc23
LC record available at https://lccn.loc.gov/2018025821

Print ISBN: 978-1-62153-676-5
eBook ISBN: 978-1-62153-710-6

Printed in the United States of America

Dedication

To my mother, Millicent, and my father, Rubin, who provided me with the gift of life and the desire to use that gift effectively. To my mother-in-law, Cumi Elena Crawford, for her faith, trust, and inspiration, and to my wife, Mary Ann, for her enduring love and continuing support.
—Leonard D. DuBoff

To my children, Random, Grey, and Scout. You are as delightful, quirky, and compassionate as I could have wished for. Your love is my greatest treasure.

—Amanda Bryan

Table of Contents

Acknowledgments

In order to assemble the vast quantity of statutes, cases, articles, and books that have become available since an earlier version of this book was published, it was necessary to enlist the aid of numerous friends and colleagues. Their help is greatly appreciated, and some deserve special recognition. I would, therefore, like to express my sincere thanks to my collaborator, Amanda Bryan, Esq., for her extraordinary help with this version. She has sacrificed many evenings and weekends to bring this project to fruition.

Amanda and I would like to thank Greg Rogers of the accounting firm of Rogers Financial Services; Sarah Tugman, Esq., and her husband, Greg; and Gregory R. Roer, CPA of Roer & Company, Inc., for their time and expertise in reviewing the tax chapter.

I am indebted to Tad Crawford of Skyhorse Publishing and his staff for their help in publishing this volume.

We would also like to thank Megan Randall for her help with some of the technical aspects of this revision. Thanks also to my paralegal Sara Cain for all of her assistance and numerous recommendations.

Amanda would like to thank her children, Random Gomm, Grey Gomm, and Scout Gomm, and her husband, Josh Congdon, for their patience and support during the writing process, giving up weekends and evenings with her, and being OK with unfolded laundry and macaroni-and-cheese dinners until this book was complete.

I am very grateful for the blurbs written by Kevin James Anderson, publisher of WordFire Press and international bestselling author of books in the Star Wars, Dune, StarCraft, Titan A.E., and X-files series; Bob Hawkins Jr., president of Harvest House Publishers; John Limb, publisher emeritus of Oregon Catholic Press; and Linda Ligon, creative director of Interweave Press.

I am grateful for the support of my children and grandchildren. My son Robert has been very helpful with technology issues, and my daughter

Colleen has been extremely creative with her graphic design skills. Her husband, Rudy, a lawyer who has recently joined our law firm, has been very helpful with research. I am also grateful to my grandson Brian for his personal assistance and to the newest member of my family, my granddaughter Athena, for her cheerfulness. I would like to acknowledge my appreciation to my daughter Sabrina and my grandsons Tony and Grant for their support.

My late sister, Candace DuBoff Jones, JD, Northwestern School of Law, Lewis & Clark College, 1977; my late father, Rueben R. DuBoff; and my late mother, Millicent Barbara DuBoff, all provided me with the inspiration to create works such as this.

I valued my mother-in-law Cumi Elena Crawford's faith, trust, and inspiration, which helped me create this project. Finally, I would like to express my sincere gratitude and acknowledge the contribution to this project by my partner in law and in life, Mary Ann Crawford DuBoff. Without her, *The Law (in Plain English)® for Publishers* would never have become a reality.

Introduction

The art of writing dates back to the very dawn of civilization. Writers were active in dynastic Egypt, as well as in the emerging civilizations in the Tigris and Euphrates river valleys. As society became more complex, the problems faced by writers increased, and, as a result, publishers were created to assume responsibility for the writers' works once they were completed. Today, the successful publisher must also be a knowledgeable businessperson.

When I first began to practice law, I realized that it was important for clients to carefully evaluate all of the options available to them and then adopt the most prudent course. Later, as a law professor, I taught my students to use this same principle in counseling their clients. Many of my publisher clients and former students have asked me to recommend a book that would aid them in understanding the legal issues faced by writers and publishers. Unfortunately, I was unable to recommend any single volume that would serve this purpose.

During my career as a practicing attorney, I became aware of the dearth of practical law books for writers and publishers. It was for this reason that I wrote *The Book Publishers' Legal Guide*, initially published in 1984 and later revised.

After a friend read and critiqued the first edition of that book, he reminded me of the plight of writers and urged me to write a text for them that would be "user friendly." I thus began work on the first edition of a writer's book, the fifth volume in my Law (in Plain English)® series. The fifth edition of that book is now available for readers. This text provides publishers with information that is intended to assist them in their extraordinarily important role in the industry. As with the other books in this series, my goal is to create an informative work that is readable, practical, and comprehensive. I collaborated with Amanda Bryan, an extraordinarily bright and experienced attorney who, among other things, teaches a course on publishing law at Portland State University. Her invaluable contribution to this work cannot be overemphasized.

As with any book on law, changes are inevitable and ongoing. The reader should therefore be careful to confer with competent legal counsel before undertaking the resolution of any issue discussed in this volume.

—Leonard D. DuBoff
Portland, Oregon, April 2018

CHAPTER 1

The Freedom to Write

The First Amendment of the United States Constitution embodies the basic freedom to express oneself in writing in the statement "Congress shall make no law . . . abridging the freedom of speech, or of the press." Censorship, called a *prior restraint* on speech because it prohibits certain expressions before they have been made, has been constitutionally disfavored since the founding of the United States. Some historians suggest that the First Amendment was written specifically to prevent the government from imposing any prior restraints on expression. Prior restraints impose an extreme burden upon the exercise of free speech, since they limit open debate and the unfettered dissemination of knowledge. It is not surprising that the United States Supreme Court has consistently found that it is unconstitutional to restrain speech prior to a determination of whether the speech is protected by the First Amendment.

However, that is not to say that all speech is permissible. The courts uphold laws that protect consumers from false advertising, prevent incitements likely to cause immediate, unlawful violence, and control the distribution of pornography. These constitutional restraints on speech impose varying degrees of control on the type of speech being made, the purpose behind the speech, and the time, place, and manner of the speech.

IN PLAIN ENGLISH

The First Amendment prohibits most *prior restraint* on speech. This means that laws will most likely be unconstitutional if the law's purpose is to stop someone from speaking or publishing some targeted content *before* the words have been spoken, published, or otherwise disseminated to the public.

POLITICAL SPEECH

The courts are very hesitant to prevent someone from expressing his or her opinion. As so much content can be construed as expressing an opinion in one form or another, it is not easy for the government to pass laws restricting speech. This is especially true when the expression goes toward *political speech*—speech that criticizes the government or otherwise questions its authority.

Any attempt by the government to prevent the publication of expression bears a heavy presumption against its constitutional validity. Even cases where national security is at issue receive *strict scrutiny*. Under the strict scrutiny standard, courts look behind any nominal justifications offered by government entities for why a restriction is necessary and apply their own judgment as to whether the alleged harm is sufficiently serious to warrant regulation. A good example of such a case is *New York Times Co. v. United States,* in which the government tried to stop the publication of the "Pentagon Papers," which detailed US involvement in Vietnam prior to 1968. The government claimed that publication of the papers violated a statute protecting government secrets and that their publication would prolong the war and embarrass the United States in the conduct of its diplomacy. The Supreme Court, although unable to agree on a single basis for its holding, found that the government's claim of potential injury to the United States was insufficient to justify prior restraint. The justices, although believing that publication would probably be harmful, were not persuaded that publication would *surely* cause the harm alleged.

More recently, when Michael Wolff wrote a very negative book about President Trump titled *Fire and Fury: Inside the Trump White House,* the president's lawyers sent Mr. Wolff and his publisher, Henry Holt and Co., a cease and desist letter threatening to enjoin the publication. Since the publisher was aware of the extraordinarily high burden to prevent a book from being published, it not only ignored the threat, but it actually accelerated the date of publication. Both Mr. Wolff and his publisher were essentially thumbing their nose at the hollow threat. The First Amendment is a particularly effective shield against threats to speech that criticizes political leaders regardless of how embarrassing that speech may be to the politicians or the political process.

Even political speech that advocates the use of unlawful force is constitutionally protected, except where such advocacy is likely to produce imminent lawless action. However, the legal standard for evaluating whether words are likely to lead to violence is very high. In such cases, the government must show that the speech is both directed to a particular person and is inherently likely to result in violent action. The mere use of expletives and offensive words, without a compelling reason to believe they will lead to imminent violence, is protected by the First Amendment.

For the most part, the constitutional battles over the right to political speech have shifted away from issues of whether citizens have the right to criticize governments or even the form of government. A more divisive issue is to what extent the First Amendment affects the right to express political views that reflect negatively on race, creed, sexual orientation, religion, or national origin. A number of schools and universities have adopted codes that prohibit statements that express any form of prejudice or bigotry, such as racism, anti-Semitism, or homophobia. Some of these codes have been struck down by courts, but many remain.

IN PLAIN ENGLISH

The First Amendment protects against censorship *by the government.* The government encompasses federal, state, and local agencies run by the government, including public universities and city councils. Private citizens and institutions, including publishers and booksellers, are not subject to the same restrictions. The choice to publish content or not, to censor certain words, or to pull offensive books from the shelves is not action that is prohibited by the First Amendment when that action is taken by a private citizen or entity.

JUDICIAL PROCEEDINGS

Courts are also reluctant to suppress information related to judicial processes because of the important constitutional interests inherent in having public trials. To justify the imposition of gag orders, parties who seek to restrict reporting and public access to legal proceedings must show that there are no reasonable alternatives. The most common situation is when the issue is the conflict between an individual's right to a fair trial and the right of the press to its First Amendment guarantee of free speech.

For example, in *Nebraska Press Association v. Stuart,* the Nebraska Press Association appealed a court order prohibiting the press from reporting about confessions and other information implicating a defendant after the murder of six family members had gained widespread public attention. The trial judge originally issued the order because he felt that pretrial publicity would make it difficult to select a jury that had not been exposed to prejudicial press coverage. The US Supreme Court struck down the trial judge's order, finding that the impact of publicity on jurors was "speculative, dealing with factors unknown and unknowable." The justices went on to suggest alternatives to restraining all publication. These included changing the location of the trial, postponing the trial, asking in-depth questions of prospective jury members during the selection process to determine bias, explicitly instructing the jury to consider only evidence presented at trial, and isolating the jury. In other words, judges must consider alternative methods of pretrial precautions and should restrict coverage only as a last resort.

Court records are generally considered public records. Even grand jury records, generally considered secret, may sometimes be obtained given a good enough reason. In *Carlson v. U.S.*, a 2016 case from the Seventh Circuit Court of Appeals, a journalist/historian and some scholarly, journalistic, and historic organizations sought access to grand jury records, sealed long ago, concerning an investigation into a 1942 *Chicago Tribune* article claiming, based on classified navy communications, that the US military had cracked certain Japanese codes. Although no one contended that secrecy was no longer necessary, the government still declined to allow access to the records, arguing that a criminal rule of court with respect to grand jury materials prohibited disclosure. The court ruled against the government, holding that the records belonged to the court, and thus, the trial court had the authority to release them. Further, the trial court was justified in doing so because of the exceptional circumstances presented, because of their historic importance, and because there was no good reason to keep them secret any longer.

The executive branch of the government is responsible for classifying information vital to national security as confidential. In late 2017, the United States released records related to the assassination of President Kennedy. These records had been withheld for reasons of national security. Among the interesting disclosures in those records was the fact that some unidentified person contacted the British Embassy shortly before the assassination to advise it of the fact that something significant would be happening very soon. The documents were released without the need for judicial intervention, since the government realized that these records would likely be made available if the court was involved and voluntarily making them available was less costly and more efficient. This illustrates that the court's tendency to release documents once held jealously by the government has influenced the government's policies and increased access to once-confidential information.

COMMERCIAL SPEECH

In areas outside of political speech, the court has been more tolerant of prior restraints. For example, prior restraints may be permissible when purely commercial speech, such as advertisements or other promotional material, is involved.

IN PLAIN ENGLISH

Commercial speech is defined as speech directed at actual or potential customers, where the speaker is offering to sell a product or service, or where the intent is to earn a profit. Publishing and selling books, newspapers, or magazines does not make the speech commercial and subject to prior restraint merely because it is sold in commerce. Rather, the content of the book, newspaper, or magazine will be evaluated to determine if that speech is intended to sell or promote a product or service.

Since commercial speech is generally comprised of objective statements, whether an advertisement is true or false can often be readily determined. Thus, there is little or no threat of prior restraints being arbitrarily imposed. Plus, commercial speech lacks the urgency that often accompanies noncommercial speech, so any delay caused by the restraint while its justification is being argued would be relatively harmless. Based on these considerations, regulation of commercial speech is generally permitted.

An aspect related to the regulation of commercial speech is whether governments may enact laws that protect commercial producers and manufacturers from the disparagement of their products. Although the common law tort of trade libel is available to address such concerns, some states have enacted laws that reduce the burden of proof needed to prevail in such a case. The government's interest is to protect state economies from being harmed by irresponsible assertions about goods. These concerns are not without merit, since there have been instances in which industries have suffered severely following media reports of questionable reliability that claimed certain products were dangerous. On the other hand, such laws can suppress speech by imposing requirements, such as having to base assertions on reliable, scientific facts. Such standards have the practical effect of discouraging controversial statements and limiting the population of qualified writers to those with science or technical backgrounds.

The best-known examples of these kinds of laws are the *food disparagement statutes* that are in effect in more than a dozen states. These statutes vary in their legal elements but generally give producers of perishable foods the right to sue anyone who disseminates statements that impugn the safety of a food product without a reasonable scientific basis for the claim. The Texas food disparagement statute was used in 1997 as the basis of a lawsuit against talk show host Oprah Winfrey for remarks she made during a segment of her program about mad cow disease. She prevailed in the suit after the court ruled that the segment may have been hyperbolic but was not defamatory, as required by the statute. The applicability of the First Amendment was not decided in the case, and the constitutionality of these statutes remains undecided.

PORNOGRAPHY

Pornographic writing is another area where the government may regulate content, although the legal standards are more difficult to apply than with commercial speech. A variety of laws are involved in regulating pornographic materials, including federal laws that prohibit the transportation of obscene material across state lines and state laws that prohibit creating, publishing, and publicly displaying obscene material. The traditional legal basis under which pornography has been regulated is the belief that obscene materials are offensive and lack sufficient social utility to deserve protection under the First Amendment. Another basis advocated in more recent times is that pornography encourages crimes and harmful conduct toward women and minors and therefore is injurious.

IN PLAIN ENGLISH

Although there is a history of writers and publishers being prosecuted for material that was considered pornographic, most (if not all) prosecutions in the last forty years have involved visual images and not written text.

In 1973, the Supreme Court set forth the modern standard governing how pornography would be addressed under the First Amendment in *Miller v. California*. The standard created in *Miller* to determine if something is considered obscene is:

- whether the average person, applying contemporary community standards, would find that the work, taken as a whole, appeals to prurient interest;
- whether the work depicts or describes, in a patently offensive way, sexual conduct as specifically defined by the applicable state law; and
- whether the work, taken as a whole, lacks any serious literary, artistic, political, or scientific value.

The intent of *Miller* was to provide much clearer guidelines for protected speech both to state legislatures enacting statutes and to prosecutors enforcing that legislation. *Miller* required that state statutes be more specific, so the states attempted to define the *Miller* test for their own communities. While the *Miller* standard has led to the enactment of laws by states that vary in their specificity, breadth, and chilling effect, the war against pornography has shifted to visual depictions, and prosecutions against creators of purely textual works seem to have virtually disappeared. Nonetheless, some states do have statutes that prohibit writings that are obscene, and publishers who describe matters related to sexual conduct should have a general understanding about how the *Miller* standards are applied.

One of the greatest difficulties courts have in applying the *Miller* test involves defining *community* for the purposes of ascertaining standards. A juror is to draw on personal knowledge of the community, but not on his or her own personal standards of what is good or bad. Separating the two is not an easy task for many.

Second, while items that are patently offensive are given little protection, items outside the definition may or may not be protected. *Patently offensive* refers to hard-core materials that, among other things, include representations or descriptions of ultimate sexual acts, normal or perverted, actual or simulated. It also refers to representations or descriptions of masturbation, excretory functions, and lewd exhibitions of the genitals. Since materials less than patently offensive may well be entitled to First Amendment protection, states' powers to arbitrarily define obscenity are limited.

The Communications Decency Act of 1996

One federal act of which publishers should be aware is the Communications Decency Act of 1996 (CDA). Through it, Congress attempted to regulate pornography on the Internet. Portions of the Act, antipornography portions, were subsequently found to be unconstitutional by the US Supreme Court in the case of *Reno v. ACLU*. Oddly, a part of the Act that remained, 47 USC Section 230, is one that insulated Internet service providers, or sites such as Facebook and YouTube, from liability for postings by others. It states: "No provider or user of an interactive computer service shall be treated as the publisher or speaker of any information provided by another information content provider." This law has been heralded as a huge boon to free speech on the Internet.

This statute is intended to promote access to information by removing any requirement that Internet hosts sort and censor every post. This statute will *not* protect publishers who edit, curate, or promote the content of others, nor will it protect hosts who knowingly allow content to remain on their sites once the specific, unlawful content has been brought to their attention.

Sometimes a law protecting freedom of speech may have unintended consequences. For example, in *Doe v. Backpage.com*, the CDA was used as a defense for a provider of online advertising that allegedly organized its website to facilitate sex trafficking. Backpage.com used the CDA to avoid liability to underage victims for posting advertisements of the victims as escorts. Since the provider was not technically the "speaker" of the contents of the advertisements, it was absolved of liability for the posting. That does not mean, of course, that the posters were not liable for their conduct, regardless of the difficulty of finding and prosecuting them.

Child Pornography

Unlike pornography that depicts adults, the standard for obscenity set forth in *Miller* does not apply to pornography that depicts children. Such materials are not protected by the First Amendment. The reason that governments are entitled to greater leeway in regulating pornographic depictions of children is that the use of children as subjects of pornography is deemed to be harmful to their physiological, emotional, and mental health. Thus, the *Miller* standards do not apply to child pornography, and governments may prohibit sexually suggestive depictions irrespective of the degree of offensiveness.

Although the ability of the government to regulate child pornography is very broad, the legislative and enforcement actions at the federal level that attempt to eliminate child pornography have targeted visual depictions rather than written ones. Further, in *Ashcroft v. Free Speech Coalition*, the Supreme Court struck a portion of a federal law because its definition of child pornography was so broad as to encompass depictions of minors by means other than using real children. The Supreme Court reasoned that computer-generated images or images of adults who look like minors do not impose the same physiological, emotional, and mental harm on children. Thus, laws that can be construed to prevent speech of this kind are overly broad and unconstitutional.

Nonetheless, the sanctions for violating the laws against child pornography are uniformly severe. Any publisher who contemplates using illustrations or descriptions of children in a sexually suggestive manner is advised to consult a lawyer to determine the legality of such use.

Violence against Women

Following the United States Supreme Court's holding that child pornography may be regulated on the grounds that it harms children, some interest groups have advocated that all pornography depicting women should be regulated. The reasoning is that it is degrading and leads to violence against women, even though it is not considered obscene under the *Miller* test. In 1984, the city of Indianapolis promulgated an ordinance that prohibited the production and distribution of materials that depicted *the graphic sexually explicit subordination of women* in words or pictures. The US Court of Appeals ruled that concerns about the debasement of women did not override the requirements set forth by the Supreme Court in *Miller*. Therefore, while children are given special protection when it comes to pornography, adult women are not.

TIME, PLACE, AND MANNER RESTRICTIONS

Laws that merely restrict the time, place, or manner of the speech are examined under a less stringent standard than is the case with laws that look to restrict specific types of content. Governmental efforts to regulate time, place, and manner must be neutral with regard to the speech's content and may not burden the flow of ideas to a substantial extent. Such restrictions must leave open ample alternative avenues of communication. The most common restrictions regulate the times and places where public performances and demonstrations may be held. Although there are instances where writing is regulated according to time and place, they are inconsequential for most publishers. Examples of content-neutral regulations include ordinances that ban posting signs and flyers on public utility poles and format requirements for documents submitted to government offices.

Another kind of restriction that has been imposed on a manner of communication is the sending of unsolicited commercial facsimiles and email, commonly called *junk faxes* or *spam email*. The rationale for the government's interest in regulating this form of commercial speech is that junk faxes and spam email interfere with the recipients' ability to receive desired communications and shift the costs of receiving advertisements to the recipient.

In 1991, Congress enacted the Telephone Consumer Protection Act (TCPA). It bans junk faxes and allows recipients to sue senders and recover their actual damages or five hundred dollars, whichever is greater.

In 2003, Congress enacted the Controlling the Assault of Non-Solicited Pornography and Marketing Act (CAN-SPAM) to impose penalties on the transmission of unsolicited commercial email. It prohibits false or misleading headers and subject lines and requires senders to identify the email as an advertisement and tell recipients where the sender is located. The Act further requires senders to provide recipients instructions on how to opt out from receiving future email and imposes tough penalties if opt-out requests are not promptly honored. At the time of this publication, these penalties are over $41,000 *per violation*. Publishers who wish to engage in email campaigns should review the FTC's CAN-SPAM compliance guide available at www.ftc.gov/tips-advice/business-center/guidance/can-spam-act-compliance-guide-business.

CHAPTER 2

Privacy Rights

Chapter 1 covered the limited power of the federal government and the states to regulate publication. As noted in that chapter, the right to freely express oneself in a publication must sometimes be balanced against the need of government to serve the common good. Similarly, the right of expression must sometimes be balanced against the rights of individuals and organizations to retain some degree of privacy and to be treated reasonably.

When a publisher works through another person or entity, the relationship is that of principal and agent. An agent acts on behalf of another, the principal. In the book publishing industry, most often the publisher is the principal and the person or entity used, be it an author, freelancer, or employee, is the agent. When this relationship exists, the laws of agency apply, and the principal, or publisher, may be liable for the wrongful acts or omissions of the agent. Therefore, the words of an author may expose a publisher to liability for privacy violations, defamation, and other negative consequences that the published book has on others.

A publisher's duty to balance his or her desire to tell a story against the rights of others is delicate. The next two chapters cover some of the instances and issues publishers must be aware of in regard to their publications and the laws surrounding privacy, defamation, and the way their books affect others.

INVASION OF PRIVACY

The right to be protected from a wrongful *invasion of privacy*, largely taken for granted today, is a relatively new legal concept. In fact, the right of privacy was not suggested as a legal principle until 1890, when arguments for developing the right appeared in a *Harvard Law Review* article written by Justice Louis Brandeis and his law partner, Samuel Warren. That article, written largely because of excessive media attention given to the social affairs of Warren's wife, maintained that the media was persistently overstepping the bounds of propriety and decency in violation of Mrs. Warren's right to be left alone.

From this rather modest beginning, the concept of a right to privacy began to take hold. Although there is no express recognition of a right to privacy in the US Constitution, state courts inferred such rights and created a body of privacy law. In addition, some states enacted right of privacy statutes to supplement the common law developed by the courts.

This is not to say that the US Constitution does not protect its citizens against invasion of privacy by the government itself. The Fourth Amendment protects citizens against unlawful search and seizure of their persons, homes, papers, and effects. Privacy rights discussed in this chapter, however, refer to the ability of a citizen to protect him- or herself from other *citizens* and *private actors*.

The general framework of privacy rights has developed over time, with some variation among the states. In general, modern privacy law is divided into four separate categories:

- intrusion upon another's seclusion;
- public disclosure of private facts;
- portrayal of another in a false light; and
- commercial appropriation of another's name or likeness.

Although there are statutes that make it a crime to violate some forms of privacy, most of the privacy rights are enforced civilly in the form of tort actions. For example, if someone feels his or her legal right to privacy has been violated, that person is entitled to file a lawsuit against the violator. Whether the complainant can prevail will depend on how closely the perceived violation conforms to those privacy rights recognized by the law.

IN PLAIN ENGLISH

There is no *right to privacy* guaranteed by the Constitution. Most privacy laws are enacted on the state level and enforced when private citizens bring a lawsuit against someone who has invaded some privacy right recognized by the state.

INTRUSION UPON SECLUSION

The best known of the violations against privacy is known as *intrusion upon seclusion*. The interest that underlies this right is the freedom to be left alone when someone is in a place where privacy can reasonably be expected. In order to establish an intrusion upon seclusion claim, the person bringing suit, the plaintiff, must show that the perpetrator, or defendant, intentionally intruded upon the plaintiff's seclusion in a way that an ordinary person would find highly offensive.

In practice, the intrusion violation does not apply directly to writing but can apply to fact-gathering, investigations, and efforts to obtain interviews that are made during a writing project. The possibility of an intrusion suit should always be weighed against the practice of aggressively pursuing facts, since the writers you deal with have no inherent right to harass, trespass, or enter a private domain using subterfuge. And if you encourage or permit them to do it, you may be liable under agency law. For example, in *Dietemann v. Time, Inc.*, journalists for *Life* magazine entered the home of Mr. Dietemann, a self-proclaimed faith healer, claiming to be seeking medical treatment from him. While there, they surreptitiously took pictures and recorded conversations. This information was used to prepare an article that appeared in *Life* exposing Dietemann as a quack. Dietemann ultimately prevailed in a lawsuit filed against the publisher of *Life* because subterfuge was used to gain access to the plaintiff's private quarters.

In egregious cases, intrusion upon seclusion can occur in public places when the level of intrusion becomes clearly unreasonable and unwanted. The best-known case is *Galella v. Onassis*, in which a freelance photographer was sued for relentlessly pursuing Jacqueline Kennedy Onassis and her children at places such as parks, churches, funeral services, theaters, and schools. One of the photographer's practices was to shock or surprise his subjects in order to photograph them in a state of distress. While taking these photographs, he would sometimes utter offensive or snide comments. The court, in a fairly scathing opinion, held that the photographer had wrongfully intruded upon the seclusion of his subjects and issued a permanent injunction that prohibited him from getting within a certain distance of Onassis and her children. However, the court did not forbid further photographs—it merely regulated the manner in which they could be taken.

On the other hand, the court found no offensive intrusion in *Bogie v. Rosenberg*, where a very short conversation between Joan Rivers and a fan backstage after a comedy performance was incorporated into a biographical film about Joan Rivers's life. The conversation was centered around the fan's comments to Rivers, sympathizing with her because of a heckler's comments critical of Rivers's jokes about Helen Keller. The fan complained that the segment containing her comments was aired without her consent, was filmed in a place in which she expected privacy, and portrayed her in a way that would be offensive to a reasonable person. Even though she did not consent to being filmed and though the film company made money on the presentation, the court refused to find that there had been a highly invasive intrusion into her privacy. The court reasoned that the statements were made in a backstage area with other people around and the segment accurately recorded her statements even though she may have later regretted making them. The issue to be determined was whether the *intrusion* was offensive, not whether the comments she made could be interpreted as offensive or embarrassing.

Neither writers nor publishers risk liability for intrusion unless they or their agents are directly involved in an intrusion. For example, in *Pearson v. Dodd*, members of a senator's staff copied some sensitive documents belonging to the senator and gave them to newspaper columnists Drew Pearson and Jack Anderson. Pearson and Anderson subsequently wrote and published a series of articles using the information the documents contained. Although Pearson and Anderson knew how the documents had been obtained, they played no role in the intrusion. Since the essence of the tort of intrusion is the intrusion itself and not the subsequent publication, Pearson and Anderson were not held liable.

IN PLAIN ENGLISH

Publishers can be held liable when authors intrude on the seclusion of others if the publisher encourages or instructs its authors or agents to aggressively gather facts or seek interviews in ways that ordinary people would find highly offensive.

PUBLIC DISCLOSURE OF PRIVATE FACTS

The second type of privacy tort, the *public disclosure of private facts*, directly affects the kinds of content publishers may reveal about others without being liable. In order to bring a case for this kind of invasion of privacy, the plaintiff must prove:

- that the publisher disclosed private facts to members of the public;
- that the disclosure would be objectionable to a person of ordinary sensibilities; and
- that there is no legitimate interest of the public in being apprised of the facts.

Whether the information disclosed involves private facts is usually a matter of common sense. Anything that one keeps to oneself and would not wish to be made public is probably a private fact. Common examples include private debts, sexual practices, and medical problems.

A major protection that publishers have against others bringing suits claiming that the publisher has publicly disclosed their private facts is that disclosures of *newsworthy* information are generally protected by the First Amendment. The newsworthy protection is not limited to breaking news one might read in a newspaper or blog. A publication is generally considered to be newsworthy when it contains information that arouses the public's legitimate interest and attention.

Truthful disclosures pertaining to public figures or public officials are almost always considered newsworthy, at least to the extent that the disclosure bears some reasonable relationship to the public role. If, however, the disclosure is highly personal (such as sexual habits, personal finances, or medical history) and has no bearing upon the individual's public role, the disclosure might be deemed not to be newsworthy and thus may be actionable. The public role of individuals who enjoy a great deal of fame or notoriety is often found to create a reasonable relationship with much more of his or her traditionally personal information. A presidential candidate or a mass murderer, for example, could expect considerably greater intrusions into, and disclosure of, his or her private affairs than a minor public official or a one-time traffic offender. Similarly, private persons who are involuntarily thrust into the public light will receive more protection than people who seek fame and notoriety.

This is illustrated by the court's decision in *Toffoloni v. LFB Publishing Group*, where the court found that a publisher had violated the right of publicity of a deceased lady wrestler who had been murdered by her husband, another professional wrestler, by publishing—in *Hustler* magazine—nude pictures of her taken twenty years earlier. Even though her murder was newsworthy and the pictures were accompanied by a biographical sketch, the photos were the selling point of the publication. The photos had no relation to the murder and invaded both her privacy rights and publications rights. Publishing the nude photos, the court believed, went too far and imparted no news or information to the public. Moreover, the commercial use of the photos to put money in the publisher's pocket, without compensating the woman's estate, made it liable for damages. The right to publish or not publish was a proprietary right, the court explained, which survived the death of its owner, was inheritable, and could be willed to another.

IN PLAIN ENGLISH

In determining whether the newsworthiness privilege applies, courts will consider the social value of the facts published, the degree to which the intrusion concerns ostensibly private affairs, and the extent to which the party voluntarily acceded to a position of public notoriety.

Even very private facts may be considered newsworthy when they bear some logical relationship to the credibility of someone who has voluntarily entered into a public debate. For example, in *Wilson v. Grant*, a person sued a radio talk show host after the host disclosed that the person had previously been confined to a psychiatric hospital. The court dismissed the claim on the grounds that there was a sufficiently logical connection between the plaintiff's long-standing vendetta against the talk show host and other media accounts describing the plaintiff as obsessed and crazy, which made the disclosure newsworthy. However, the disclosure of private facts, such as a high school student's suspected medical condition, will not be considered newsworthy if a person is not in the public eye and has previously kept that information private.

Get Permission

When in doubt, the best way to avoid liability when publishing about a person's private life is to obtain written permission from that person to disclose the information. This is one of the reasons why publishers sometimes prefer to publish *authorized* biographies. While many biographies are published without the consent of their subjects, these works assume a greater risk that they will disclose facts in violation of the subject's privacy rights. However, there is no legal requirement to obtain authorization. Courts will generally allow a great deal of latitude when works relate to persons whose lives are a matter of interest to the public.

Getting permission is not always as difficult as it may seem. Publishers who do not know the subject personally can often find ways to contact them, known associates, or employers through the Internet. However, a publisher should be careful when communicating through a third party that no personal or private information be disclosed to that third party, lest the publisher become the target of a lawsuit. In most cases, it will suffice, and protect you from the risk of accidentally disclosing private facts, to let the third party know whom you wish to contact and to provide information on how that person can get in touch with you.

PORTRAYAL OF ANOTHER IN A FALSE LIGHT

The third type of privacy tort is the portrayal of another in a *false light*. To bring a suit for false light, a plaintiff must prove that (1) the publisher publicly portrayed the plaintiff falsely; and (2) the portrayal would be offensive to reasonable people. In cases where a public figure is portrayed in a false light, the plaintiff must also prove that the portrayal was done with malice.

One of the better-known cases involving portrayal in a false light is *Leverton v. Curtis Publishing Company*. In this case, a photograph of a young girl who had been struck by an automobile was used by the *Saturday Evening Post* to illustrate an article about child safety. The article stated that most injuries to children are the result of carelessness on the part of the parents. The girl's parents successfully sued the *Post*, alleging (among other things) that it had portrayed them as negligent, when they had in fact been completely without fault in the accident.

Another way to be liable for portraying someone in a false light is to attribute statements, views, or opinions that the person does not actually hold. For example, in *Cantrell v. Forest City Publishing Company*, a newspaper published an article concerning the destitute condition of a family following the death of the father in a bridge disaster. Among other things, the article contained fabricated excerpts from an interview with the mother of the family, when she had never actually been interviewed. The newspaper was held liable for portraying the family in a false light by attributing statements to the mother that she never made.

IN PLAIN ENGLISH

Publishers of narrative nonfiction should be particularly careful with regard to false light portrayals, especially if they engage in the genre commonly known as *creative nonfiction*, which sometimes relies on speculation rather than ascertainable facts.

Factual works, especially those concerning newsworthy figures or events, are rarely actionable. Fictionalizations, however, are vulnerable to claims of false light invasion of privacy. Generally, courts will not impose liability if the publication merely contains insignificant distortions or errors. In *Carlisle v. Fawcett Publications, Inc.*, for example, the court refused to impose liability for minor inaccuracies about actress Janet Leigh's age at the time of some romantic relationships during her marriage. Although these mistakes tended to portray the plaintiff in a false light, the court nevertheless ruled that the article did not constitute an invasion of privacy, since the errors in that case were of little or no consequence.

At the other extreme is the case of *Spahn v. Julian Messner, Inc.*, in which the defendant published a biography of Warren Spahn, a renowned baseball player of his day. Unlike the work in *Carlisle,* this biography was replete with fictionalized events, dramatizations, distorted chronologies, and fictionalized dialogues. Although the biography tended to glorify Spahn, it nevertheless placed him in a false, albeit radiant, light. As a result, the publisher was held liable for invasion of privacy.

IN PLAIN ENGLISH

False light can be either positive or negative and still be actionable.

When dealing with false light issues, it is difficult to predict where liability will lie. Distortions or inaccuracies involving insignificant events, places, and dates are likely to be safe, provided the errors are not pervasive. However, false statements pertaining to significant aspects of someone's life are more likely to result in liability, particularly if they involve highly personal or sensitive matters. The crucial question is whether the false portrayal would be offensive to a reasonable person in the position of the person portrayed.

A false light publication might be objectionable to the average person for a number of reasons. For instance, the plaintiff might be humiliated, estranged from friends or family, or simply embarrassed. In *Carlisle*, the plaintiff failed to prove that the infrequent and trivial inaccuracies were offensive. In *Spahn*, on the other hand, it was deemed reasonable to suppose that the player would have been highly embarrassed by the glorified but largely inaccurate version of his life.

In cases involving the false light portrayal of public figures, plaintiffs must also prove that the publisher knew of the falsity or recklessly disregarded the truth before they can recover damages. This is known as the *malice standard*. If the publisher acted without malice, innocent or negligent misstatements are not sufficient to support a finding of liability. However, when the plaintiff is a private person, defendants can be held liable for defamation based on mere negligence.

Get Permission

Just as in the case of disclosing private facts, the best way to avoid liability when publishing content involving an actual person is to obtain written permission from that person prior to publication. Some plaintiffs bring lawsuit because the surprise robbed them of the ability to prepare friends and family for the publication. Giving an individual fair warning prior to publication may be all that is needed to avoid a costly lawsuit.

In the event that the person who is the subject of a publication denies permission, you should seek advice from an experienced attorney and develop and document a strategy prior to publication. The strategy may include things like obtaining a legal opinion that the content is newsworthy or not an invasion of privacy, clarifying that the author will indemnify the publisher for any liability, or reviewing your business insurance policy to ensure you are covered in the event of a lawsuit of this kind.

COMMERCIAL APPROPRIATION

The fourth kind of privacy right is the right not to have one's name or image used to endorse a product or service without permission. *Commercial appropriation* of someone's name or likeness as an invasion of privacy bears little resemblance to cases based upon wrongful intrusion, public disclosure of private facts, or portrayal in a false light. In all of these other situations, the plaintiff must prove that the defendant's words or conduct caused the plaintiff to suffer humiliation, embarrassment, or loss of self-esteem, focusing on the injury to the plaintiff's sensibilities. In contrast, the law against appropriation is designed to protect someone's proprietary interest in one's own name or likeness. Celebrities, such as professional athletes and entertainers, frequently receive a considerable amount of their income from the controlled exploitation of their names or likenesses. The monetary benefits from such exploitation would be minimal without some legal protection. However, a person need not be a celebrity to have a cause of action if his or her name or likeness is misappropriated, even though the compensation to which that person is entitled might not be great.

In order to bring a suit for this type of invasion of privacy, one only needs to prove that the publisher wrongfully appropriated the plaintiff's name or likeness for commercial purposes. Appropriation in this sense means *use*. The fact of appropriation is rarely at issue in these cases, since the use will be obvious. However, determining the purpose of the use is not always a simple process, because it is not always clear whether the intent is expressive, commercial, or a combination of both. Uses that are informative and cultural are not actionable. However, if the use primarily exploits the individual portrayed, then courts will likely rule that the person's identity was appropriated.

As with the other kinds of invasion of privacy, any use that is considered newsworthy will likely not be actionable, even though some commercial gain might result from the use. Determining whether a use is newsworthy is often difficult. For example, the case of *Rand v. Hearst Corporation* concerned a book written by Eugene Vale. A review of the book appearing in the *San Francisco Examiner* maintained that Vale wrote with the same "mystique analysis" as author Ayn Rand. This excerpt comparing the two authors was printed on the front cover of Vale's book. Rand did not object to the original review, since it was clearly privileged as being newsworthy, but she did object to the publisher's use of her name to advertise Vale's book. The appellate court, in ruling that the publisher was privileged to quote from the review, stated that "a review concerning a book offered for sale is a matter of great public interest," at least to the extent that the review is of public interest and informative. Thus, although the publisher's use of Ayn Rand's name was clearly motivated by a desire to increase sales, the use was nevertheless privileged as being newsworthy.

Other lawsuits brought by celebrities have unsuccessfully attempted to claim commercial appropriation. In one, the heirs of Agatha Christie's estate were unable to stop the distribution of a book and film that speculated about what the mystery writer did during an actual eleven-day disappearance. In another case, Ginger Rogers was unsuccessful in her suit against a movie distribution company, based on wrongful commercial appropriation of her name in the title of Federico Fellini's film *Ginger and Fred*.

In general, when celebrity names and likenesses are used in forms of expression protected by the First Amendment, such as movies or books, no action will lie for wrongful commercial appropriation. This general rule seems to extend to advertisements for magazines as well, but only if a commercial appropriation is held by a court to be for a newsworthy purpose. For example, Joe Namath was unable to collect damages when *Sports Illustrated* used his photograph to advertise an upcoming issue of the magazine. The court held that the use of Namath's photograph in the advertisement was informative of the magazine's contents and thus not a wrongful commercial appropriation of his likeness.

What these cases point out is the balance that has been struck between celebrities on one hand and the free press on the other. The unauthorized use of a person's name or likeness is not allowed when the use is primarily for the purpose of selling a product or service. But when the use is for the purpose of informing the public of newsworthy events or matters of interest to a segment of the population or for the purpose of providing information about a performance, the First Amendment will supersede the right of a person to claim the monetary benefits of celebrity status.

Get Permission

A commercial appropriation will not be actionable if the person portrayed has consented to the use. If a publisher plans to use someone's name or photograph for endorsement or for any other commercial purpose, written permission that clearly defines the terms of the allowed use should be obtained in order to avoid accidentally exceeding the scope of the permission.

IN PLAIN ENGLISH

It is risky to rely on a third party, such as a photographer or illustrator, to obtain consent.

RIGHTS OF PUBLICITY

In recent years, the area of commercial appropriation has evolved to include a *right of publicity*. This right endows a celebrity or public figure with a proprietary interest in his or her public reputation and allows the celebrity to control the exploitation of his or her name for commercial purposes.

The right of publicity has been the subject of much litigation in recent years, and courts continue to rule inconsistently on its scope and extent. The right of publicity traditionally has been viewed as protecting only the appropriation of names and likenesses (i.e., drawings or photographs) of celebrities or other public figures. However, some cases have held the right to extend to famous voices, nicknames, and verbal slogans. In a Michigan case, comedian Johnny Carson brought a suit against a company that rented portable toilets for appropriating his famous opening line, "Here's Johnny." The federal court found a right of publicity and granted a nationwide injunction and damages.

Recall the case involving the murdered wrestler discussed earlier. The court recognized the woman's right of publicity and its monetary value and found that she or her estate had the right to publish or not publish the nude photos, but it was not permissible for someone else to do it without permission. As will be discussed later, these rights should be carefully considered in the estate plan of people with such valuable rights.

CHAPTER 3

Defamation and Other Content Issues

Although the First Amendment protects free expression, it does not go so far as to allow publishers the unfettered right to harm other people through false statements that injure their reputations. However, the First Amendment does permit some leeway in particular circumstances that protects publishers from being liable for some kinds of opinions and unintentional misstatements.

DEFAMATION

Defamatory statements may be written or oral. Written defamatory statements are known as *libel* and oral ones are *slander*. However, the same laws and principles govern all defamatory statements, irrespective of whether they are libel or slander.

IN PLAIN ENGLISH

Formal organizations, such as associations, partnerships, and corporations, have the same right to sue for defamation as do individuals.

A statement will generally be considered defamatory if it subjects a person to hatred, contempt, or ridicule, or if it results in injury to that person's reputation in the community. To be legally actionable, a claim for defamation must meet three elements:

1. it must say something that is defamatory about an identifiable person or organization;

2. it must be untrue; and
3. it must have been published.

Depending on the jurisdiction and the circumstances in which the statement was made, a plaintiff may have the burden to prove that the statement was false. However, *truth* may always be asserted as a defense in any defamation case.

It is not always simple to determine whether a statement is actually defamatory. Since defamatory statements must be false to be legally actionable, they must be sufficiently definite to be capable of being proven true or false. They must also be reasonably understood to be statements of fact rather than opinion. For example, statements in a magazine article that asserted investors would become disillusioned with a company's stock once they realized one of its primary products performed less effectively than claimed did not constitute defamation because the statements were subjective opinion. Generic insults such as "loser" or "chicken-butt" tend not to be subject to defamatory inference, because they are more appropriately characterized as taunts than statements of fact. Even derogatory terms such as "sleazy attorney" are generally considered subjective expressions of disapproval that have no factual content.

Although legitimate opinions are protected by the First Amendment, disguising factual statements in the form of opinion may not be sufficient to avoid liability for defamation. For example, the statement *In my opinion, John Jones is a liar* can cause as much damage to reputation as stating that *Jones is a liar.* The test for whether a statement that purports to be opinion may be actionable for defamation is whether it:

- implies an assertion of fact; and
- is sufficiently factual to be susceptible of being proved true or false.

Context

The context in which the statement is made must also be considered in determining whether a statement is defamatory. When considering context, statements are considered in conjunction with the entire publication to determine the sense and meaning that were likely conveyed to the readers. A false statement that is defamatory on its face may not be defamatory when read in context. Likewise, a statement that is not defamatory on its face may be defamatory when read in context.

For example, assume that a person named Ronald McGorge has recently published a memoir called *My Life as a Con Man*, in which he falsely claims to have rendered several widows destitute by defrauding them of all their assets. If you wrote that *Ronald McGorge is a despicable con man*, the statement would be false because he never actually committed the frauds he claims. However, it would not be defamatory in this context, because McGorge is trying to develop a reputation as a criminal and asserting that he has committed crimes does not damage his reputation.

Conversely, a statement that *McGorge is an honest man who can always be trusted to do the right thing* could be construed as defamatory. Such a statement is false, because honest people do not knowingly make false claims in their memoirs. It also has the effect of damaging Ronald McGorge's reputation by mitigating the notoriety he is trying to cultivate. Note that a statement that *McGorge is a cream puff who is falsely claiming to have defrauded several widows* would likely not be considered defamatory in this context, because part of the statement is opinion and the other part is true.

IN PLAIN ENGLISH

In general, statements made in serious works are more likely to be construed as defamatory than those in works that are clearly communicating hyperbole, parody, or jest.

Reputation

Adding to the ambiguity as to what constitutes defamation is whether the substantive content of the statement is the kind that damages reputation. Since the question of whether the allegedly defamatory statement adversely affects the plaintiff's reputation in the community is a critical element, the mores of the community can be important in determining whether words are defamatory.

In addition, certain states have passed statutes that describe certain kinds of characterizations as defamatory. Making a characterization that the state has ruled as defamatory could subject you to liability in that state—even if the comment would not be defamatory elsewhere. For example, some states have statutes that dictate that false statements regarding sexual promiscuity are defamatory, although the courts in some states are tending to hold that the usage of terms such as "slut" and "whore" have come to be understood as generic insult and thus are not actionable at law.

Per Se Versus Per Quod

Courts have historically categorized defamatory statements as defamation *per se* and defamation *per quod*, although some jurisdictions no longer follow this approach. In *defamation per se*, the defamatory meaning is apparent from the statement itself. In *defamation per quod*, the defamatory meaning requires additional evidence to show how the statement is injurious. For example, falsely accusing John Doe of stalking Mary Smith would be defamation per se, since stalking is a serious crime. Falsely accusing John Doe of talking to Mary Smith in a public park would be defamation per quod, if John Doe was subject to a court-issued restraining order that prohibited him or her from interacting with Mary Smith.

The distinction between defamation per se and defamation per quod is important primarily because it determines whether the plaintiff has to prove his or her damages. If the statement is defamation per se, the damage to reputation will be presumed, and the plaintiff need not prove it. With defamation per quod, the traditional rule has been that specific injuries to reputation must be proved, unless the innuendo conforms to one of the kinds of statements that have traditionally constituted defamation per se. The kind of statements that constitute defamation per se are those that:

- adversely reflect upon someone's professional competence;
- impute serious sexual misconduct;
- accuse someone of committing a serious crime; or
- accuse someone of having a serious infectious disease or mental illness.

Many of the categories are rooted in history when such statements could have serious repercussions on a person's economic prospects or social standing. For example, under the social mores in effect fifty years ago, stating that an unmarried woman was unchaste could affect her prospects for marriage, and identifying someone as a communist or homosexual could severely impair his or her ability to gain or sustain employment. These areas are becoming increasingly gray as social mores change but are still considered actionable in many jurisdictions.

IN PLAIN ENGLISH

There is a trend among the states to eliminate presumed damages and require plaintiffs in all defamation cases to prove an actual injury to reputation.

Defamation Per Se

One example of defamation per se is an accusation of criminal or morally reprehensible acts. An accusation of criminal conduct is defamatory per se, even though it is not explicitly stated. If an author stated facts that describe a crime or cast suspicion by innuendo, it is sufficient for defamation per se. On the other hand, it is never defamation per se to accuse someone of exercising a legal right, even though some members of the public may disapprove. For example, it is not defamation per se to say that a man killed someone in self-defense, that he brought a divorce suit against his wife, or that he invoked the Fifth Amendment forty times during his trial. Although these statements may cast suspicion, they cannot be defamatory per se, because they merely report the exercise of a legal right.

It is usually deemed defamation per se to impute to a professional person a breach of professional ethics or general incompetence to practice a profession. Falsely stating that a doctor was suspended from a hospital for malpractice or incompetence would be one example of such a statement.

There is a gray area concerning statements about certain business practices that may not be illegal but nonetheless could give a business bad publicity. To say someone is selling goods at very low prices would not be defamation per se, but to say someone is selling goods below cost to drive a competitor out of business might be.

Defamation Per Quod

In defamation per quod, since the defamatory meaning of a statement is conveyed only in conjunction with other statements, the plaintiff who sues for defamation must introduce the context of the statement and demonstrate to the court how the writing, as a whole, results in a defamatory innuendo. For example, the statement that someone intentionally burned down his barn is not sufficient to constitute defamation, since such an act by itself would not normally subject someone to contempt or ridicule. A plaintiff contending that the statement is defamatory would have to show that it was accompanied by other information, such as a statement that the barn was heavily insured. This might well constitute defamation per quod, since the implication of these statements might be that the person is trying to defraud an insurance company.

Defamation by Implication

In some cases, true statements can result in liability for defamation if they create a misleading impression that defames the plaintiff. This is known as *defamation by implication*. For instance, a newspaper that reports that Jane shot Mary upon finding her husband at Mary's home could be liable to Mary if it left out information that Mary's husband and several neighbors were present, and that the shooting had been an accident. Even if the fact of the shooting was true, the manner in which the newspaper reported the story implies that marital infidelity between Jane's husband and Mary had occurred.

Publication

As stated earlier, a defamatory statement must be published to be actionable. In the legal sense, the term *publication* has a broader meaning than in the conventional sense. A statement is considered to be published when it is communicated to a third person. For example, if you tell someone in private that he is a promiscuous, herpes-infected child molester, the statement would not be considered to have been published, since it has not been communicated to other people. If you make the same statement to others, the publication requirement is satisfied.

In addition to the person who initially publishes a defamatory statement, persons who restate or repeat such a statement may also be liable under the *doctrine of republication*. If the republication was foreseeable, the person who initially made the statement can also be liable for the republication. For example, if a private person writes a letter to the editor of a newspaper expecting that it will be published, then both that person and newspaper might be liable for any defamatory statements in the letter. While someone who republishes a defamatory statement may have defenses that are not available to the original publisher, merely attributing the statements to a particular source will not protect one from liability.

Generally, the person who is defamed can bring a separate lawsuit for each repetition of the defamatory remark. However, a majority of courts have adopted what is known as the *single-publication rule* to cover situations in which a remark is contained in a book, magazine, or newspaper. Under this rule, a person cannot make each copy of the book grounds for a separate suit. The number of copies is instead taken into account only for purposes of determining the extent of damages.

Identification

In order for someone to sue for defamation, the statement at issue must identify that particular person or entity. This proof is easy, of course, when the plaintiff is identified by name. However, if a plaintiff is not identified by name, the plaintiff can prove that he or she was nonetheless *identified* by showing that a third party could reasonably infer that the statement was about the plaintiff.

If a defamatory statement is made about an identified group of people, the possibility of each member of that group having a valid cause of action will depend on the size of the group and whether the statement defames all or only a part of the group. Statements made about large, loosely defined groups are less likely to be actionable. For example, if someone states that *all publishers are thieves*, an individual publisher could not prevail in a defamation suit, since it can hardly be said that the one publisher's reputation was damaged as a result of the statement. On the other hand, if that same statement was directed to the members of a particular publisher's group, they probably could prevail, since they would be more likely to have their reputations damaged by the defamatory statement.

The individual members of a group are not likely to prevail if the allegedly defamatory statement referred only to a portion of the group. If, for example, someone states that an unidentified employee at a restaurant is infected with HIV, the employees probably could not prevail in a defamation suit since the statement does not implicate all the employees or identify a particular individual. On the other hand, if an accusation has the effect of implicating all the members of a group, such as accusing one or more members of a small work crew of stealing, then courts are more likely to sustain a defamation claim. Again, the size of the group is an important factor. Statements made about small groups are more likely to damage the reputations of the individual members than statements about a few members of large groups.

Public Officials and Public Figures

An important aspect of defamation law that increases the freedom of expression is that *public officials* are required to meet a higher burden of proof when they bring defamation cases. This requirement, known as the *malice standard*, was created by the US Supreme Court in 1964 in *The New York Times Co. v. Sullivan*. This case involved an advertisement in a newspaper that implied that a police chief was responsible for abusive police action directed against students who participated in a civil rights demonstration and against civil rights leader Reverend Martin Luther King Jr. The US Supreme Court held that the First Amendment provides some protection to writings that criticize *public officials* for anything they do that is in any way relevant to their official conduct. In these cases, the public official must prove that defendants either knew that the statements were false or recklessly disregarded whether they were true or false.

In *Rosenblatt v. Baer*, the US Supreme Court further defined public officials to be those among the hierarchy of government employees who have, or appear to the public to have, substantial responsibility for or control over the conduct of governmental affairs. Persons who qualify include officials who are elected or appointed to office (judges and military commanders are obvious examples). Courts have ruled that lower-level public employees, such as police officers, teachers, and municipal managers, qualify if they exercise discretion in ways that affect the public. However, public employees whose duties do not require them to exercise such discretion are unlikely to be considered public officials.

The coverage of the malice requirement was expanded in *Gertz v. Robert Welch, Inc.* to include persons who are *public figures*. One way that persons may become public figures is to achieve such pervasive fame or notoriety that they are deemed to be public figures for all purposes. This category includes people who are frequently in the news but are not public officials, such as major television personalities and entertainers. Persons who are public figures for all purposes must satisfy the malice standard for any statement made about them.

The other way to become a public figure is to thrust oneself into a public controversy in order to influence the resolution of the issues involved. These persons are deemed public figures for a limited purpose and are required to meet the malice standard when statements relate to the controversy in which they are involved.

The second requirement in this public figure category is that the person must have voluntarily thrust him- or herself into the controversy in order to influence the issues. This requirement would be met if someone's actions

were calculated to draw attention to that person or to arouse public senti-
ment, but not if the person was merely arrested, sued, or a victim of a crime
or accident. A student who makes a speech during a protest demonstration
would be considered a public figure with respect to the subject of the demonstration, but a student who was pepper-sprayed while listening would not be.

Private Persons

Individuals who do not qualify as public officials or figures are private persons, even if they are involved in a newsworthy event. Private persons generally do not have to prove actual malice in their defamation claim. However,
the Supreme Court has placed the burden of proof on the plaintiff—not the
newspaper—to determine the truth or falsity of the statement for which the
private plaintiff is suing the newspaper if it was writing about matters of public concern. In media cases, the plaintiff must always prove that the statement
is false. In nonmedia cases, some states still follow the doctrine in which the
plaintiff need only show that the statement was defamatory and published to
establish a claim, and then put the burden on the defendant to prove that the
statement was true.

Defenses

In addition to the higher standard or proof required of public officials and
figures, there are several defenses available to defamation claims. The practical effect of these defenses is to allow publishers to avoid liability when
they address issues of public concern. Unlike the malice standard set forth
in *Sullivan*, defenses apply to private persons as well as public officials and
figures.

Truth is an absolute defense to a charge of defamation, although it may
not protect against other charges, such as invasion of privacy. Furthermore, it
is not necessary for a potentially defamatory statement to be correct in every
respect in order to be considered true. As long as the statement is materially
true, the defense will likely be acceptable. For example, stating that someone
robbed a bank on a cloudy day in June 2005 would not be actionable even if it
were sunny at the time the person committed the robbery. The essential fact
is that the person robbed the bank—the weather is immaterial to the person's
reputation.

Another defense to defamation actions is that the statement was *opinion*
rather than fact. The rationale for this defense is that an opinion can never

be false, and therefore it cannot defame. However, it is not always easy to distinguish between statements of fact and opinions. For example, in the early 1970s, Gore Vidal sued William F. Buckley Jr. for calling Vidal's book *Myra Breckenridge* pornography. The court held that, in this context, this statement did not assail Vidal's character by actually suggesting that he himself was a pornographer. Thus, the statement was not defamatory.

Someone accused of defamation may also raise the defense of *consent*. It is not defamatory to print material about a person who has given permission for the statements to be published. In this situation, the terms and context of the consent govern the extent of the material that may legally be published.

IN PLAIN ENGLISH

Consent may be obtained indirectly, without the subject knowing the extent of the consent he or she has given.

A major exception to the rule that a party may be liable for republication of a defamatory statement is reporting on *official proceedings* or *public meetings*. As long as the context is a *fair and accurate* account of those proceedings, there can be no liability—even if the statement being reported is defamatory. The requirement that the publication be fair and accurate means that whatever was written must be a balanced and unbiased account. For example, a publisher may not quote only one side of an argument if there was also a rebuttal. However, such accounts need not be literal. It is permissible to include background material to provide context. Nonetheless, extraneous information, such as editorial commentary, is not protected by this defense.

It is not always clear what constitutes an official proceeding or public meeting. Proceedings filed in court definitely constitute official proceedings, while comments made outside of court may not. A newsletter sent by a legislator to constituents does not generally constitute an official proceeding, whereas a political convention probably does.

Reply is another defense to an accusation of defamation. If someone is defamed, that person has a right to reply, even if the original defamer is defamed in the process. This privilege is limited to the extent necessary to meet the original charges and cannot be used to bring fresh accusations. For example, if someone calls another person a communist, that person has a right to reply that the accuser is a liar or a right-wing extremist, because these comments bear some relation to the original comment. But if the person called the accuser a thief, the statement would bear no relation to the accusation and would not be covered by the reply defense.

Defamation in Fiction

Works of fiction can also be subjects of defamation suits and, as such, have presented somewhat different problems for courts and juries. A fictional work, by definition, depicts imaginary events. However, if a real person can be sufficiently identified, he or she may be able to bring a defamation suit against the author and publisher. Disclaimers, such as *any similarities to persons living or dead are purely coincidental*, will likely not protect the author if readers reasonably understand otherwise.

IN PLAIN ENGLISH

Publishers may still be liable for works of fiction if a real person can be sufficiently identified. Disclaimers that similarities are purely coincidental will *not* protect the publisher from liability in such a case.

When the work claimed to be defamatory is fictional, courts will look at the similarities and dissimilarities between the plaintiff and the character and will determine whether a person who knew the plaintiff and who read the book could reasonably conclude that the plaintiff is the person depicted by the character. There are no clear standards that apply, but courts have held that neither mere similarity in names nor strong similarities in the context of a preposterous plot are sufficient to support a defamation claim.

In 1971, author Gwen Davis Mitchell wrote a novel, *Touching*, that told the story of a fictional therapist, Simon Herford, who conducted nude group therapy sessions. Before writing the book, Mitchell attended nude marathon group sessions with Dr. Paul Bindrim. Even though the fictional Dr. Herford and the real-life Dr. Bindrim had different names, physical characteristics, and professional backgrounds, the court found that the fictional doctor was recognizable as Dr. Bindrim to at least some of Mitchell's colleagues. The *Bindrim v. Mitchell* court ultimately held that although the novel was never a commercial success, Mitchell and her publisher, Doubleday, were liable to Dr. Bindrim for $100,000.

To prevail in an action for defamation in a fictional work, the plaintiff must demonstrate that readers will be convinced that the book describes the plaintiff in its defamatory aspects. However, when the allegedly defamatory statements create such a profound alteration of the plaintiff that a reasonable reader could not possibly attribute the defamatory aspects of the character to the plaintiff, there can be no defamation.

Since statements must be capable of being reasonably understood to imply statements of fact, the more obvious it is that a work is exaggerated or not to be taken literally, the less likely it is that a defamation claim will be supported. For example, a court has held that an article in a men's magazine that attempts to humorously describe sexually explicit but fictional acts by Miss Wyoming during the Miss America pageant could not reasonably be understood to depict the person who was the real Miss Wyoming at the time.

Social Media and Defamation

Courts have had differing opinions on whether tweets on Twitter or postings on Facebook constitute defamation. Courts apply standard defamation law and have attempted to divide such cases into general statements of opinion, which are not actionable, and actionable factual claims that damage a person's reputation. As technology evolves, publishers should think carefully about the nature and tenor of speech and counsel authors, employees, and anyone who might be considered an agent of the publisher to fact-check statements and set processes in place to filter out potentially defamatory statements. Savvy publishers should contact an experienced attorney to help establish a social media policy that can educate authors and employees alike in methods and practices to avoid publishing defamatory statements.

NEGLIGENCE

The general principle of negligence in a publishing context is that someone who provides information to another without taking the appropriate amount of care when publishing that information may be liable for any injuries caused by reasonable reliance on that information. However, publishers are generally not liable for providing bad information. In general, publishers have no legal duty to investigate the accuracy of contents of books they publish. Further, publishers are not liable under product liability law unless a book itself causes injury—as distinguished from the information in the book. For example, people who pick and eat mushrooms based on the descriptions provided in a publication may have a cause of action against the author but will have no cause of action against the publisher—even if the mushrooms are poisonous and cause serious harm. However, there will likely be liability if the publisher guarantees the accuracy of the publication, contributes to content, or circulates the information knowing it to be false.

Unfortunately, the law is not so clear when it comes to authors. Some courts have suggested that authors may owe such a duty to readers since they are the persons primarily responsible for ensuring the accuracy and safety of their materials. The circumstances surrounding an author's duty may depend on the nature of the publication, the intended audience, the role of the information in causing the injury, and whether the damage was foreseeable. Generally, the rule is that persons who are in the business of providing information are liable only if they fail to exercise reasonable care or competence in obtaining or communicating the information and know that others will rely on the information. This rule is further tempered by the requirement that it apply to information that is intended to be relied upon by a limited group of persons.

Appropriately drafted disclaimers can reduce both the publisher's and author's risk of liability. In general, blanket disclaimers, such as *the publisher and author assume no liability for the use of the information in the book*, run the risk of being legally ineffective, since one cannot absolve oneself of legal liabilities through simple declarations. The text of a disclaimer should consider the nature of the publication, the role of the information, and the intended audience. For example, this book is written to provide general educational information about legal issues to publishers and is not intended to provide specific legal advice to readers. The laws that affect publishers vary, often in significant detail, throughout the United States and may also change over time. Therefore, while a book such as this one can provide useful information to publishers, it is an inappropriate source of information for addressing the legal matters that may affect the individual affairs of readers. An appropriate disclaimer might state:

> This book is written to provide general educational information about legal issues to a broad audience of publishers and is not intended to provide specific legal advice to individual readers. The laws that affect publishers vary, often in significant detail, throughout the United States and may also change over time. In the event you

have an issue for which you need specific legal advice or services, you should consult an attorney regarding your matter and should not rely on the information in this book.

INCITING OR ABETTING A CRIME

Publishers are generally not legally responsible for the acts of readers who either use the information in their works to commit a crime or are inspired to imitate the acts. Some recent cases have departed somewhat from that rule, but the legal standard for imposing liability remains high.

In 1993, Paladin Press was named the defendant in a lawsuit that asserted it aided and abetted the murders of three people. The essence of the claim was that the person convicted of the contract killing of the victims had relied on the information in the book *Hit Man* to perpetrate the murders. This book provided guidance on how to operate a contract murder business and instructions for killing people and avoiding apprehension. The murders committed were consistent with the book's instructions. The US Court of Appeals ruled that the lawsuit could be tried before a jury because Maryland, unlike most other states, recognized a civil tort for aiding and abetting. The facts of the case led the court to decide that whether the publisher had aided and abetted the murders was question for a jury to decide. It will never be known whether the jury would have found Paladin Press liable, because its insurance company settled the case over the publisher's objections.

A related concern is whether publishers can be liable for copycat scenarios, wherein people emulate depictions of violent or dangerous behavior and injure themselves or others. Courts have consistently held that no liability exists where the depictions were merely copied.

CHAPTER 4

Access to Information

For many authors, conducting their craft depends on getting access to information in the form of interviews, documents, images, and site visits. Although it would be nice for authors if they could legally compel anyone to provide information, the general rule is that individuals and private entities have no obligation to disclose information to other private parties. For example, if the chairman of General Motors declines an invitation to be interviewed, there is not much the author can do about it—except, of course, note that fact in the published work.

This does not mean that authors are always precluded from obtaining the information that most individuals and businesses would prefer to keep hidden from public view. Even though private parties cannot compel others to disclose information, the government has substantial power to collect information from the parties it regulates and is also required to make most of it available to the public. For instance, while a publicly traded corporation would most likely decline a request from an author to describe its most significant litigation matters, it is required by law to disclose this information to the US Securities and Exchange Commission in periodic reports. These reports are available online to the public. Similarly, most industries are reluctant to disclose information about the pollutants they release into the environment, but they are required by law to provide such information to the US Environmental Protection Agency. State and local agencies also collect sensitive information from private entities. Knowing how to use federal and state laws regarding public disclosure can, in many cases, offer an excellent means of obtaining information.

Another aspect of getting information is the right to access sources and laws that govern how you make a record of your information. For example, if an author's writing practice requires him or her to interview people who are not interested in being interviewed, you might want to know how persistent that author can be in seeking information from them before crossing the line and becoming vulnerable to legal action. Similarly, when is it acceptable to walk onto someone else's property to investigate a scene or witness an event taking place on that property? Authors who use tape recorders and similar devices need to know what laws govern the recording of conversations either in person or by telephone. Understanding the legal aspects of collecting and retaining information is important, because failing to comply with the law in this area can inadvertently get the author into trouble, as well as keep him or her from gathering important facts. Remember, if the author is acting on your instructions or if you ratify the author's conduct, you, the publisher, may very well be liable.

THE FREEDOM OF INFORMATION ACT

The Freedom of Information Act (FOIA), enacted in 1966, requires federal agencies to make their records available to the public, with some limited (but significant) exceptions. One of the reasons FOIA can be a powerful research tool is that records held by federal agencies can provide significant information about entities whose activities are subject to the jurisdiction of those agencies. For example, the *Chicago Tribune* used FOIA to collect information to prepare a story about the increase in illness outbreaks associated with school food programs. Specifically, the newspaper requested the computer files on all US Department of Agriculture inspections of meat plants between 1997 and 2000. Using statistical software to analyze 80 million inspection records, the *Tribune* determined that meat plants that sold to the National School Lunch Program had a significantly higher rate of violations than the meat plants that did not. Considering the sensitive nature of the subject, this information would have been almost impossible to collect from private sources.

The Freedom of Information Act can also be used to gather information about individuals. A good example of such a use of FOIA is the way B. G. Burkett and Glenna Whitley used it to gather information for their book *Stolen Valor: How the Vietnam Generation Was Robbed of Its Heroes and Its History*. By using FOIA to obtain the publicly available portions of military records for many prominent activists who claimed to have been veterans of the Vietnam conflict and to be suffering from posttraumatic stress syndrome, the authors discovered that many had never served in Vietnam or been in the military at all. This information served as the foundation for the authors' premise that the media has inaccurately portrayed Vietnam veterans in a negative manner. Absent access to the information provided through FOIA, it is doubtful the authors could have supported their premise with the degree of credibility they established.

Using FOIA, you can access not only paper records, but also film, tape, and electronic files. FOIA requires that federal agencies post guidelines on their websites on how to make requests under FOIA. It also requires agencies to make frequently requested records available in electronic reading rooms on websites.

Agencies are permitted to charge for the copying and time needed to respond to requests, although the first two hours of search time and 100 pages of copying are free of charge to noncommercial requesters. Persons who are affiliated with an educational or noncommercial scientific institution whose purpose is scholarly or scientific research, or who are representatives of the news media, are entitled to a waiver of all search and review fees. In addition, agencies may waive fees if the material requested is likely to contribute significantly to public understanding of the operations or activities of government and is not primarily for the commercial benefit of the requester.

In theory, the use of FOIA should be straightforward. Although some agencies have set up formal procedures for making requests, all the Act requires is that the requester make the request in writing and allow the agency twenty working days to respond. In reality, most agencies take far longer than twenty days and often fail to provide all the information required by law. The remedy for an agency's failure to respond is to file a lawsuit in federal court. Although plaintiffs who prevail in such cases are eligible to recover their attorney fees, bringing an action is time-consuming and often impractical. In addition, if the complainant does not prevail, then the legal fees are likely to be extraordinarily high.

Scope of FOIA

It is important to understand that FOIA's scope is limited to the records kept by federal agencies. For example, it does not apply to records held by the US Congress, federal courts, state and local government agencies, or private persons and entities. However, many congressional and court records are publicly available, and all of the states have public disclosure laws that grant the public the right to access—with some limitations—state records.

There are nine statutory exemptions to FOIA that relate mostly to national security, personal privacy, and proprietary commercial information, such as trade secrets. The following are the nine specific exceptions:

1. National security information concerning national defense or foreign policy, provided that it has been properly classified in accordance with government procedures

2. Records related solely to the internal personnel rules and practices of an agency

3. Information specifically exempted by statute from disclosure

4. Trade secrets and commercial or financial information (that is privileged or confidential), obtained from a person

5. Interagency or intra-agency memoranda or letters that would not be available by law to a party in litigation with the agency

6. Information about individuals in personnel, medical, and similar files, when the disclosure of such information would constitute a clearly unwarranted invasion of personal privacy

7. Records or information compiled for law enforcement purposes, but only to the extent that production of such law enforcement records or information could reasonably be expected to:
   - interfere with enforcement proceedings;
   - deprive a person of a right to an impartial adjudication;
   - constitute an unwarranted invasion of personal privacy;
   - disclose the identity of a confidential source and information furnished by a confidential source;
   - disclose techniques, guidelines, and procedures for law enforcement investigations or prosecutions, if such disclosure could reasonably be expected to risk circumvention of the law; and
   - endanger an individual's life or physical safety

8. Matters that are contained in or related to examination, operation, or condition reports prepared by, on behalf of, or for the use of an agency responsible for the regulation or supervision of financial institutions

9. Geological and geophysical information and data—including maps concerning wells

When a requested document contains some information that falls under an exemption, FOIA requires agencies to release the nonexempt portions. This is important, since it prohibits an agency from withholding an entire document merely because parts are exempt.

Making a Request

When you make FOIA requests, it is important to be clear in your communication and to be reasonable in how you deal with the agency. The request should be made in a letter sent to the FOIA officer at the agency most likely to hold the records. While the Department of State and the Central Intelligence Agency have centralized FOIA offices, most agencies have designated FOIA officers assigned at each unit. For example, if you are seeking the environmental compliance records of a business located in Alaska, you should submit the request to the FOIA officer at the regional office of the US Environmental Protection Agency in Seattle, Washington, which oversees the agency's Alaskan operations. You should not submit the request to the headquarters office in Washington, DC, which handles matters of a national scope.

A FOIA request letter should state that it is a request under the Freedom of Information Act, 5 USC §552, to ensure that the person receiving it will understand that the agency has a legal obligation to respond.

The information sought should be described clearly and with specificity. Providing information such as the dates, authors, recipients, subjects, or titles of documents sought will help the agency expedite the request. Vague and overly broad descriptions are likely to impede efforts to obtain the requested materials. Be sure to ask for a fee waiver if you are eligible.

Most agencies have specific guidelines for making FOIA requests that can be obtained from their websites and online forms that streamline and simplify the process. However, federal agencies are required to comply with FOIA requests irrespective of whether the agency guidelines are followed or whether their online forms are used. A template for a FOIA request letter is provided on the next page and can be used for noncommercial requests. In the event the information is for commercial use, delete the paragraph regarding the fee waiver.

FOIA Officer
[Name of Agency]
[Address of Agency]

Re: Freedom of Information Act Request

Dear Sir or Madam:

This is a request made pursuant to the Freedom of Information Act, 5 USC §552. I request that a copy of the documents containing the following information be provided to me:

[Describe the documents or information sought as specifically as possible.]

[Alternate provisions when information is requested for noncommercial use:

(personal) I am an individual seeking information for a noncommercial use and request that fees associated with complying with this request be waived.

(news media) I am a representative of the news media affiliated with (name of publication, radio station, or television station) and make this request as part of news gathering and not for a commercial use.

(scientific or academic) I am affiliated with an educational or noncommercial scientific institution, and this request is made for a scholarly or scientific purpose and not for a commercial use.]

I request a waiver of all fees for this request because disclosure of the requested information is in the public interest. Specifically, the information is likely to contribute significantly to public understanding of the operations or activities of the government and is not primarily in my commercial interest for the following reasons:

_____

_____

If a fee is assessed, I am willing to pay up to a maximum of $_____. If you estimate that the fees will exceed this limit, please inform me first.

Thank you for your consideration of this request.

[Signature]

IN PLAIN ENGLISH

Visit www.foia.gov for guidance in preparing a request, identifying the appropriate department, and for links to online submission forms.

FOIA and Privacy Issues

A significant and not altogether clear type of FOIA exemption deals with personal privacy. The government maintains a great deal of personal information about the lives of most citizens, which can be relevant to persons writing about matters of public interest. Although Congress included the privacy provisions in FOIA to protect the legitimate interests of individuals, there has been a growing concern that government agencies are improperly using these exemptions to justify the withholding of information.

Congress enacted the Privacy Act of 1974, amending the Freedom of Information Act in order to protect the privacy of information about people contained in records kept by federal agencies. It prohibits disclosure of personally identifiable information without the consent of the person affected unless the disclosure was permitted by twelve statutory exceptions. The Act also allows individuals to get, and then amend, their own records along with other provisions. Disclosure is permitted for certain US governmental statistical purposes, routine uses by a US government agency, archival purposes, law enforcement purposes, congressional investigations, pursuant to court orders, and other limited purposes.

In recent years, about two-thirds of FOIA denials have been based on exemptions relating to privacy. The most significant expansion of the privacy exemptions occurred in 1989. The US Supreme Court ruled that whether disclosure of a private document is warranted depends on the nature of the requested document, as well as its relationship to FOIA's central purpose of allowing public access to official information that sheds light on an agency's performance of its statutory duties. Under this holding, the disclosure of information about private citizens can be denied unless the requester shows that it will reveal something material about an agency's conduct.

In *World Publishing Co. v. U.S. Dept. of Justice*, a Tenth Circuit case, a newspaper publisher appealed from an adverse lower court ruling denying disclosure under FOIA of booking photographs (mug shots). Finding that disclosure of the photos was unlikely to contribute significantly to the public's understanding of how a governmental agency was doing its job, and that the implication of criminal activity associated with mug shots was an unwarranted invasion of the privacy of the arrested parties that outweighed any public interest in disclosure, the appellate court upheld the denial. The same conclusion was reached in *Detroit Free Press Inc. v. U.S. Dept. of Justice*, a Sixth Circuit case overruling a ten-year-old determination to the contrary, finding no privacy interest—ever—in such photos, recognizing the fact that such photos were taken in very humiliating and embarrassing circumstances, and ruling that each case would need to be determined on its own facts in the future.

A good example of how courts balance privacy against public access to government information can be seen in the litigation commenced for the purpose of obtaining the death scene photographs of Vincent Foster. A White House deputy counsel and close friend of President Bill Clinton, Foster was found dead from a gunshot wound in a Virginia park. The local law enforcement agency deemed the death an apparent suicide. However, in light of the attention given to the allegations of scandals committed by the Clinton administration, Foster's death became the subject of five separate official investigations and several private ones. There were numerous FOIA requests made to obtain the records held by the Federal Bureau of Investigation, the Office of Independent Counsel, and the National Park Service.

Although many of the records were provided, the National Park Service withheld ten color photographs of Foster's body taken at the scene of his death, contending that they were exempt on the basis of their exceptional sensitivity and potential to cause pain to Foster's surviving family.

FOIA establishes a higher threshold for determining the entitlement to obtain information with regard to privacy issues. In the normal FOIA request, the requester does not have to provide reasons for wanting the information. However, when seeking information that pertains to the private affairs of individuals, authors should be careful to explain the relevance of the information they seek and should provide some sort of evidence as to why the information is needed to uncover official misconduct.

IN PLAIN ENGLISH

The exact nature of the evidence required to show that the public need for the information overcomes the privacy interests associated with exempting its disclosure is not defined.

Once a request involves a privacy issue, the government must consider whether a public interest is involved. To enhance the chance that your request will be fulfilled, it is important for you to make clear how the disclosure would benefit the general public and how the information would shed light on an agency's performance of its statutory duties. Should the government withhold the information on privacy grounds, it can sometimes help to renew the request and ask that the government redact or delete the identifying information in order to protect the privacy interests at issue.

In 2011, in *FCC v. AT&T, Inc.*, the United States Supreme Court confronted the issue of whether, for purposes of FOIA, corporations were entitled to the same privacy protections that individual people were with respect to the disclosure of law enforcement records. The court ruled that they were not: only individual people were entitled to this privacy, as only people were entitled to privacy protection with respect to their personal and medical information, but corporations were entitled to maintain the privacy of trade secret, commercial, and financial information.

What to Do If Your Request Is Denied

In the event an agency denies the FOIA request made by you or one of your authors, there is a right to appeal to the courts. Agencies denying a request are required to provide a written response describing the reasons for the denial, names and titles of each person responsible for the denial, and the procedures required to invoke judicial assistance.

The general rule when dealing with government agencies is that you must give the agency an opportunity to correct its errors through administrative review or appeal processes before you can file a judicial action to compel performance. This is known as the *doctrine of exhaustion of administrative remedies*. However, FOIA treats an agency's failure to comply with the time limits for responding to a request as a constructive exhaustion of administrative remedies. If an agency does not respond within twenty working days (as required by FOIA), the requester may seek immediate judicial review without the necessity of filing an administrative appeal. Because it is common for agencies to not meet the statutory time limits, in many cases, it is possible to file a judicial action without waiting to see the response. This approach is not justified in most routine cases but could be an effective way to compel compliance with FOIA when the requester believes it likely that the agency will not respond substantively.

If the agency responds to the FOIA request before a judicial action has been filed, FOIA requires that the requester administratively appeal a denial and allow the agency at least twenty working days to decide the appeal before the requester can commence a lawsuit. Some agencies have formal rules that govern to whom the appeal must be filed and what information must be provided. In such cases, a request for an appeal will not be deemed received if the requester does not follow those regulations. Should the agency fail to decide the appeal within the twenty working days or decide the appeal against the requester, then the requester is legally entitled to file a lawsuit to compel compliance.

Any FOIA lawsuit can be filed in the District of Columbia, but filing outside that jurisdiction requires there be some connection between the FOIA request and that jurisdiction. In most cases, the connection can be as simple as the jurisdiction in which the requester resides. However, filing suit in a jurisdiction in which the agency maintains a regional or local office requires that a substantial amount of the activity related to the request took place at those offices.

What the Court Can Do

Whether an agency has improperly withheld records most often depends on whether an exemption applies to the documents at issue. Other common issues include whether any other responsive records exist or whether the agency has released all responsive records to the requester. If the court finds that documents have been improperly withheld, it will order the agency to release them.

Another important FOIA provision allows the trial court to award reasonable attorney's fees and litigation costs when the requester has substantially prevailed in the case. This award is limited to fees and costs incurred in litigating the case brought pursuant to FOIA and does not apply to costs or legal services rendered at the administrative level. In deciding whether to award fees, the court will consider first whether the plaintiff is in fact eligible for an award of fees and costs, and second whether the plaintiff is entitled to the award.

Plaintiffs (requesters) are generally found eligible as long as they actually incurred attorney fees. Parties representing themselves, even if they are attorneys, are generally ineligible to recover fees for their labor—although they can still recover costs.

Entitlement is evaluated according to four factors:

1. the public benefit derived from the case;
2. the commercial benefit to the complainant;
3. the nature of the complainant's interest in the records sought; and
4. whether the government's withholding had a reasonable basis in law.

Keep in mind that even if a plaintiff is found to be eligible and entitled to recover attorney fees, the actual award of fees and costs remains within the discretion of the court. In most instances, it will be unlikely that a court will award attorney's fees in the absence of a judgment in favor of the plaintiff or a court-ordered consent decree.

Plaintiffs who settle a FOIA case after the court orders the agency to release documents but before the court rules on the attorney fees request will usually lose their right to request an award of such fees. From a practical standpoint, plaintiffs in FOIA cases should negotiate the recovery of attorney's fees as part of any settlement and should insist that the court consummate the settlement in the form of a consent decree.

FOIA requesters sometimes need to demonstrate great patience and persistence and seek redress in court before getting what they want. This was demonstrated in the case of *Coleman v. DEA*, in which an author made a FOIA request to the Drug Enforcement Administration, asking for records concerning the government's regulation of a drug. Although federal agencies are supposed to respond to such requests within twenty days, the DEA took over sixteen months to respond in any way and then responded by denying the request because the author had not paid what it considered the right amount for a processing fee. The author appealed the fee determination, arguing that he was not a commercial requester, that he was a published author of academic and technical materials, and that the information would contribute to the public's understanding of how the agency enforced the Controlled Substances Act. It took seven more months before the Department of Justice sent the request back to the DEA for reconsideration. After waiting another four months and still hearing nothing, the author sought help from the lower court. Even after the case was filed, the DEA still refused to eliminate or reduce the fee it wanted and refused to give him the requested documents.

The lower court then refused to order the DEA to grant his request, saying that he had not paid the fee or waited for the DEA to make a determination on reconsideration before he filed his case. The appeals court ruled that because the author had already waited almost two and a half years and because of the "extended and inexcusable agency delay" that he was entitled to come to court for help when he did. The case did not end there, however; the appellate court sent the case back to the lower court to reconsider its decision. Since there were no more reported decisions on this case, it is unknown whether the author ever got his documents.

STATE PUBLIC INFORMATION LAWS

Individual states have their own public disclosure laws. In *Bainbridge Island Police Guild v. City of Puyallup*, an author sought disclosure, under Washington state law, of police investigative reports pertaining to a case in which a woman alleged that a police officer sexually assaulted her. The reports found the claims to be unsubstantiated, and the officer claimed privacy rights in his identity. After analysis, balancing the interest of the public in disclosure, including information about how the complaint was handled and the officer's right to privacy, the court ordered production of the report with the officer's name redacted. As can be seen, many of the same exceptions and analyses that apply in FOIA cases also apply under these state laws.

Many states also have open meeting laws that allow members of the public to observe certain kinds of government meetings. These laws are commonly referred to as *sunshine laws* or *open records laws*. They are mostly modeled after FOIA and typically require that records maintained by state, county, and city governments be made available to members of the public for inspection and copying, subject to some limited exemptions. The exemptions tend to protect the same kinds of interests that underlie the exemption from disclosure under FOIA but are more related to state matters, such as student records at public schools.

The exemptions under state laws can sometimes be narrowed or broadened, depending on the interests involved and the wording of the state statutes. For example, a county in Arizona passed an ordinance that required nude dancers to obtain work permits. The applications for the permits required the registrants to provide to the county their real names, addresses, telephone numbers, and previous aliases. Because of this, a commercial establishment that hired such dancers challenged the ordinance on the grounds that it unconstitutionally interfered with their free expression. The information was available to the public under the state public records law and thus could subject the dancers to unwelcome harassment and stalking. The court refused to strike down the ordinance as unconstitutional but did hold that the personal information in the nude dancer work permits cannot be revealed under Arizona's open records law.

Most open meeting laws do not provide the public with the right to ask questions at meetings but do allow citizens to observe the proceedings and provide reasonable comment. The typical open meeting statute describes the kinds of meetings that are open to the public and mandates that any person be permitted to attend any meeting, with the exception of executive sessions held to discuss sensitive matters, such as employee discipline, litigation, and security. Other typical requirements include providing prior notice of meetings to the public and maintaining minutes of meetings. These statutes generally encompass those meetings that are held for the purposes of briefing, discussion of public business, formation of policy, or the taking of any action by a public body. Examples include the meetings of planning commissions, school boards, and public library trustees. Open meeting laws do not, however, allow access to all meetings in which state business is conducted. For example, they do not encompass informal meetings of agency staff held in the routine course of their duties.

ACCESS TO PEOPLE AND PLACES

Being able to conduct interviews is an important way for authors to obtain information, and being able to obtain access is critical for many kinds of writing. Just because someone needs information for a writing project does not necessarily give them any special legal right of access. In other words, publishers and their authors must obey the same laws that apply to the general public.

Publishers and authors also need to be aware that property owners are free to place express or implied limits on what takes place when they allow others to enter their premises. For example, authors can generally assume that a restaurant owner will not object to an author inviting and interviewing a person over lunch, because these kinds of activities are compatible with the nature of the restaurant business. It would, however, be unreasonable to assume that a restaurant owner would tolerate your uninvited and unwanted attempts to interview a celebrity patron that you encountered there by chance.

In the event you encounter someone in a public place, you are free to ask questions, provided that you do not persist to an unreasonable extent if the person indicates that he or she does not want to be interviewed. The line between appropriate and inappropriate persistence is not always clear, but repeatedly asking questions in the face of objections from a clearly unwilling subject can violate privacy rights (and possibly criminal laws directed against harassment and disorderly conduct). Extreme efforts to pursue unwilling individuals for interviews may even run afoul of stalking statutes. Many states have passed laws that make it a crime to repeatedly engage in activities such as following, surveying, and harassing, with an intent to either harm a person or cause a material level of fear or emotional distress.

Misrepresentations

One aspect of interviewing that publishers need to be careful about is misrepresenting the reasons why they or their authors want to interview a person. Irrespective of the ethical ramifications, falsely representing one's purpose for requesting an interview may (depending on the circumstances) invalidate the subject's consent and expose the publisher to liability for fraud or invasion of privacy. The *doctrine of fraud* is somewhat technical, and succeeding on a claim requires a party to prove the following elements:

- there was a representation of a material fact
- the falsity of that representation
- intent to deceive
- a justifiable reliance upon the misrepresentation by the party deceived, which induces him or her to act thereon
- injury to the party deceived as a result of his or her reliance on the misrepresentation

All these elements can be subject to subtle legal nuances, and it is not always easy to discern when or how they will be applied to a particular set of facts.

This doctrine was used when two undercover reporters were hired as food workers in the meat departments at two Food Lion supermarkets. Although the reporters worked at Food Lion supermarkets for only a short period, they gathered a considerable amount of information about unsanitary meat handling practices and helped produce a *Prime Time Live* broadcast that was sharply critical of Food Lion. The supermarket chain sued on the grounds that it had been defrauded, because the employment applications had not been completed by the reporters with the intent to work as bona fide employees of Food Lion.

When your authors are interviewing a subject, you should also be careful to caution them not to affirmatively misrepresent that they will make or refrain from making particular statements and then fail to live up to their end of the bargain. For example, if your author told a celebrity that he intended to write a favorable magazine article when he intended the opposite, it would be improper to elicit and publish private facts that would tarnish the celebrity's reputation. This does not mean that an author is required to tell a person ahead of time that she may be writing something they will find unpalatable. Your author can even engage in a bit of flattery if that encourages the subject to open up. But if the author makes a false promise to induce the person interviewed to say something he or she would not have otherwise said, there may be potential liability. Remember, if you authorize or ratify an author's improper conduct, you may be liable for those wrongful acts.

Trespassing

Obtaining access to places in order to view scenes and events is governed by property laws, which include the ability of landowners to prevent individuals from trespassing on their property. Property owners have the legal right to exclude others from their property and to limit the activities of those they allow to enter. This means they are free to exclude anyone from their property irrespective of the reason. Should an author ignore or disregard the owner's right to exclude them from their property or to limit their activities, authors can be held liable for trespassing.

Although the law against trespassing prohibits entry onto another's property without the owner's permission, the law recognizes that in many cases, people may rely on the customs of the community that establish implicit permission to enter someone else's property. For example, members of the public are allowed to enter the public areas of commercial businesses, such as restaurants and stores, during business hours. Conversely, it is well recognized that the public generally may not enter places such as residences or industrial properties without getting explicit permission to do so.

Public Places

Another category of places where authors may reasonably assume they have the right of access are public places. The most open public places are those where the public has an established right to express themselves politically, the most obvious being city sidewalks and public parks. Some cities have gone so far as to enact ordinances that encourage the maximum public use of facilities, such as parks. While the government can impose restrictions when necessary to protect public welfare, these are typically addressed to the public at large and rarely affect publishers or authors specifically. The primary restrictions for activities on public sidewalks are prohibitions against obstructing free passage and access to properties adjoining the sidewalk. The ordinances and rules that apply to city parks typically prohibit things such as littering and unreasonable noise.

It is sometimes difficult to determine whether the property owner allows public access to property, and judgment must be exercised. A good example is an open field that shows obvious signs of public use, such as paths or recreational structures, and is not posted against trespass. Although such activities may indicate that the owner allows the general public to enter the property, there is no legal presumption that the landowner has consented to people entering the property. Furthermore, owners are not required to post signs prohibiting trespassing even though they want to exclude the public from entering the property. Whether it is reasonable to enter such properties is a judgment call to be made at your own risk. A good-faith—but mistaken—belief that you have permission may not protect you from a claim of trespass.

Consent

Individuals are always free to enter a property when owners or their agents knowingly consent. It is, however, important that you understand that there can be significant legal limits on the effect of consent. In some cases, even the knowing failure of an owner to object to someone's entry can invalidate a defense to a trespassing claim, such as when the owner mistakenly believes that an individual was accompanying the police to record evidence as part of an investigation. If the author is actually working for the media and did not obtain permission from the owner, he or she could be liable for committing trespass. As previously pointed out, when an author is authorized by you or you ratify the author's improper conduct, you may very well be liable for those wrongful acts. Therefore, you should be careful not to assume that the absence of objections implies consent if the circumstances suggest that the property owner could reasonably misunderstand why the author is present. Caution is important, and when in doubt you should advise the authors you work with to determine whether their activities are proper. Working with an experienced publishing law attorney in questionable situations is very important.

It is important to determine whether the person giving permission to enter a property has the legal capacity to do so. The legal capacity of a person to consent on behalf of the owner depends on his or her relationship to the owner, as well as the ability to appreciate the nature, extent, and consequences of the consent. People such as very young children and the mentally impaired are generally presumed not to have the legal capacity to give permission to enter a property, because they lack sufficient judgment to consider the effect of any consent.

When seeking entry to a property, it is prudent to obtain permission from people who appear to be competent adults who have the kind of relationship to the owner that indicates their authority to authorize entry. In many cases, you can reasonably infer that people such as the managers of commercial establishments have such authority. Specific factors to consider include the stature of the party, the nature of the property, and the general customs that apply. It is equally important to understand that not all employees have the authority to allow entry. For instance, it would be unreasonable to expect that the janitor at a bank would have the legal authority to let someone in after hours and inspect the contents of a safety deposit box. When in doubt about a person's authority, permission should be sought from someone who is more certain to have authority.

A related issue is whether public officials, such as police and fire officers, can allow the media and other publishers onto private property to report on searches, firefighting, and similar activities. Although there is some authority supporting the proposition that it is customary in parts of the country for law enforcement to invite the media to cover police activities, it is generally unwise to assume that government officials have the authority to allow access without the owner's permission. Most courts that have considered this issue have ruled the other way.

Sometimes you may encounter a situation where the person who objects to entry to a property may not have the authority to exclude anyone. In such cases, the scope of authority to refuse entry is the same as the scope of authority to grant it, and third parties have no rights to order someone off a property unless the owner has given them the right to do so. An example of this kind of situation would be a store manager who tries to expel a reporter from a common area at a shopping mall to keep them from covering an event associated with the store. In general, tenants do not have control over the common areas of buildings normally accessible to the public.

Damages

Finally, although landowners and their agents may use force to evict a trespasser, the law generally requires them to first ask the trespasser to leave unless the circumstances indicate that the request would be futile. They can, however, still sue a trespasser for damages in civil court even if that person leaves willingly after the owner's request to do so. The amount of damages that may be awarded will vary, depending on the circumstances of each case. The damages might be only a few cents for a technical trespass that causes no real harm but can be significant when the trespass results in actual injury, such as the destruction of property. In cases in which the trespasser enters property posted against trespassing or willfully disregards an owner's request to leave, they may be liable for criminal trespass, as well.

In the Food Lion case previously discussed, a claim was also made that the undercover reporters had trespassed onto the supermarkets' premises, because its consent was voided as a result of the reporters' misrepresentations about their purpose for entry. The court in that case ultimately ruled that because the reporters went into areas of the stores that were not open to the public and acted adversely to the interests of their second employer, Food Lion, they had breached their duty of loyalty and thereby abused their authority to be on Food Lion's property. Although the court upheld the judgment as it pertained to the trespassing claim, the damages awarded to Food Lion were only $2.00.

IN PLAIN ENGLISH

The law of trespassing as applied in these kinds of situations varies substantially among the states.

RECORDING INTERVIEWS

Whether it is lawful to record a conversation depends on the circumstances of each case. It is always legal to record conversations when all the parties are aware they are being recorded and give their consent. Such consent can be explicit, such as when a person verbally acknowledges that the conversation is being recorded, or implicit, such as when the person sees the recorder operating in front of them and does not object. Of course, authors and publishers are better protected by obtaining explicit consent, since whether a person has implicitly consented can be a matter of interpretation.

Federal and state statutes govern the use of recording equipment, and unlawful use can result in civil liability and criminal prosecution (in some cases). Some states permit people to record telephone conversations to which they are a party without informing the other parties. In other words, as long as you are a party to the call, it is legal for you to record it. Other states require that all the parties know they are being recorded and provide their consent, including California, Connecticut, Florida, Illinois, Maryland, Massachusetts, Michigan, Montana, New Hampshire, Pennsylvania, and Washington. This number may change, as bills are pending for changes in some states. Careful research should be undertaken with respect to the status of your state at the time you consider recording any conversation.

In situations in which the parties to the call are in different states, the law of the state in which the recording device is located will likely apply. This is a fairly common situation when people are talking by long-distance telephone. For example, if two people are participating in a call between telephones in Oregon and Washington, the party in Washington could not lawfully record the conversation unless both parties know they are being recorded and give their consent. The party in Oregon, however, could lawfully record the conversation—even if the party in Washington is unaware that the call is being recorded. The laws among the states vary, and it is possible that nuances in their drafting could affect how the laws apply in an interstate context. The rules on recording apply to Internet calls, Skype calls, as well as any other form of interstate communications.

IN PLAIN ENGLISH

In situations in which the law of one state conflicts with that of another on the issue of whether all parties need to consent, it is advised that you seek specific legal advice before recording without the consent of all parties.

The law regarding recording in-person conversations tends to follow those that apply to telephone conversations in most, but not all, states. For example, Oregon law allows the recording of telephone calls when a single participant consents but prohibits the recording of face-to-face conversations unless all parties consent. Therefore, it is important for you to determine what the law is in your jurisdiction before you record conversations either in person or by any form of electronic communication.

SEEKING HELP

For many authors and publishers, obtaining access to information or to locations is essential, yet the law establishes rules that must be adhered to. The rights of individuals and property owners must be balanced against those of the publisher. The guidelines are often blurry, and publishers may be forced to risk both civil liability and perhaps penal sanctions. By working with competent, experienced publishing attorneys, you can reduce your exposure and likely achieve most, if not all, of your publishing objectives.

CHAPTER 5

Copyright Basics

Copyright is a double-edged sword. On the one hand, copyright is the primary vehicle for protecting a publisher's literary creations. Unless publishers have the legal ability to prevent others from copying the works they publish, it would be very difficult to preclude others from using the fruits of the publisher's labor without compensation. Fortunately, there are strong copyright laws that enable publishers to prevent others from wrongfully appropriating their works. On the other hand, overly restrictive copyright laws may chill a publisher's creative endeavors. Authors frequently use the works of others as the basis for research and literary development, sometimes to the extent of quoting portions of other works *verbatim*. From this perspective, unless the copyright law provides some flexibility, many publishers could be inhibited for fear that an author's work may infringe on another work and expose the publisher to liability.

Copyright law in the United States has its foundations in the Constitution, which provides, in Article I, Section 8, that Congress shall have the power "to promote the progress of science and the useful arts, by securing for a limited time to authors and inventors the exclusive right to their respective writings and discoveries." The first Congress exercised this power and enacted a copyright law, which has been periodically revised by later Congresses.

In 1909, Congress passed the Copyright Act. It remained in effect for more than half a century but had some fundamental problems affecting its usefulness. The 1909 Act was not the exclusive source of copyright law. Copyright protection or its equivalent was also provided by common law (that body of law developed by the courts, independent of statutes) and various state statutes. This caused considerable confusion, since copyright protection, and avoiding copyright infringement, varied among the states and careful examination of a variety of different laws was required. Further, new technology, such as radio, microfilm, television, videotape, and computer software, created the need for a revision that would provide more appropriate copyright protection for newer information systems.

The Copyright Act was substantially revised in 1976, and its provisions became effective on January 1, 1978. Under the Copyright Revision Act of 1976, the extent to which works are protected by copyright depends on whether they were published before 1978, created before 1978 but published thereafter, or created during or after 1978. It is important to be aware of the basic differences in the two laws and which law applies to a given work.

The 1976 Act largely resolved the problem of conflicting state laws by preempting and nullifying them. In other words, the copyright of all works created after 1978 are governed solely by the 1976 Act and may not be regulated by the states. However, the Act does not preempt the common law or the statutes of any state for copyright claims that are not within the scope of the federal statute.

In 1988, the Act was amended to facilitate the United States becoming a party to the international copyright treaty known as the *Berne Convention*. One important aspect of the revisions for publishers is that copyright notices are no longer required as a condition for copyright protection. However, as discussed in chapter 6, such notices are strongly recommended.

WHAT IS COPYRIGHT?

A copyright is a collection of five exclusive intangible rights. These are

1. the right to reproduce the work;
2. the right to prepare derivative works;
3. the right of distribution;
4. the right to perform the work; and
5. the right to display the work.

Under the Copyright Act of 1976, the general rule is that protected works may be reproduced only with the permission of the copyright owner. There are some significant exceptions, however, which are discussed in chapter 6.

Copyright also covers the right to prepare *derivative works* based on the copyrighted work. A derivative work is one that it based on another work. Under copyright law, the holder of the copyright has the sole right to prepare such works or license that right to others. Examples of derivative works include dramatizations, fictionalized versions, film versions, abridgments, condensations, annotated editions, and any other work that is recast, transformed, or adapted from an original.

Authors can even obtain a copyright on a work derived from a work in the public domain if a distinguishable variation is created. For example, the Latin text of Virgil's *Aeneid* cannot be copyrighted, but an original translation can be. As a result, no one would be able to legally reproduce the translation, whereas anyone may copy Virgil's original or create other translations.

The copyright holder has the *initial right to control distribution* of copies of the protected work to the public. However, once an author conveys a copy of the protected work, the right to control the further distribution of that copy, by virtue of the copyright law, ends. This rule, known as the *first-sale doctrine*, does not apply if the work is intended to be in the temporary possession of someone, such as by a rental or loan. In these instances, the copyright owner retains the right to control the further sale or other distribution of the work. In addition, the first-sale doctrine does not apply if the author or copyright owner contracts with the purchaser to restrict the purchaser's freedom to distribute or dispose of the copy. Application of the first-sale doctrine to digital books will be discussed further in chapter 13.

The next aspect of copyright is the *right to display or perform the work in public*. Once the copyright owner has sold a copy of the work, however, the owner of the copy generally has the right to display that copy.

WHAT CAN BE COPYRIGHTED?

The Copyright Act provides protection for a limited time to creators of works that meet certain legal requirements. (Issues surrounding that protection are discussed in chapter 6.) The scope of works that can be protected is very broad and encompasses, but is not limited to, writings, images, music, architectural design, recordings, and choreography.

To qualify for protection, the work must be independently created by an author and show at least some minimal creativity. For example, an alphabetical list of customers published by a telephone company was held not to be entitled to copyright protection by the US Supreme Court in *Feist Publications, Inc. v. Rural Tel. Serv. Co.*, but a directory that arranged the subscribers' information in an original way—for example, into categories such as net worth or age—likely would be.

The requirement that the work show some creativity to qualify for copyright protection does not require that the work be of a particular quality or suited to particular tastes. In the past, the Copyright Office occasionally denied registration to works considered immoral or obscene, even though it had no express authority for doing so. This practice has changed. The Copyright Office will not attempt to decide whether a work is obscene, and copyright registration will not be refused because of the questionable character of any work.

Nonetheless, the Copyright Office is authorized by the Copyright Act to draft regulations that define the scope of copyright coverage and has chosen to deny protection to *blank forms and similar works, designed to record rather than convey information*. This category includes time cards, scorecards, address books, and the like. Even items such as these, however, have been granted copyright protection for certain creative embellishments. Short phrases, such as titles, slogans, or mottoes, cannot be copyrighted. However, these types of works may be protectable under trademark law.

The other critical requirement for copyright protection is that the work be *fixed in a tangible medium of expression*. For publishers, this requirement is generally simple to meet. A literary work is protected by copyright as soon as it is handwritten, typed, or entered into a computer. Spoken words are not protected unless they are fixed into a recording of any kind or read from text. In the first case, the protection extends to the contribution of the person whose voice is captured and the contribution of the person responsible for capturing and processing the sounds to make the final recording, if any. In the second instance, the text being recited is protectable—extemporaneous speech is not.

The 1976 Copyright Act expressly exempts from copyright protection any *idea, procedure, process, system, method of operation, concept, principle, or discovery*. In other words, a copyright extends only to protect the expression of creations of the mind and not to the ideas themselves. Frequently, there is no clear dividing line between an idea and its expression—a problem that is considered in greater detail in the section on infringement in chapter 6. For now, it is sufficient to note that no matter how original or creative a pure idea such as a mathematical equation is, it cannot be copyrighted.

Basic plot ideas or themes are not protected by copyright. Fictional characters, when sufficiently developed and expressed, can be protected by copyright. Cartoon characters, which are visual works, are sufficiently delineated to qualify for copyright protection. Unfortunately, the standard is more difficult to apply to characters described in written works. Clichéd characters of the type that naturally flow from a common theme are considered to be ideas and therefore cannot be copyrighted. An example would be a waiter in a short story who is incidental to the plot and does nothing more than take an order.

As plots become more developed and characters become more idiosyncratic, at some point they cross the line into expression and may be protected by copyright. A good example of such a character is James Bond, as developed in the works by Ian Fleming and various screen publishers.

Compilations may also be copyrighted, provided that the preexisting materials are collected and arranged in a new or original form. Compilations such as magazines can be copyrighted as a whole, even though individual contributions or articles may also be individually copyrighted. Similarly, compilations of works that are not otherwise protected by copyright may be copyrighted if the requirements for minimum creativity and originality are met in selecting and arranging the pieces included in the compilation.

OWNERSHIP

The general rule regarding ownership of copyright is that the author of a work is the initial owner of the copyright in that work. Unless there is a written agreement that transfers the copyright to another, the author retains the copyright.

The authors of a *joint work* are co-owners of the copyright in the work. A joint work is a work prepared by more than one author with the intention that their contributions be merged into inseparable or interdependent parts of the whole. If there is no intention to create a unitary work, then each author may own the copyright to that author's individual contribution. For example, one author may own the rights to the written text and another the rights to the illustrations. Theatrical works, for example, are generally considered joint works, coauthored by the script publisher, composer, lyricist, set designer, choreographer, director, and others who have contributed to the final production. The owner of the copyright may be determined by a contract entered into by the contributors. In order for there to be a joint work, each author's contribution must be independently *copyrightable*. Mere ideas, directions, and suggestions are not sufficient to entitle a person to the status of being a joint author.

Work for Hire

The exception to the rule that the author owns the copyright in a work is the *work for hire* doctrine. If the work was created by an employee as part of his or her job duties, it is considered a work for hire. The copyright in these works belongs to the employer, and the parties cannot directly contract otherwise. An employment contract may provide that creating such material not be part of the scope of employment. In this case, it is probable that the employee will be considered the owner of the copyright. Care should be exercised in drafting such a contract so that it will produce the desired result. Another way to accomplish this is for the employer to assign the copyright to an employee.

Under the Copyright Act of 1976, a work created by an independent contractor (as opposed to an employee) may be considered a work for hire only if

1. the contractor and employer agree *in writing* that the work performed is to be a work for hire; and
2. the work is specially ordered or commissioned to be a contribution to a collective work, translation, supplementary work (one that introduces, revises, comments upon, or assists a work by another author), compilation, instructional text, answer material for a test, atlas, motion picture, or audiovisual work.

In the absence of a written agreement, the independent contractor will own the copyright in a commissioned work.

Determining whether a particular work qualifies as a work for hire can be difficult. It is not always clear whether the author was an employee or a contractor of the party claiming the copyright. An author is more likely to be considered an employee the closer the relationship resembles regular, salaried employment. For example, the copyright in articles written by a journalist working on the staff of a newspaper will be owned by the newspaper, but the copyright to articles written by a freelancer will not be, absent a written agreement to the contrary. When evaluating whether a party is an employee or an independent contractor, courts look to factors such as:

- the degree of control the employer had over the work (its content or style);
- the employer's ability to control the employee (working hours and schedule); and
- the conduct of the employer (the nature of the employer business and method of compensation, such as lump sum payment or paycheck).

These can be complex issues. Contracts should be drafted by experienced and knowledgeable attorneys in order that the desired outcome be achieved.

TRADEMARK ISSUES

Trademark laws prohibit using marks in ways that might confuse consumers over the origin or sponsorship of a product or service. For the most part, trademarks do not pose significant legal issues with regard to publishers and individual books, although misconceptions are not uncommon. Absent using a trademark in a way that would likely confuse consumers, the authors you work with are free to refer to trademarks in their works. Similarly, there is no requirement that your author place a trademark symbol, such as ™, after a brand name when mentioned in a work. For example, an author of a cookbook is free to describe a recipe in which an ingredient identified as "Rice Krispies" is mixed with another ingredient identified as "Coca-Cola," instead of the more traditional ingredient of milk. There is no need to identify the ingredients as puffed rice cereal or as cola beverage, nor must a trademark symbol be placed next to the product names. Although the Coca-Cola Company and the Kellogg Company might find the use of their products in the recipe unappetizing, the recipe does not imply that either company is endorsing the book and they would, therefore, likely have no basis for claiming infringement. On the other hand, using *The Coca-Cola Company Book of Breakfast Ideas* as the title would imply an endorsement and thus would be actionable if not authorized by the company.

Trademark disparagement can be a complicated issue, since some states have laws regarding use of trademarks to malign or ridicule products and companies. It is not unlawful to mention a trademark in truthful critical evaluation of a product or company. For example, one is free to state that the safety of ephedra products such as Metabolife has been questioned by federal regulators. On the other hand, false or unflattering depictions of a trademark can constitute disparagement under some circumstances. For example, a screenplay in which the main character donned a uniform similar to that worn by the Dallas Cowboys Cheerleaders and engaged in various sex acts while clad, to various degrees, in the uniform was found to disparage the trademark of the Dallas Cowboys Cheerleaders organization.

Publishers should be sensitive to trademark issues. In fact, it is a good idea to check Books In Print and to do a trademark search before adopting the title for a book. If the title is identical to the title of another book or if there is a likelihood that the desired title will result in market confusion, then you should adopt another title. Book titles are protectable as trademarks, though, only when there are two or more titles in a series; then that title can be registered under the federal trademark law, known as the Lanham Act. For example, the title of this book, *The Law (in Plain English)® for Publishers*, is a registered trademark, since there are numerous books in the Law (in Plain English)® series.

CHAPTER 6

Copyright Protection

A copyright is a form of property that can be created by individuals and transferred to others. Unlike most property that exists in tangible form, there are nuances that affect the ability to assert claims of ownership. Publishers need to understand the nature of their rights and how licensing agreements can affect their ability to profit from and market their work. Otherwise, they are at risk of needlessly yielding their rights to other parties.

CREATION OF COPYRIGHT

Under the 1909 Copyright Act, a statutory copyright was created when the work was published with a copyright notice (at which time it was required to be registered promptly with the US Copyright Office). Unpublished works could be protected by common law copyright doctrines developed under state law. The 1976 Copyright Act dramatically changed the law in that respect by making works automatically copyrighted once they were created. There are no formal requirements of notice or registration for a work to be protected. However, prior to March 1, 1989, copyright protection could be lost if the work was published without the proper notice.

TRANSFERRING OR LICENSING COPYRIGHTS

On death, a copyright may be willed to another by the owner of the copyright, or it may be distributed as personal property from the estate of someone who dies without a will.

During lifetime, a copyright owner may transfer the entire copyright or any part of it to another person or may grant limited permission to others to copy the work. The transfer of all the exclusive rights in a copyright is commonly known as an *assignment*. It must be made in writing and be signed by the copyright owner or the owner's agent. Once the rights are assigned, the party who receives the assignment is entitled to all of the protection and remedies accorded to the copyright owner by the statute. This means that the assignee can give permission to others to copy the work and enforce against infringements. The party that assigns the copyright relinquishes its rights altogether. For example, an author who assigns all rights to an article to a magazine can no longer grant permission to others to use the text or sue parties who reproduce the work without his or her permission.

It is also possible to assign only a particular subset of the exclusive rights encompassed by a copyright, such as the right to prepare derivative works. Such transfers are commonly called *exclusive licenses* or *partial assignments*. For example, an author might assign the right to publish a book to a publishing house and the right to prepare screenplays to a movie producer. Once a particular right is assigned, the author may no longer legally prepare screenplays based on the work or grant permission to others to do so. Such permission must come from the party that acquired the exclusive right.

Giving another person limited permission to reproduce a copyrighted work is known as granting a *nonexclusive license*. Another term commonly used in the publishing business for a nonexclusive license is a *permission*. These kinds of licenses allow the recipient of the license to reproduce the work without potential liability for infringement but generally do not give the recipient the right to take action against infringers or grant permission to others to copy the work.

Courts typically construe licenses narrowly. For example, in the case of *New York Times Co. v. Tasini*, the United States Supreme Court held that, in the absence of an agreement that allowed for the continued electronic reproduction of particular works, publishers are not entitled to republish, on the Internet or on CD-ROMs, articles written by freelancers that were licensed for publication in printed periodicals.

Both exclusive and nonexclusive licenses can be limited as to time, geographical area, and media. This allows copyright owners to exploit their rights more broadly than would otherwise be possible. For example, an author can sell the exclusive right to publish an article for the first time in North America to a magazine publisher. Having done so, the author is also free to sell the right to publish the article outside North America. Once the article is published, the author will still have the right to license publication of the article in other magazines, incorporate the material in a book, or prepare a derivative work.

Many publishers demand that authors transfer their entire copyrights to the publisher. Publishers favor such transfers because they make it easier to republish (or resell) material in other media, such as on the Internet, without having to further compensate the author. Holding the copyright also provides the publisher with the assurance that competing publishers cannot legally use the material. In general, authors resist transferring copyrights and instead attempt to license the rights. Even when an author foresees no additional personal use for the material, transferring the copyright precludes the author from incorporating the material in a future work or giving others permission to publish it.

Publishers should seek the license that most effectively preserves their rights to use the material in the time, geographic area, and media that they need. In many cases, a permission or a limited exclusive license will meet the publisher's legitimate business needs. However, if a publisher's business model includes worldwide distribution, sublicensing movie or translation rights, producing audio books, or creating derivative works and marketing materials, it is important to request a complete transfer of copyright as part of the publishing agreement with the author. Regardless of what kind of license or transfer is granted, it is vital that the terms of the licensing agreement be in writing and the agreement reflect the full scope of the rights transfer.

IN PLAIN ENGLISH

Courts are reluctant to extend the transfer of rights beyond the explicit terms of licensing agreements.

Recording Transfers

Both an assignment of ownership and a licensing agreement can be recorded with the Copyright Office. When the transaction is recorded, the rights of the assignee or licensee are protected in much the same way as the rights of an owner of real estate are protected by recording a deed. A critical fact to remember is that before a transferee (either an assignee or licensee) may sue a third party for infringement, the document of transfer must be recorded.

Involuntary Transfers

One section of the 1976 Copyright Act pertains to the involuntary transfer of a copyright. This section, which states that such a transfer will be held invalid, was included primarily because of problems arising from US recognition of foreign copyrights. For example, if a country did not want a dissident author's works to be published, the country could claim to be the copyright owner and thereby refuse to license foreign publication. Under the 1976 Copyright Act, the foreign government must produce a signed record of the transfer before its ownership of the work will be recognized.

Another situation covered in this section of the Act deals with a transfer that at first glance might appear to be involuntary but is not. For example, a transfer of a copyright in a bankruptcy proceeding or in the foreclosure of a mortgage secured by the copyright is valid. Such a transfer is considered voluntary rather than involuntary because the copyright owner freely chose to declare bankruptcy or to mortgage the copyright, even though the owner may not have chosen the consequences.

Alternative Licensing Schemes

In recent years, there have been some alternative licensing schemes. These include, for example, Creative Commons, Copyleft, and other vehicles whereby material may be used without additional permission of the copyright owner, who by publishing it without reserving all rights gives such permission as to those rights expressly relinquished, provided that any modification, enhancement, or the like remains part of the work and that the enhanced, modified, or altered work must be available for others to freely use, as well. There are some technical restrictions imposed by the different alternative licensing schemes, and attribution may be required. For example, some Creative Commons works do not permit modification, others impose economic restrictions on use, etc. It is therefore important for anyone relying on these alternative licensing schemes to carefully read the terms of use and strictly comply with them. A significant issue that should be considered before taking advantage of one of these forms of alternative licenses is that once the material is available, it cannot be withdrawn. This means that, for example, someone who has published material and identified it as Creative Commons or Copyleft will not be able to then publish it commercially, since it is highly unlikely that anyone would purchase material when it is already available for free. If questions arise, an experienced publishing lawyer should be consulted.

Termination of Copyright Transfers and Licenses

It is not unusual for authors, confronted with an unequal bargaining position with respect to a publisher, to transfer all rights in the copyright to the publisher for a small amount, only to see the work become valuable at a later date. The 1976 Copyright Act, in response to this situation, provides that after a certain period has lapsed, the author or certain other parties in special cases may terminate the transfer of the copyright and reclaim the rights. Thus, the law grants the author a second chance to exploit his or her work after the original transfer of copyright. This right to terminate a transfer is called *termination interest*.

In most cases, the termination interest will belong to the author or authors. If the author is no longer alive, however, and is survived by a spouse but no children, the surviving spouse owns the termination interest. If the deceased author is not survived by a spouse, ownership of the interest belongs to any surviving children in equal shares. If the decedent is survived by both a spouse and children, the interest is divided so that the spouse receives 50 percent and the children receive the remaining 50 percent in equal shares.

When the termination interest is owned by more than one party, be they joint authors or an author's survivors, a majority of the owners must agree to terminate. Under the statute, the general rule is that termination may be effected at any time within a five-year period, beginning at the end of the thirty-fifth year from the date on which the rights were transferred. If, however, the transfer includes the right of publication, termination may go into effect at any time within a five-year period, beginning at the end of thirty-five years from the date of publication or forty years from the date of transfer, whichever is earlier.

The party wishing to terminate the transferred interest must serve an advance written notice on the transferee. This notice must state the intended termination date and must be served not less than two but no more than ten years prior to the stated termination date. A copy of the notice must be recorded in the Copyright Office before the effective date of termination.

In service to the underlying purpose of the termination interest provision, the termination interest cannot be contractually avoided. However, courts have held that a subsequent agreement in which an author capitalizes on his or her increased bargaining power to renegotiate the original transfer will effectively revoke the original agreement and replace it with the new one. Publishers should be aware of works that are approaching the thirty-five-year window for termination and consider renegotiating the publishing contract if the work is still viable.

In fact, rights to several Beatles songs were demanded back by the original grantor of the license. Paul McCartney was in a dispute with Sony, who had purchased the rights from the Michael Jackson estate. The dispute was for the purpose of regaining the rights initially sold under the Copyright Revision Act's reversionary provision which allows copyright owners to reclaim their rights in accordance with the termination clause discussed above. The dispute went on for some time until it was confidentially settled.

DURATION OF COPYRIGHT

Determining when the copyright to a work expires can be somewhat complicated, because the rules vary depending upon when the work was created and when it was published. They also vary depending on whether the work was created by a natural person or is anonymous, pseudonymous, or a work made for hire. Under copyright law, the date of creation is the date when the work was first fixed in a tangible medium. The date of publication, with a limited exception, is determined by when the work was first distributed (sold, rented, or loaned) to the public or offered for further distribution. The exception is that limited distribution, made with the understanding that such copies are not to be further reproduced and distributed, is not considered publication. Examples include showing a manuscript to a friend for review and submissions to publishers for purposes of consideration. A public performance or display of a work does not of itself constitute publication.

For a work created on or after January 1, 1978, by identified natural persons, the copyright will last for a term consisting of the life of the author, plus seventy years. If the work was created by two or more authors and is not a work for hire, the copyright endures for a term consisting of the life of the last surviving author, plus seventy years. With regard to works created anonymously, pseudonymously, or for hire, the duration of the copyright depends on the creation and publication dates. The copyright will endure for ninety-five years from the year of first publication or for 120 years from the year of its creation, whichever expires first (this is sometimes called the *95/120 rule*). However, the life plus seventy years rule will apply if the identity of one or more of the authors of an anonymous or pseudonymous work is revealed in a registration filed with the US Copyright Office during the term of the copyright.

There are special rules for works that were created before 1978, including the requirement of renewals. Renewal is not required under the 1976 Act.

Once the copyright on a work has expired, or been lost, the work enters the public domain, where it can be exploited by anyone in any manner.

Copyright Duration

Date of Work	Term or Status of Copyright
Published before 1923	Public Domain
Published 1923–1963	*If never renewed:* Public Domain *If renewed before October 27, 1998:* 95 years after first publication
Published 1964–1977	95 years after first publication
Created prior to 1978 but never published or registered	*Individuals:* Life plus 70 years, or 120 years from creation if date of death is unknown *Works for hire; anonymous or pseudonymous works:* 120 years from date of creation
Created prior to 1978 and published or registered before 2003	Life plus 70 years, or December 31, 2047, whichever is later
Created prior to 1978 and published or registered during or after 2003	Life plus 70 years
Created 1978 or later	*Individuals:* Life plus 70 years, or 120 years from creation if date of death in unknown *Works for hire; anonymous or pseudonymous works:* 95 years after first publication or 120 years from the date of creation, whichever comes first

COPYRIGHT NOTICE

Works published under the 1909 Copyright Act had to contain the proper notice in order to be protected by the federal copyright law. With few exceptions, any omission, misplacement, or imperfection in the notice on any copy of a work distributed by authority of the copyright owner thrusts the work forever in the public domain. Thus, savvy copyright owners often insisted that any license to publish was conditioned on the publisher's inclusion of the proper copyright notice. That way, if the publisher made a mistake in the notice, the publication might be deemed unauthorized, but the copyright would not be affected. The publisher could be liable to the copyright owner for the loss of the copyright if it did occur.

Notice remained a requirement until March 1, 1989, when the United States became a party to the Berne Convention. The intent of the Berne Convention is that copyright notice is not a legal requirement for protection. Notice is optional for works published after March 1, 1989. The Copyright Office does not take a position on whether reprints published after March 1, 1989, of works first published with notice before March 1, 1989, must bear the copyright notice. It is likely that such notice is not required.

A proper copyright notice on a written work has three elements. First, there must be the word *copyright*, the abbreviation *copr.*, or the symbol ©. Courts may show some leniency with respect to minor variations, but departures do carry legal risk.

Second, the notice must contain the year of first publication (or, in the case of unpublished works governed by the 1909 Copyright Act, the year in which the copyright was registered). This date may be expressed in Arabic or Roman numerals, or in words. Under the 1909 Copyright Act, it was not clear when a derivative work, such as a substantially revised textbook, was first published. To be safe, the general practice was to include in the notice both dates—that of the original work and that of the revision. The 1976 Copyright Act makes it clear that the date of the publication of the derivative work is sufficient. The year of the first publication can be omitted on certain works specified in the Act, but this category is extremely narrow. Since the date is necessary for some forms of international protection, it should always be included.

The third necessary element is the name of the copyright owner. If there are several creators, one name is sufficient. Usually, the author's full name is used, but if the author is well known by a last name, the last name can be used alone or with initials. A business that owns a copyright may use its trade name if the name is legally recognized.

Errors in a Copyright Notice

Failure to provide a copyright notice or publishing an erroneous notice had serious consequences under the 1909 Copyright Act. Under that Act, the copyright was lost if the wrong name appeared in the notice. If the author sold the copyright and recorded the sale, either the author's or the new owner's name could be used. If the sale was not recorded with the Copyright Office, however, using the subsequent owner's name in the notice destroyed the copyright.

Under the 1976 Copyright Act, a mistake in the name appearing in the notice is not fatal to the copyright. A person who is honestly misled by the incorrect name can, however, use this as a defense to a suit for copyright infringement if the proper name was not on record with the Copyright Office. This is another incentive for registering a sale or license of a copyright with the Copyright Office.

Under the 1909 Copyright Act, a mistake in the year of the first publication could also have serious consequences. If an earlier date was used, the copyright term would be measured from that year, thereby decreasing the duration of protection. If a later date was used, the copyright was forfeited, and the work entered the public domain. Because of the harsh consequences of losing a copyright, a mistake of one year was not penalized.

Using an earlier date under the 1976 Copyright Act will not be of any consequence when the duration of the copyright is determined by the author's life. When the duration of the copyright is determined by the date of first publication, however, the earlier date in the notice will be used to measure how long the copyright will last. If a date that is later than the year of publication is used, the work is considered to have been published without notice. While this is not fatal to the actual copyright itself, it will preclude the recovery of statutory damages and attorney fees in the event of an infringement action.

The 1909 Copyright Act contained complicated rules for placing the copyright notice within the work. Improper placement was one more error that was fatal to the copyright. Although the 1976 Copyright Act gives the Copyright Office the authority to promulgate regulations as to where the copyright may be placed, failing to follow them will not invalidate the copyright. For example, the regulations specify that the copyright notice for a book should go on the cover, title page, or the back of the title page.

IN PLAIN ENGLISH

The back of the title page is traditionally designated as the copyright page in the book-publishing industry. This is where you will generally find the copyright information.

Failure to comply with these regulations does not automatically void the copyright notice but does put the burden on the copyright holder to prove that the notice was placed so as to give reasonable notice of the claim of copyright. The public is not expected to search high and low for a copyright notice. Should a court determine that the placement did not give reasonable notice, the work will be treated as if it were published without any notice.

Digital books should also contain copyright notices. If the ebook retains pagination, such as with a PDF or fixed-layout ebook, the copyright notice can follow the title page. If the ebook does not retain pagination, such as in a reflowable EPUB or MOBI file, the copyright notice can follow the title page, if included, or it can be shifted to the end of the ebook or to some other location that makes sense in the overall flow of the work. To increase the likelihood of giving reasonable notice to readers, the copyright notice can be included in the digital file's metadata, and a link to the copyright page can be included in the table of contents. Digital distributors and retailers often provide copyright information on the webpage where the ebook is sold. While it is yet unclear what the legal implication of this information might be, ensuring this information is complete and correct can only help protect the copyright and bolster any argument that notice was reasonably given.

Under the 1976 Copyright Act, if a work was published prior to March 1, 1989, without notice, the copyright owner could still be protected for five years. During those five years, the owner must have registered the copyright with the Copyright Office and made a reasonable effort to place a notice on those copies published without notice and distributed within the United States. If this was done, full copyright protection is granted for the appropriate duration of the published work. This is known as the *savings clause*.

A copyright owner is always forgiven for an omission of notice if the omission was in violation of a contract that made inclusion of the proper notice a condition of the right to publish. Also, if the notice is removed or obliterated by an unauthorized person, this will have no effect on the validity of the copyright or the notice.

Even though any work published after March 1, 1989, is not required to have a copyright notice affixed, it is nevertheless important to continue to provide notice. One reason is that an adequate notice is one of the prerequisites for eligibility to recover statutory damages and attorney fees in an infringement case. Another reason is that providing notice tends to better deter casual infringers from unauthorized copying, and one who relies on good faith on the omission of notice may argue that the copying was an innocent infringement. Innocent infringers may not be held be liable for damages, or damages may be limited to as little as $200, and they may be permitted to continue copying if the court upholds their claim of innocence if the infringer has made a sizable investment for future production, or the court may compel the copyright owner to grant a license to the infringer. In other cases, the innocent infringer may be compelled to give up any profits made from the infringement.

DEPOSIT AND REGISTRATION OF COPYRIGHTS

Works published after March 1, 1989, are protected by copyright irrespective of whether they contain a copyright notice or have been registered with the US Copyright Office. Nonetheless, providing an adequate notice and registering the work are critical, since enforcing against an infringement may be impractical otherwise. Even though registration is not a strict condition to copyright protection, copyright owners cannot file a lawsuit to enforce their copyrights until a work has been registered. More important, if the copyright was registered prior to the infringement, the owner may be entitled to recover attorney fees and statutory damages. In the absence of prior registration, the legal costs associated with bringing the action and the difficulty of proving actual damages will usually make an infringement action impractical from an economic perspective, since the costs to bring the action will typically exceed the damages awarded.

Registration is a fairly straightforward process. The most current information on how to do this can obtained from the US Copyright Office. Contact the Register of Copyrights, Library of Congress, Washington, DC 20559, or go online to www.copyright.gov. A registration fee is required. To be eligible to recover attorney fees and statutory damages from infringers, the owner of the work must register the copyright before the infringement occurs or within three months of publication. Moreover, there is a statutory presumption that a copyright is valid if the work has been registered within five years of its first publication. Thus, the copyright owner has a strong incentive to register the copyright at the earliest possible time.

In addition to completing the registration application form, the applicant must deposit two copies of the best edition of the work if published and one copy if unpublished. The best edition of a work will be the highest quality of a work that is publicly circulated. For example, the hardback version is considered better than the soft cover. The version with archival quality paper, a slipcase, or special features will be considered better than those without. If the book is circulated in print, it must be deposited in print, not digitally. However, if the book is only circulated digitally, the digital version is sufficient. When a publisher circulates multiple versions of a particular work, it can be difficult to determine which is the "best" edition. An experienced attorney can assist the publisher in determining which edition must be deposited.

The deposit must be made within three months after the work has been published. If the copies are not deposited within the requisite three-month period, the Register of Copyrights may demand them. If the copies are not submitted within three months after demand, the person upon whom demand was made may be subject to a fine for each work that was not submitted. In addition, such person or persons may be required to pay the Library of Congress an amount equal to the retail cost of the work, or if no retail cost has been established, the costs incurred by the Library in acquiring the work (provided such costs are reasonable). Finally, a copyright proprietor who willfully and repeatedly refuses to comply with a Register demand may be liable for a significant additional fine. While depositing copies under the deposit section of the law is not a condition of copyright protection, in light of the penalty provisions, it would be foolish not to comply.

When your claim to copyright has been accepted by the Copyright Office, you will receive a certificate of registration, which will include the registration number as well as the effective date of registration. That date is when the form, fee, and deposit are received together at the Copyright Office. This is an important legal document. You cannot bring a lawsuit to enforce your rights until the copyright has been registered.

LIBRARY OF CONGRESS

There are several additional noncopyright registrations that publishers may be interested in obtaining. The registrations available through the Library of Congress (LC) are the Library in Congress Catalog Number and the Cataloging in Publication record number.

The LC Catalog Number is a unique identification number given to each book that is cataloged by the Library of Congress. The number is useful for librarians and researchers who wish to use the Library of Congress indexing system and is therefore advantageous for most publishers to obtain but does not establish or affect any legal right. The publisher may obtain the LC Catalog Number by sending one copy of the work to the Library of Congress with an application. If the publisher desires to obtain the LC Catalog Number before the book is in print, the publisher can apply for a Preassigned Control Number (PCN) by submitting the application only and agreeing to forward the book when it is actually published. The publisher can then print the control number in the book to facilitate cataloging and book processing. Applications for LCCNs and PCNs are available online through the Library of Congress website available at www.loc.gov.

The Library of Congress also administers the Cataloging in Publication (CIP) program. Like the PCN, this program aids libraries by making cataloging information available even before the book is published and can be included in the book prior to printing. To participate in the CIP program, the publisher must be eligible for membership. Only US publishers that have at least three titles by three different authors that have been widely acquired by US libraries are eligible for membership. Each new imprint must apply for a separate membership and be independently eligible. Other publishers who are ineligible for the CIP program may still be eligible for the PCN program. Publishers must send a complimentary copy of the book to the Library of Congress immediately upon publication. Failing to send this copy may result in disqualification from the program.

CHAPTER 7

Copyright Infringement

It is important for publishers to understand the nature of the property interest encompassed by a copyright, as well as how copyrights are created and registered. It is equally important to understand how the ownership interest in a copyright is protected. Federal law provides individual copyright owners the legal right to sue infringers in federal courts to stop the infringing activities and recover damages. However, not every instance of copying is actionable, because the copyright statute provides a defense for certain uses deemed to be in the public interest.

INFRINGEMENT

The unauthorized copying of a work protected by copyright constitutes infringement. This is commonly referred to by the lay term *piracy*. When copyright infringement occurs, copyright law gives the copyright holder the right to sue for damages, and the copyright holder can obtain a court order prohibiting further copying and distribution of the work. Such actions must be brought in a federal court within three years of the date of the infringement or within three years of the last infringement, defined as the last sale of the infringing copy.

To prevail, the copyright owner must prove

- that the work is copyrighted and registered;
- that the infringer had access to and improperly used the copyrighted work; and
- that the infringer copied a "substantial and material" portion of the copyrighted work.

To demonstrate the extent of the damage caused by the infringement, the copyright owner must usually provide evidence showing how widely the infringing copies were distributed. Proof of copyright may be provided through evidence about how and when the work was created. In cases involving works created in 1978 and after, proving that the work is covered by copyright is rarely difficult because copyright attaches when the work is put in a tangible form.

The copyright owner must prove that the infringer had access to the protected work, because an independent creation of an identical work is not an infringement. Some creators include minor errors in their works as a means of proving that others copied their works. For example, the plaintiff in a landmark case included a few fictitious entries in its telephone directory to facilitate the detection of copiers.

IN PLAIN ENGLISH

The likelihood that two literary works will be identical is so slight that a jury will likely infer that one was copied from the other—if they are identical.

Infringement can occur short of a verbatim copy of an entire work. Any unauthorized copying of a substantial portion of a work may constitute an infringement. The quality of the writing copied is considered, as well as the quantity. If one sentence in a scientific work states a principle in a mundane way, another scientist using the same statement might not be considered an infringer because short, straightforward statements of fact are not protectable. On the other hand, one line of poetry can be so highly creative that it may be protectable.

Similarity of ideas alone is not enough to show infringement. There must be a substantial similarity. The court first looks at general similarities like subject matter, setting, and the like. This is known as the "extrinsic test." Expert testimony may be used here. The court next applies a "subjective" or an "intrinsic test," questioning whether a lay observer would recognize that the allegedly infringing work was copied from the original. No expert testimony is permitted at this phase.

The most difficult infringement suits to prove are those in which a copyright owner asserts that someone has copied the original by paraphrasing it. In such cases, the text of the original work has not been copied, but the

overall creative pattern of the work has been copied. To constitute infringement, it must be shown that the two works are sufficiently close that the
similarity in the expression is due to the appropriation from the original
and not caused by the independent expression of similar ideas. For example,
most romance novels follow a general type of plot, where a man and woman
overcome some obstacle to forming a relationship. This kind of generalized
pattern is not protected by copyright. As similarities such as the characteristics of the settings, characters, and events become closer, it becomes easier
to prove infringement.

In *Shame on You Productions v. Banks*, a California federal court declined
to find any actionable infringement of a screenplay. Although there were
similarities between the plots—for example, the lead characters, attractive
young women, were helped by a "nice guy" male character, as well as other
similarities such as a "walk of shame" theme—the court found that the two
screenplays told fundamentally different stories and that the themes were
not substantially similar and that there were other differences between the
stories.

Works that are based on the expressions contained in another work can
sometimes be considered derivative works, even if they are different in character and nature from the original. In *Castle Rock Entertainment, Inc. v. Carol
Publishing Group*, a trivia quiz book about the television series *Seinfeld* was
determined to infringe on the television series because it incorporated short
expressions from the series. The court took special note that the book did not
quiz about true facts, such as the identity of the actors, the number of days it
took to shoot episodes, or biographical information about the actors. A book
dealing with that kind of information would not have infringed on the copyright of the series. However, a book that contained detailed summaries of the
plots to the episodes likely would infringe.

If a work is held to be an infringement, the court can order the destruction of all copies and enjoin further infringement. In addition, the copyright
owner may be awarded damages. The copyright owner may elect to recover
either actual or statutory damages, although the choice must be made before
the final judgment is entered. Actual damages are the amount of the financial
injury sustained by the copyright holder plus the profits made by the infringer
that are not included in the copyright holder's financial injury. As to profits,
the copyright holder needs only to prove the infringer's gross revenue; it is up
to the infringer to prove his or her legitimate deductible expenses. Statutory

damages are decided by the court and may range from $750 to $30,000. If the infringing party did not intend to improperly use protected rights or did not know that the work was protected by copyright, that innocent intention or lack of knowledge may be used as a defense to lessen the damages awarded. If the infringement is shown to have been willful, the maximum possible recovery is increased to $150,000. The court has the option to award the prevailing party its costs and attorney fees. As previously noted, statutory damages and attorney fees cannot be awarded in cases where the copyright was not registered prior to infringement, provided such infringement occurred more than three months after the copyrighted work was published.

In 2005, Congress amended the copyright statute to create a rebuttable presumption that an infringement was committed willfully if it involved a website that the violator registered or maintained using false contact information. The intent of the amendment was to deter Internet fraud, but it could possibly enhance the exposure to copyright damages of publishers who use fictitious identities to maintain their privacy for legitimate reasons. Examples might include publishers who want to report anonymously on political corruption or corporate malfeasance, as well as those publishers who simply want to avoid identity theft or being stalked. These publishers, if found to have infringed a copyright, could be subjected to the much higher damages for willful infringement if a court finds that their websites were registered using false contact information. At the time this book was published, it was not entirely clear what constitutes false contact information. Misleading names and false addresses would clearly qualify. However, it was unclear whether writing under a pseudonym but otherwise providing correct information would be considered false contact information under the statute.

Criminal Infringement

Egregious cases of infringement can result in criminal prosecution as misdemeanors and felonies. In such cases, the US Department of Justice will bring charges in federal court. The size of the fines and possible duration of imprisonment depends on whether there have been repeated offenses and the retail value of the infringing items. It is also a criminal violation to falsely represent the copyright status of a work by placing a false copyright notice or removing or obliterating the notice. In addition, it is a federal crime to knowingly make a false material statement in an application to register a copyright.

COPYRIGHT INFRINGEMENT 83

Online Infringement

If the infringement occurs on an Internet website, the *Digital Millennium Copyright Act of 1998* (DMCA) provides a notification requirement whereby the Internet Service Provider (ISP) must remove or block access to material if it receives a proper notice from the copyright owner, or else risk liability as an infringer itself. Under the DMCA, the notification of a claimed infringement must contain:

- an electronic or physical signature of the owner, or of the person authorized to act on behalf of the owner, of the copyright;
- identification of the copyrighted work (or works) about which infringement is claimed;
- a description of the material claimed to be infringing and the location where the original or authorized copy of the copyrighted work exists (for example, the URL of the page of the website where it is lawfully posted; the name, edition, and pages of a book from which an excerpt was copied; the music album or single; etc.);
- a clear description of where the infringing material is located on the infringer website, including (as applicable) its URL, so the material can be located;
- the claimant or agent address, telephone number, and email address;
- a statement that the claimant has a good-faith belief that the disputed use is not authorized by the copyright owner, its agent, or the law; and
- a statement by the claimant, made under penalty of perjury, that the above information in the notice is accurate and that the claimant is the copyright owner or is authorized to act on the copyright owner's behalf.

The identity of registrants for domain names can be found by searching the WHOIS database at www.whois.icann.org/en.

This is important for you to be aware of whether you are responsible for the allegedly infringing website or whether you are the complainant. In either case, you should evaluate potential claims and determine whether the work you are posting or the work you are complaining about actually infringes. If so, you should deal with the problem diligently.

Recent amendments to the DMCA require service providers who host content posted by other users to designate an agent to receive and respond to take-down notices and register that agent with the Copyright Office. The Copyright Office maintains a centralized online directory of designated agents and can be searched at dmca.copyright.gov/osp.

There are subscription services available to publishers and copyright owners that can assist you in monitoring for online infringement. Services like Digimarc's Copyright Protection Solutions and Cyber Alert's Media Monitoring use web crawlers, bit torrent trackers, and even human researchers to identify infringing uses of your copyrighted content. In this way, you can monitor the Internet with respect to the works you are interested in without relegating your own personnel to this time-consuming task.

Filing Suit

Copyright owners whose works have been infringed should take prompt action upon discovery. First, they should request that the party infringing the work cease from further infringement. If the infringing use appears willful and is associated with a commercial venture, many publishers will enclose an invoice requesting payment for the unauthorized use.

If the infringer refuses to compensate the copyright or refuses to stop using the protected material, it will be necessary to file a lawsuit in federal court, since the Copyright Act does not provide for filing in state courts. It will also be necessary to register the copyright if that has not already been done. It is possible to obtain an expedited registration, but doing so is expensive. As of the date of this writing, the cost of expediting a registration was $800, as compared to a mere $35 for a single author registration for one work (not for hire) or $85 for a paper filing. Cases that involve the infringement of works that were registered before the infringement, or within three months of being published, tend to settle quickly, because the infringing party does not want to bear the risk of having to pay the copyright owner's attorney's fees. Conversely, cases involving unregistered works are often dropped because the attorney's fees and the difficulty of proving actual damages make them uneconomical. Although registration is not a legal requirement for copyright protection, the associated economics tend to make it a practical one.

FAIR USE

As noted at the beginning of this chapter, the overly restrictive application of copyright protection could unduly prevent the creation of socially valuable works. For example, works such as book reviews, biographies, and news articles sometimes must necessarily use or paraphrase other copyrighted material. Since permission in such cases is often burdensome or impossible to obtain, a strict prohibition on copying would make some kinds of writing very difficult. Fortunately, not every unauthorized copying of a copyrighted work constitutes infringement. The two exceptions are known as *fair use* and *exempted use*.

The *fair use doctrine* was developed by courts to mitigate the harsh effects of the 1909 Copyright Act and allow for limited uses of copyrighted material for purposes such as criticism, comment, news reporting, teaching, and research. Under the doctrine, four factors are considered in determining whether a particular use is fair:

1. the purpose and character of the use, including whether it is for commercial use or for nonprofit educational purposes;
2. the nature of the copyrighted work;
3. the amount and substantiality of the portion used in relation to the copyrighted work as a whole; and
4. the effect of the use upon the potential market for, or value of, the copyrighted work.

The 1976 Copyright Act explicitly recognizes the fair use doctrine, although it neither ranks the four factors nor does it exclude other factors in determining the question of fair use. In effect, all the Act does is leave the doctrine of fair use to be developed by the courts. Questions of fair use are decided on a case-by-case basis, and it is sometimes difficult to determine whether a particular use will be considered infringement or fair use. Although uses that significantly reduce the value of the copyright or intrude on the scope of the author's right to prepare derivative works are more likely to be found to infringe, there are no *bright line tests* defining what constitutes a fair use.

A recent case from the Second Circuit Court of Appeals, *Authors Guild v. Google, Inc.*, confronted the question of whether Google's publicly available, searchable, digital copies of books received from major libraries infringed the copyrights of the book's authors or whether this use was a fair use permitted by copyright law. Since the practice contributed to the public knowledge and was unlikely to cause loss to the authors' protected market opportunities, the court determined that there was no actionable infringement.

On the other hand, in *New York Times Co., Inc. v. Tasini*, freelance authors of articles that appeared in the *New York Times* and other publications sued due to the publisher's reproduction of the articles, without the authors' permission, in an electronic database. Finding that the use of the articles was not fair use or a permitted revision as the publisher claimed, the US Supreme Court found an infringement of the authors' copyrights.

Using small portions of a copyrighted work tends to favor fair use, except when such use has a major effect on the market for the work. Excerpting large portions of a work can sometimes constitute fair use, depending on the nature of the excerpting and excerpted work. In one case, a theology professor wrote a book that criticized the published accounts of women who had obtained abortions following unwanted pregnancies. He maintained that the book was aimed at the relatively small audience interested in the public debate on abortion. The book quoted about 7,000 words from another book titled *Pregnant by Mistake,* which consisted of interviews with women who had experienced unwanted pregnancies. The author of *Pregnant by Mistake* had previously refused permission to quote from her book and sued the professor for infringement. Although the professor's book excerpted almost 5 percent of the other work, the court upheld the defense of fair use on the grounds that he used the material for the purpose of criticism and comment, and the excerpted material was verbatim interviews and, therefore, essentially reportorial in nature. The court also noted that readers of the professor's book would not confuse his work with the original, nor did it find that the professor intended to supplant that work with his own.

As is apparent in this brief discussion, fair use is a complex subject, and it would be wise to consult with a knowledgeable copyright lawyer before relying on this defense in an infringement case.

Parody and Satire

Parody can fall into the category of fair use because it is a form of criticism and comment. Legally, a *parody* is a work that uses some elements of a prior work to, at least in part, comment on the prior work. In *Sun Trust Bank v. Houghton Mifflin*, the court found that Alice Randall's work *The Wind Done*

Gone commented on *Gone with the Wind* and was a fair use of the original. She appropriated its characters, plot, and major scenes and flipped them as a rejoinder to the way it depicted slavery and the relationships between blacks and whites. Although the fair use defense can be viable in parody cases, it should be emphasized that the four-factor analysis must be applied to each parody, and that parodies are not always exempt from findings of infringement.

It is also important to distinguish parody from *satire*, in which the copyrighted work is merely used as a vehicle to poke fun at another target. The reason is that satire is not as readily protected by the fair use doctrine as is parody, since it does not constitute comment on the original work. An example is *Dr. Seuss Enterprises, LP. v. Penguin Books USA, Inc.*, which involved a book that used the rhyming style of *The Cat in the Hat* to summarize the highlights of the O. J. Simpson murder trial. Although the court found that the book did broadly mimic Dr. Seuss's characteristic style, it did not hold his style up to ridicule or make any other type of comment about it. Instead, it was targeted at the trial of O. J. Simpson. Because the purpose of borrowing Dr. Seuss's creative style was to attract attention to an issue unrelated to the works of Dr. Seuss, incorporating it into their book was not considered to be fair use.

Statutory Exemptions

In some instances, the ambiguities inherent in the fair use doctrine have been resolved by statutory exemptions. Exempted uses are those specifically permitted by statute for situations in which the public interest in making a copy outweighs any harm to the copyright proprietor. Perhaps the most significant of these exemptions is the *library and archives exemption*. Libraries and archives may reproduce and distribute a single copy of a work, provided that

- such reproduction and distribution is not for the purpose of direct or indirect commercial gain;
- the collections of the library or archives are available to the public, or available to researchers affiliated with the library or archives, as well as to others doing research in a specialized field; and
- the reproduction and distribution of the work includes a copyright notice.

The exemption for libraries and archives is intended to cover only single copies of a work. It does not generally cover multiple reproductions of the same material, whether made on one occasion or over a period of time, and whether intended for use by one person or for separate use by the individual members of a group. Under interlibrary arrangements, various libraries may provide one another with works missing from their respective collections, unless these distribution arrangements substitute for a subscription or purchase of a given work.

Governmental Works

In addition, works created by the US government are precluded from being copyrighted. The government is not precluded from receiving and holding copyrights transferred to it. Therefore, it is risky to assume that all works published by the federal government are in the public domain. For example, text on a government website could be subject to copyright if it was created by a nongovernment employee or entity under circumstances where it was not a work for hire.

PLAGIARISM

While copyright infringement is the unauthorized use of another's copyrighted material, plagiarism occurs when an author poses as the originator of the work of another. Plagiarism can be copyright infringement; however, there are several legal distinctions.

First, a work does not need to be protected by copyright to be considered plagiarism. For example, a student who copies work from the public domain and turns it in as his own has not committed copyright infringement but has plagiarized the public domain work.

Second, plagiarism is a violation of moral, ethical, or organization rules but is not illegal. Our student from the above example may be punished by the school according to the school's guidelines but will not be liable in court for what he has done.

Third, plagiarism can occur even if there is permission from the copyright holder to use the work. Our plagiarizing student, for example, could have copied his assignment from a willing participant that originated the work. While the agreement between the co-conspirators means there was no copyright infringement, the student has still plagiarized the work by claiming to be the author.

The remedy for plagiarism is often institutional—defined by the policies and practices of the school or organization where the plagiarism occurred. Whether the remedy be expulsion or failing grades for students or dismissal for employees, reputational damage and shame can occur when an accusation of plagiarism becomes public. It is important, therefore, that any claims of plagiarism be verified before an author or publisher makes a public allegation in order to avoid liability for defamation.

Even though there is no cause of action recognized for plagiarism, there may still be legal remedies in the form of breach of contract, fraud, unfair competition, or false designation of origin claims.

CHAPTER 8

Authors and Literary Agents

Writers have traditionally relied on licensing their works to publishers, who in turn edit, print, market, and distribute the works. Some authors deal with publishers through agents, while others deal with publishers directly. Although the Internet and the expanded opportunities for self-publishing have made some inroads, conventional publishing remains the dominant pathway for most writers. There are three things publishers should consider when dealing with authors and other industry professionals (such as literary agents)—protocol, legal issues, and handling the transactions. Various parts of the industry have different standards by which they do business. For example, magazine publishers follow somewhat different practices than book publishers. Understanding how to deal with authors and agents can help expedite the evaluation of a work and avoid unpleasant situations.

SUBMISSION PROTOCOL

While publishers sometimes solicit projects from writers, in most cases it is the writers who approach publishers to solicit consideration of their work. Different segments of the publishing industry follow generally accepted protocols with regard to submissions, although individual publishers often have their own variations. Protocols have evolved to make the process of evaluating submissions more efficient. Failing to follow these protocols does not violate any laws, and publishers should feel free to vary their submissions process when a more efficient method is discovered.

While the decision to change the submission process belongs to the publisher alone, expectations should be made clear to inquiring authors, and recent changes to the process should be noted. It must also be clear that the publisher is under no obligation to read, respond to, or accept submissions even if all of the procedures are followed. Including these kinds of disclaimers will prevent zealous authors from asserting that the publisher's submission process is more akin to an offer to contract that an author can accept by complying with the rules.

Query Letters

Most publishers prefer to be first contacted through a query letter or email. The purpose of a query is to ascertain whether an editor is interested in seeing more material and often contains the underlying idea of a book. As mentioned in chapter 5, ideas are not protected by copyright, so as far as copyright law is concerned, an unscrupulous publisher could take the idea presented in a query letter and hire another author to write the book.

Some authors may be cautious when submitting query letters, knowing that an idea may be taken without copyright repercussions, and may seek to enter a contractual relationship with the publisher prior to submitting anything. While most publishers will not contemplate such an agreement, there may be circumstances where a particular author makes such an agreement desirable. A contract between an author and publisher prohibiting publication by any other author on a specific topic is likely to be enforceable. Before signing any such contracts, it is advisable to discuss the contract with an attorney to avoid unwanted consequences.

Besides the obvious reputational harm that can occur when a publisher makes it a habit to co-opt ideas from pitches and query letters, publishers may become liable for breach of an implied contract. Under an implied contract theory, creators in the television and movie industries have successfully sued production studios for "idea theft" when their original pitches were rejected but later created and attributed to others. In the publishing industry, authors have usually sought a remedy through a theory of misappropriation, discussed more fully below.

IN PLAIN ENGLISH

Copyright law does not protect ideas; however, stealing a book concept from an author can still result in legal liability.

LEGAL ASPECTS OF SUBMISSIONS

The legal obligations of publishers to writers are not extensive, although some exist. Absent a specific contract, publishers are not legally required to review submissions, give them good-faith consideration, respond in a reasonable amount of time, or even respond at all. In some instances, a publisher who accepts a submission with the understanding that it will be returned after review may be liable for the materials if they are damaged or lost. Such situations are known as *bailments* and exist when a person accepts the property with the understanding that it will be returned, kept until reclaimed, or otherwise disposed of in accordance with the understanding of the parties.

Bailments of submission materials rarely rise to the level of legal disputes because their replacement value is rarely high enough to warrant legal action. Furthermore, the custom in the publishing industry is that publishers are not expected to return materials, such as manuscripts, unless return postage is provided by the writer if a manuscript is mailed. In today's publishing world, manuscripts are customarily submitted electronically, and thus, return of that manuscript is not an issue. The submission of original artwork and photographs can be a different matter, since some works are very valuable. The better practice is to advise the authors you deal with not to submit originals if at all possible. Most publishers will accept (and even prefer) digital copies of artwork or photographs over the originals. Failing that, valuable materials should be requested only after the publisher agrees, and then only with a delivery memorandum that specifies that the publisher accepts the submission on the terms contained in the memorandum, and that materials will be returned promptly and undamaged. You should have an experienced publishing attorney assist you in preparing this kind of memorandum if you intend to request valuable original material.

MISAPPROPRIATION

An issue that occasionally arises is that authors claim publishers have misappropriated the author's idea and arranged to have another author prepare competing work using that idea. As a practical matter, reputable publishers should not engage in such activities. Although confidentiality agreements are occasionally used in highly sensitive areas, such as celebrity exposés and sensational crime stories, they are not a standard practice in publishing. Writers who request them for routine submissions are generally not invited to submit their work.

In any case, establishing a case for misappropriation of ideas is very difficult. The law concerning misappropriation of ideas varies among the states, but generally, the elements include that the idea:

- must have been fully novel and original;
- was understood to be for sale; and
- was misappropriated by a party with a fiduciary or contractual duty not to do so.

The requirement for the idea to be fully novel and original demands a fairly high degree of specificity, and deriving something from existing knowledge will suggest a lack of sufficient originality.

For example, as one litigant found out, proposing an idea to a television network for a comedy in which Anthony Anderson stars as the head of a wholesome African American family is not sufficiently novel to support a misappropriation claim, even if the network eventually produces such a program. The reasoning in that case was that given the plethora of situation comedies that feature families, the concept was not specific enough to be novel.

DEALING WITH COMMON ISSUES

Publishers should be aware of the fact that writers may negotiate for more favorable terms than initially offered, though new writers may be reluctant to risk losing the opportunity to work with a publisher by attempting to modify the author-publisher contract. Their most significant fear is that publishers have an abundance of other works to choose from and will seek other projects if a writer balks at an offer. Given the breadth within the industry, there are elements of truth and falsity to this fear. It is true that some publishers look for the lowest cost materials and obtain most of their material from less sophisticated writers. Typically, these kinds of publishers have a readership that is captive, such as publications of professional organizations, or that deals with a limited audience, such as books dealing with niche hobbies. On the other hand, many publishers face competitive markets, where the quality of content is critical to their success.

When it comes to negotiation, knowledge is power, and it helps to understand industry practices. Organizations such as the American Society of Journalists and Authors and the National Writers Union post information about bad publisher practices on the Internet. Writers often exchange information about publishers on Internet forums. Safeguarding your reputation as a publisher may garner better author submissions. If a publisher feels that a post on one of these sites rises to the level of defamation and is harmful to its reputation, the publisher should seek advice from a lawyer to determine what action is appropriate.

No reputable publisher should withdraw an offer merely because a writer asks for better terms. The publisher may refuse to accede to those terms, but they should not risk losing a good author merely because the writer asks a question.

Issues concerning such terms should be dealt with tactfully and professionally. For example, a request for more compensation can be dealt with by explaining that the financial arrangement the writer is requesting will not work for the publisher. Where a writer is confident about the value of a work, a statement about needing a specific amount is not unreasonable.

LITERARY AGENTS

Many publishers prefer to deal with authors through literary agents. Agents provide the service of submitting work to publishers, negotiating contracts, and handling matters such as monitoring payments and working out issues between the publisher and the author. They also are familiar with the terms of publisher contracts and may negotiate these terms on behalf of the authors they work with. Some literary agents are lawyers, and many will have ongoing relationships with lawyers to review and draft contracts.

FEES

Most reputable agents charge for their services by taking a commission on advances and royalties. In addition, many agents will deduct direct costs, such as editing or postage, from the writer's portion of the proceeds. Some agents will charge clients an up-front fee to cover direct costs, and some require their clients to reimburse them for such costs even if the work does not place.

IN PLAIN ENGLISH

Very few ethical agents charge any sort of fee to read or evaluate submissions from prospective clients.

Publishers who work with agents they have not worked with before should be aware that there are many unethical agents who take advantage of the inexperience and naïveté of some authors. Many such agents charge reading fees to evaluate submissions. Others prey on writers' hopes by talking favorably about submissions but then ask for a fee to revise a work or else refer the writer to a supposedly independent editing service that kicks back part of the fee to the agent. Such agents make their money by preying on writers and rarely succeed at placing works with publishers, and publishers should be careful not to deal with them. A particularly notorious example was the Edit Ink agency, which closed in 1999 after criminal convictions and levied fines were affirmed by an appellate court in New York. Edit Ink worked with several literary agents who were paid kickbacks after encouraging writers to seek professional editing from Edit Ink. About $4.75 million was obtained by Edit Ink from 3,600 potential writers who had been deceived by agents' representations that their works showed great commercial promise yet were rejected by publishers after editing.

THE DUTIES BETWEEN AGENT AND CLIENT

The agent's ability to succeed depends in large part on maintaining the good graces of the publishing industry. Even though this can create a conflict of interest between the agent and the writer, agents cannot legally put the interests of publishers above those of their writers. Literary agents are *fiduciaries* and thus owe a duty of loyalty and good faith to their clients. This means that literary agents may not disclose confidential information, make deals that are essentially self-serving, or receive secret profits. It also means, among other things, that the agent cannot represent writers whose commercial interests conflict with each other, except with the consent of both writers. For example, an agent should not take on books that are so similar that they compete directly for prospective book contracts. As a publisher, you should be aware of these issues so that you do not wind up in the middle of a dispute between an agent and the author represented by that agent.

Should an agent act in such a way as to interfere with the writer's best interests, the agent may be liable for breach of the fiduciary duty. For example, the agent's role in contract negotiations will normally be to get the best contract possible for the writer without unduly antagonizing you, the publisher. Many publishers prefer to negotiate with agents because agents are familiar with the legal and trade aspects of the industry, and this tends to facilitate the process. Moreover, since agents are constantly involved in negotiations between various writers and publishers, they are usually in the best position to identify an acceptable contract and can be trusted to moderate unreasonable or unrealistic demands made by writers. Publishers should be wary of agents who cross the line and attempt to ingratiate themselves with a publisher by giving the publisher a better deal at the expense of the writer. In such cases, the agent might be liable to the writer, and the publisher could wind up in the middle of this legal dispute. Fortunately, this is rare, and many agents who are highly respected by publishers have reputations for zealously advocating the interests of their clients.

Agents serve the important function of getting publishers interested in books and have the duty to act diligently in submitting their clients' materials to publishers. While agents are given considerable leeway in how they allocate and schedule their time, they are not free to ignore clients. Should a publisher make an offer, the agent is obligated to inform the client promptly even if the agent does not feel the offer is worthy of consideration.

IN PLAIN ENGLISH

Agent's Duties to the Publisher:

- Duty to provide manuscripts that are believed to be acceptable
- Duty to effectively communicate on behalf of the author
- Duty to negotiate an acceptable contract
- Duty to deal with authors who have unreasonable demands
- Duty to transmit all communications between publisher and author

LIABILITY FOR THE ACTS OF AN AGENT

Since literary agents are not agents of a publisher, the publisher should not be liable for the wrongful acts of a literary agent. In fact, disputes between authors and agents should not legally affect the publisher, though occasionally publishers wind up in the middle of those disputes as witnesses, or as possible parties, because one party or the other may believe that the publisher was responsible for the wrongful conduct. For this reason, publishers should be careful to deal with experienced agents with good reputations and should be concerned when it appears likely that a dispute between a literary agent and the author is brewing.

CHAPTER 9

Working with Other People

Authors and publishers frequently work with other people. Common situations include working relationships between coauthors, editors, ghostwriters, illustrators, photographers, book designers, and employees. Given the expected degree of cooperation and contribution inherent in ventures where two or more people work together, it should not be a surprise that these kinds of relationships can be fertile grounds for conflict. Moreover, problems can escalate when contributors encounter situations they did not anticipate. For example, disputes can develop over issues as simple as which party's name is listed first on the cover or as complex as sorting out what happens if one party becomes incapacitated or disenchanted before the project is completed.

Publishers who are unaware of the underlying agreements between co-creators can be caught in the middle of a dispute that ultimately leaves the publisher with a project that will never reach bookshelves. It is vital, therefore, for publishers to understand the relationships between co-creators and, as third-party beneficiaries of their agreements, know who owns rights in the work, how disputes will be resolved, and what will happen if the collaboration dissolves.

The publishing industry uses several distinctions to describe people who collaborate to produce a work. Although these distinctions are useful for conducting business, they do not define the legal relationship between the parties. They can be helpful factors in deciding what kind of relationship exists between them. A common relationship in the publishing industry is that of coauthors, in which two or more writers collaborate to produce a joint work, such as an article or book. Another type is that of editor and contributing authors, in which the editor solicits individual works from several writers and compiles them into a single work. There are also relationships in which one person is identified as the author, although someone else does most or all of the actual writing. *Ghostwriting* is a situation in which the actual writer is never identified as such. The *as told to* work is another variation, where the speaker is identified as the primary author, but credit is provided to the actual writer in the form of *as told to*.

Writers also collaborate with visual artists (typically photographers, graphic artists, and fine artists). As with literary collaborators, the descriptions customarily used in the publishing industry do not define the legal relationship between the parties. For example, contributions by illustrators and photographers can range from a minor portion of a book, such as the author's photograph on a dust jacket, to the majority of the book, such as one that consists of dozens of photographs and a short, written narrative. In such cases, the legal relationship will be determined by factors such as the parties' intentions, agreements, relative contributions, and business practices.

Publishers should be aware of these industry norms, and they should be sure that appropriate agreements defining them are in place. Before a writing project begins, it is important to fully discuss each party's expectations and to be sure they have all reached a consensus regarding all significant terms. Written agreements are strongly recommended, since memories about the parties' agreement can (and often do) blur when a dispute arises. Oral contracts are not worth the paper they are written on. Furthermore, the mere act of preparing a written agreement tends to encourage the consideration of issues that might otherwise be overlooked. Specific issues that should be discussed are described in the remainder of this chapter.

SCOPE OF THE AGREEMENT

It is important for the parties to describe the scope of the project and define their relationship. Most parties to a writing project will limit the relationship to a particular work. If this is not the case, the parties should clearly distinguish what kinds of projects they intend to perform jointly and which ones each can perform alone. Likewise, the parties should specify how they intend to work with each other on subsequent editions, derivative works, and related projects. For example, if the parties work together on a magazine article, they should decide what happens when one of them wants to revise the article to sell to another magazine or wants to incorporate the material into a book authored by that person alone.

The nature of the relationship should also be described with specificity. If two writers decide to write a book together and agree to share the profits, they will usually be considered to be a partnership or a joint venture if they do not incorporate or form a limited liability company. There is nothing inherently wrong with being partners or joint venturers, so long as this is the intended relationship. On the other hand, it is always better to be clear about the nature of the relationship, because it affects issues such as control over the product, liabilities, and tax obligations.

Another kind of relationship that writers can enter into as collaborators is that of employer/employee. For example, if a writer pays an illustrator to provide a drawing for a chapter in a book, this relationship is most likely one of employer and employee, or employer and independent contractor. If a writer and illustrator agree to work jointly to produce an illustrated book and share the royalties equally, the relationship is more likely to be construed as a joint venture or a partnership. However, unless the parties take measures to define their relationship, they run the risk of operating in the gray area where the relationship could arguably be considered either a partnership or that of employer and employee or independent contractor. If a dispute or legal question arises in such cases, courts and government agencies will look to various factors in making the determination. In such cases, the determinations can profoundly affect issues such as copyright ownership and how profits are distributed, liabilities are shared, and taxes are assessed.

A major difference between a partnership and an employer-contractor relationship is that an employer has control over what the employee produces, whereas partners share control over management decisions. If the relationship is that of employer and independent contractor, the control is over the product, but not over how the result is achieved. The amount of control is the key factor in determining whether an employee is considered to be an independent contractor or a statutory employee (also known in common law as a *servant*). This distinction is important because the consequences of having a statutory employee are significantly different from those associated with independent contractors. For example, there are no requirements to withhold income tax or comply with employee protection laws when working with an independent contractor. Whether a particular person is a statutory employee or an independent contractor will largely depend on

- the amount of control over the method of performing the assigned task;

- the understanding between the parties;
- the agreement they have worked out; and
- other factors that have been articulated in the tax and labor laws.

A person who receives extensive instructions or is trained by the employer to perform the required tasks is likely to be considered a statutory employee. Similarly, someone who invests in the equipment needed to do the work, is not reimbursed for all of his or her expenses, can incur a profit or loss, and who performs similar work for others is more likely an independent contractor.

While the above analysis applies to authors and the parties they deal with, it also applies to publishers, as well. As a publisher, you will be dealing with cover illustrators, book designers, editors, and a number of other professionals to assist in preparing a manuscript for publication. It is also vital to understand who is entering the contract with the publisher. In the event that a work is coauthored, the publisher must be sure that the party to the contract has the legal right to enter the contract and make all of the promises the contract requires.

WARRANTY AND INDEMNIFICATION

Collaborators who are partners or joint venturers will be legally liable for the misdeeds of the other collaborators. One way to ameliorate, but not eliminate, the liability is to have each collaborator agree that the others will be reimbursed if that collaborator does something that gives rise to a liability. In addition, publishers should request indemnification provisions from all collaborators. Normally, collaboration agreements first have each party warrant to the others that he or she will not do anything in connection with the work that infringes a copyright, defames any person, violates a right of privacy, or injures any personal or property right of another. Second, they have each party agree to indemnify the others for loss, liability, and expense arising from any breach of the warranties. This means that the collaborator whose actions caused the liability will agree to not only pay any damages that might be awarded to the injured person, but also pay the legal expenses of the other collaborators in defending the action. Typically author/publisher agreements contain similar provisions, as well. This, unfortunately, has limitations, since a party agreeing to pay these expenses must have the resources to fulfill that obligation. Another method of dealing with these issues is for the parties to purchase insurance. Regrettably, the cost of such insurance is fairly steep.

TERM OF THE AGREEMENT

Written works can remain in print for a long time, so the collaborators should define how long they intend to be bound by their agreement. A common provision for coauthored books is for the agreement to last for the period of the copyright in the book and any subsequent revisions thereof. This period is measured by the life of the longest-living collaborator plus seventy years, when the copyright is owned by the authors. In such cases, the writers are legally bound to cooperate with each other in the event that the publisher requests that the book be revised. If the writers wish to have different obligations, these should be expressed in the agreement. Publishers should be aware of the arrangement between the parties, and if the publisher believes another arrangement would be more beneficial for the book in question, the publisher should attempt to work with the parties in order to achieve the maximum benefit for the work.

OWNERSHIP OF RIGHTS

The rights to a work can be valuable. The agreement should make clear who will own the rights to the work and the manner in which they are owned. It is vital that the publisher be certain of which party owns the rights in the work so that the publishing contract is formed with the proper party.

The most common situation for coauthors who produce a unitary work is joint ownership of the copyright. That is, the parties will jointly own the copyright in a single work. If each writer wants to be the sole owner of the portions he or she contributes to a work, this should be specified in the agreement. Under copyright law, a contributor to a work must provide copyrightable material in order to be a joint owner.

Since mere ideas cannot be copyrighted, persons who work with ghostwriters or *as told to* authors cannot own the copyright, except in works for hire or if the copyright is transferred by the actual writer through a written agreement. To qualify as a work for hire, the work must be written by an employee within the scope of his or her employment (i.e., a statutory employee). If written by an independent contractor, the contractor and employer must agree in writing that the work performed is to be a work for hire, and the work must be specially ordered or commissioned to be a contribution to one of the following:

- a collective work
- a translation
- a part of a motion picture or other audiovisual work
- a compilation
- an instructional text
- a test or answer material for a test
- an atlas
- a supplementary work (one that introduces, concludes, explains, revises, comments upon, or assists, etc., a work by another author)

In the absence of a written agreement, the independent contractor will own the copyright in a commissioned work.

When the work is not unitary, such as when an illustrator contributes a few drawings to a book, the contributors will separately hold the copyrights to their individual contributions. Even so, it is a good idea to confirm this in the written agreement, since ambiguities can affect the ability to control how the rights to the individual contributions are licensed in future transactions. For example, an illustrator may not want the writer to claim part ownership of the copyright in the illustrations, and the writer may not want the illustrator to claim any rights in the text.

MANUSCRIPT ISSUES

The collaboration agreement should describe the role of each party and their agreed contributions to the work. It should also state that the contributors are required to use their best efforts with respect to their contributions. Another important issue, particularly when working as coauthors, is to include in the agreement who has control over the content. Typically, it is best to require the parties to agree to consult with each other in good faith regarding issues concerning content, but to specify that one of the contributors will have the final say in such matters. This can greatly simplify the publishing and editing process for the publisher, as trying to get approval from a group of authors can be impossible. If one author is designated as the ultimate decision maker, compromises are more likely to be reached efficiently.

Another issue that should be addressed is how revisions will be handled once the manuscript is completed. Often the agreement will forbid one party from making changes to the manuscript without the consent of the other contributors once they agree it is complete. It may also specify how the contributors will respond to revisions recommended by the publisher. Editors have been known to make substantial changes to works, and publishers often provide writers with short time frames in which to review edited manuscripts and galleys. Therefore, a good agreement will allocate the responsibility to review and address revisions proposed by the publisher. Similarly, if the book contract requires the writers to prepare an index, the contributor agreement should address on whom that responsibility falls.

In addition, it is a good idea for the contributors to discuss and agree on the schedule of production, when the contributions will be provided to each other, and who has the final approval. For example, writers should decide whether they want to see the work as chapters are completed or whether they want to wait until all contributors have completed their assignments. Reaching agreement regarding the logistics of preparing the manuscript can be particularly important when one contributor needs to see the work of another to complete his or her assignment.

These issues are important to publishers, since they do not want to become embroiled in disputes between the writers they deal with and the individuals or entities with whom those writers have relationships. It is therefore important for the publisher to confirm that their authors have appropriate agreements in place before launching a publishing venture.

When a publisher agrees to publish a manuscript prepared by collaborators, such as coauthors or authors and illustrators, the publisher should be sure that the arrangement is sufficiently detailed between the parties so that problems should not arise. In fact, if the publisher does not make these arrangements, then there is a good chance that the publisher could wind up in the middle of a dispute between the other parties. A publisher is well-advised to work with an experienced publishing attorney in order to be sure that the arrangement is adequately worked out between the parties and that the publisher is protected. Among other things, the publisher should insist that the parties work out their financial arrangements, what will happen if one party is unable to continue because of death or incapacity, whether either party has a right to use any of the material in the manuscript for other purposes, and if so, how that material will be attributed when used elsewhere. There should also be a provision dealing with resolution of any disputes between the parties. A careful publisher should review a collaboration agreement with an experienced lawyer before agreeing to publish any collaborative work. If the collaboration agreement does not address all of the vital issues, an attorney can include such provisions in the publishing agreement to protect the rights of the publisher and ensure the publisher doesn't wind up in the middle of a dispute with no way to finish the project.

CHAPTER 10

Contracts

Publishers need to understand the basics of contract law, since many aspects of publishing—including arrangements with authors, agents, illustrators, freelancers, employees, printers, binders, and distributors—involve contracts. The terms of a contract vary depending on the situation, but in every case, the nature of legally binding agreements is the same. This chapter describes the basic elements common to all contracts.

The word *contract* commonly brings to mind lengthy, complicated documents replete with legal jargon, but this need not be the case. A simple, straightforward contract can be just as valid and enforceable as a complicated one. A contract is nothing more than a promise or set of promises that become enforceable because the parties have agreed to provide something of value to each other. The promises are known as *offers* and *acceptances,* depending on which party has made them, and the *something of value* is known as *consideration.* Once a contract is formed, both parties have a legal duty to perform it and may be subject to liability in the event they fail to perform.

OFFERS

The first stage of the formation of a contract is the *offer.* An offer is a statement that indicates the willingness of a party to enter into a binding agreement. Once an offer has been accepted, the contract is considered formed, and the person making the offer cannot afterward alter the terms without the consent of the other party.

Offers should be distinguished from expressions of intent, predictions, opinions, or statements indicating the desire to conduct preliminary negotiations. For example, a statement by a publisher to a writer expressing the opinion that a manuscript is excellent and will likely warrant an advance of $25,000 is not an offer, because it merely expresses the publisher's opinion. At most, it suggests an interest in negotiating a publishing agreement. Conversely, if the publisher states that it will publish the book on the terms set forth in a proposed agreement, this will constitute an offer that the writer may either accept or reject.

Typically, a writer's submission of material to a publisher for review will be considered an invitation to the publisher to make an offer. If the price and publishing terms are specified in the submittal—for example, *North American First Serial Rights for $5,000*—then the submission could be construed as an offer.

Sometimes the distinction between an offer and a nonoffer is unclear, so determining if a given statement is an offer will depend on whether a reasonable person would consider it to be an offer. Such considerations depend on the content of the statements, as well as the circumstances under which they were made. In addition, reasonableness is to be viewed from the perspective of the person to whom the statements are made. So if you know a statement is not truly an offer or is being made by someone without the ability to actually make an offer, then even though someone else might not be sure if the statement were an offer, it is not an offer to you.

Length of Time an Offer Stands

Once an offer is made, unless it states otherwise, it is considered to be open for a reasonable amount of time, unless it is revoked by the person who made the offer prior to its acceptance. What constitutes a reasonable amount of time will depend on the circumstances. At some point in time, an offer will be considered so stale that the person making it will no longer be legally bound.

In some cases, an offer will be irrevocable for a period of time. The most common instance of this for publishers is the *option contract*. An option contract is one in which the person who made the offer agrees not to revoke the offer for a given length of time, perhaps indefinitely. Common situations in which option contracts are used are in book publishing contracts, where the writer agrees to submit his or her next work exclusively to a particular publisher for evaluation. That publisher, in turn, is given the right to make an offer regarding the work. If the manuscript is rejected, the writer is free to have it published elsewhere. However, the initial publisher usually retains the right to match any other publisher's offer. This type of offer is irrevocable for the time stated in the option clause.

Another situation, not common in the publishing industry, is *irrevocable offers* under Article II of the Uniform Commercial Code (UCC). These are written offers made by sophisticated parties for the sale of goods that provide some assurance that the offer will be open for a stated time, or if no time is stated, for a reasonable time. However, Article II of the UCC is limited to tangible goods and does not apply to intellectual property. Most publishing agreements involve the sale of rights, which are not considered goods under the UCC. Transactions between a publisher and a distributor or book retailer may, however, fall under the UCC.

IN PLAIN ENGLISH

The Uniform Commercial Code is a body of commercial law that has been adopted in every state for the purpose of unifying the business relations between parties subject to it.

ACCEPTANCE

An *acceptance* is a statement agreeing to the terms of the offer. Once the acceptance is made, the parties have created a legally binding relationship. Both the offeror and the acceptor are legally bound to do what they have promised to do, as long as there is consideration, which is discussed below. One party or the other may refuse to go through with the deal, but that would be a breach of the contract and would make the refusing party liable to the other for any damages caused by the refusal.

The manner in which the offer may be accepted is subject to a few fundamentals. The general rule is that an acceptance is valid as long as it is made by a reasonable method of communication. The exception to this rule is when the offer places conditions on how the acceptance must be communicated. For example, if a publisher specifically requires that an author accept an offer to publish a work within five days by singing telegram, the author must comply with that direction for the acceptance to be valid.

The question of whether acceptance was made within a *reasonable time* is determined by common sense. A writer who waits for a year before responding to a publisher's offer probably has not accepted within a reasonable time. However, a writer who responds within one month has likely met this requirement. Whether an acceptance has been made within a reasonable time may also be affected by the business customs within the book publishing industry or by past dealings between the parties.

The issue of whether an acceptance is made in a *reasonable manner* is also determined by common sense. If, for example, the writer submits an offer by mail, a reasonable manner of communicating the acceptance would include not only mail, but also telephone, email, or facsimile. In addition, acceptances may be communicated by actions, such as beginning performance of the contract, provided that the other party reasonably understands that such action is being taken to reflect acceptance. For example, a celebrity who offers a writer several thousand dollars to ghostwrite his memoir would likely understand that the offer has been accepted when he becomes aware that the writer is working on the project.

CONSIDERATION

Consideration is a legal term meaning something of value. For a contract to be valid, the parties must agree to exchange consideration. Each side promises to give something of value. The most obvious example is the agreement to pay money, but consideration can also consist of things such as an agreement to waive one's legal right (e.g., the right to file a lawsuit or to compete against a former employer), an agreement to alter a legal relationship, or an agreement to provide a service. Consequently, in the vast majority of agreements, a promise made by either party will be considered sufficient consideration to support a binding contract.

The requirement of consideration is what distinguishes legally enforceable contracts from unenforceable promises. For example, an offer by a distinguished writer, such as Kevin, who wrote a blurb for this book, to his unpublished nephew to present the nephew's manuscript to his own publisher constitutes nothing more than a promise, because the nephew has provided no consideration. If the writer fails to present the manuscript, the nephew will not be able to legally enforce the writer's promise.

For a contract to be binding, however, the consideration does not necessarily have to be substantial or even equivalent to the fair market value of the promise received. For example, if the nephew in the previous example offered to wash the writer's car in exchange for the writer presenting the nephew's manuscript to the publisher and the writer accepted, the writer would be legally bound to present the manuscript. In this case, a contract is created because consideration (the service of washing the car) was provided in exchange for the presentation of the manuscript.

FORM OF CONTRACTS

In most instances, once the requirements of offer, acceptance, and consideration are met, a contract is formed and is legally binding. There are generally no legal requirements that the contract contain specific terminology, be printed in a particular way, or be arranged according to a particular format. However, the practical aspects associated with enforcing contracts make it easier to enforce those that clearly describe the obligations of the parties and are memorialized in writing.

Implied Contracts

Contracts that are not explicitly stated in words may be implied by conduct. For example, suppose that a writer submits a manuscript to a publisher, which publishes the manuscript but does not compensate the writer. Even though they did not sign a contract, there is an *implied contract* between them. The terms of that contract depend upon the relationship between the writer and the publisher. If the facts indicate that the writer submitted the manuscript with no expectation of payment, then none would be due. On the other hand, if the writer has historically submitted manuscripts to this publisher and received payment from the publisher for publishing them, it is likely that the writer expected to receive compensation and that a promise by the publisher to pay would be implied. The implied terms of the contract would be legally enforceable. But absent a clear written agreement, the parties could be faced with lengthy and expensive litigation to determine the amount due and other issues.

Oral Contracts

An *oral contract* is one in which the parties have verbally agreed to something but have not recorded the agreement in writing. Most oral contracts are valid and enforceable, although some kinds of agreements are legally required to be in writing to be enforceable. As a practical matter, oral contracts are often difficult to prove in court, since the main evidence is usually the conflicting testimony of the parties. It has been said that *oral contracts are not worth the paper they are written on*. While not technically correct, this adage does reflect the harsh reality that many worthy claims cannot success-fully be enforced because oral agreements lack the strength of written ones.

Written Contracts

Written agreements should adequately describe the obligations of the parties and the consideration involved. The practice of some drafters to describe the consideration in generic terms (*for just and valuable con-sideration*) should be avoided. Such language can create ambiguity about whether consideration was involved at all. Courts generally will not enforce agreements that describe a fictitious consideration or one that was not actually exchanged. Custom dictates that written contracts be signed and dated by the parties.

Under the Electronic Signatures in Global and National Commerce Act (ESIGN) and various state laws, transactions executed electronically, such as by email, cannot be invalidated solely because an electronic signature or electronic record was used in their formation. An electronic signature is any identifying mark, such as the sender's name at the end of an email or email address in the header. Some kinds of documents, such as wills, are typically covered by these laws, as are most publishing agreements.

Some types of agreements are legally required to be in written form. The Statute of Frauds, a law adopted to inhibit fraud and perjury, provides that any contract that cannot be fully performed within one year must be in writing in order to be legally binding. This rule has been narrowly construed to mean that if a contract can conceivably be performed within one year of its making, it need not be in writing. Assume that a writer has agreed to submit two manuscripts to a publisher—one within eigh-teen months after the contract is signed and the second within eighteen to twenty-four months thereafter and no earlier. In this situation, the terms of the agreement make it impossible for the writer to complete performance within one year. If, however, the writer agrees to submit both manuscripts within twenty-four months, it is possible that the writer could submit both manuscripts in the first year and the requirements of the Statute of Frauds would be satisfied.

The fact that the writer might not actually complete performance within one year is immaterial. So long as complete performance within one year is possible, the agreement need not be made in writing. The Statute of Frauds applies to other kinds of contracts as well, but these rarely involve writing activities. For instance, the UCC requires that contracts for the sale of goods costing over $500 must be in writing, but there is no such requirement for service contracts (such as publishing agreements). The UCC would apply to agreements between publishers and, for example, paper companies and other suppliers of materials. It would also apply to agreements between publishers and their distributors or book retailers.

CAPACITY TO CONTRACT

For a contract to be enforceable, the parties must be capable of understanding their contractual obligations. Minors are deemed by law to have *diminished capacity* to contract. A person is legally a minor until the age of majority. This age varies from state to state but is either eighteen or twenty-one years of age in most states. This fact is relevant to publishers, since a publisher might wish to contract with a minor author or illustrator. A contract entered into by a minor is not necessarily *void*, but such a contract is generally *voidable*. This means that the minor may be free to rescind the contract until he or she reaches the age of majority, but that the other party is bound by the contract if the minor elects to enforce it. In some states, a minor over eighteen years of age must restore the consideration or its equivalent as a condition of rescinding or getting out of the contract.

Persons who are so disabled by mental illness that they are unable to understand the nature of the transaction in a reasonable manner also lack the legal capacity to enter into a contract. However, the fact that a person may suffer from a mental disorder does not necessarily preclude their ability to understand the nature of a contract, so not all such agreements are voidable. Persons afflicted with temporary incapacity, such as intoxication, may be able to void some contracts, especially if the other party was aware of the incapacity. Courts are reluctant, however, to void contracts with fair terms when the other party was unaware of the incapacity.

Persons who have the capacity to enter into contracts and who sign written agreements are generally bound to the terms of those agreements, irrespective of whether they read or understood the agreement before signing. The law imposes the burden on the parties to read proposed agreements and understand the terms prior to signing them. The fact that an agreement was lengthy, obtusely drafted, or complicated will seldom justify rescission, except when the terms are unconscionable or against public policy.

ACCEPTABLE FORMS FOR WRITTEN CONTRACTS

Written agreements do not have to be in any particular form to be legally effective. Courts have upheld memoranda, letters, and telegrams as valid and enforceable writings, as long as they adequately describe the agreement, identify the parties, and are signed. Many contracts contain considerably more information than the bare minimum necessary to comply with the Statute of Frauds. The typical contract will recite the basic terms of the agreement and may also include various covenants, conditions, and warranties.

A *covenant* is an absolute, unconditional promise to perform. Failure to perform a covenant is a breach of contract in and of itself. In a writer-publisher contract, the writer's promise to submit a manuscript is generally a covenant. Failure to submit a manuscript by the specified date will result in a breach of contract and provides the publisher with the right to cancel the contract (unless he or she has agreed to an extension).

A *condition*, on the other hand, is a fact or event that creates the duty to perform the contract at its occurrence, and the failure of which to occur extinguishes the duty. Conditions can be either precedent to an agreement or subsequent to the agreement. A *condition precedent* is one that must occur before the agreement becomes effective or binding. A *condition subsequent* is a future event, the nonoccurrence of which may give one party the right to abandon its contractual promises.

For example, in addition to being a covenant, the writer's promise to submit a manuscript for publication may be a condition precedent to the publisher's promises to pay and publish. In such a case, the publisher's promises to publish and pay are not enforceable until the writer has, in fact, submitted a manuscript. Once the writer submits a manuscript, however, a failure to pay or publish would be a breach and would likely make the publisher subject to liability. This would not be true in a situation in which the publisher has agreed to give the writer an advance before the manuscript is completed. In this type of arrangement, the agreement to submit the manuscript might be seen as a condition subsequent, which, if not performed, could result in a revocation of the writer-publisher contract.

Warranties are statements that provide some sort of assurance about the quality of the subject of the contract. They may be either express or implied. When making a warranty, a writer is assuming all responsibility that the work contains the represented quality, irrespective of the writer's absence of actual knowledge.

For example, a writer who warrants that her work is original and that she is the copyright owner will be liable if this is not the case, even if she unconsciously copied another work or believed in good faith that her work was not derivative of another. Such a warranty can be (and often is) made explicit by inserting it into a publishing agreement. If the parties are commercially sophisticated, such as an established publisher and an experienced freelance journalist, this kind of warranty would likely be considered made by implication. This is because both parties realize the importance of originality and ownership of the copyright.

All warranties, express or implied, can be *disclaimed*. Express warranties can be disclaimed by words or conduct that negate the warranty when it would be reasonable and fair to do so. For example, a warranty of originality could be disclaimed by inserting text into the publishing agreement that reads, "the writer has disclosed to the publisher a list of his sources in preparing the work." Publishers should be very careful when this type of provision is used. In fact, it is a red flag for the publisher, who may very well request more information from the writer before publishing the identified work.

Mere statements of opinion, called *puffing*, will not create a warranty. If a publisher, when offering a book contract to a writer, exclaims that the book is a potential best-seller, then such a statement would likely be construed as puffing—not a warranty. The publisher is not making a statement of fact but is merely stating an opinion. The distinction, however, may not always be clear, and publishers should be careful when making such statements.

In ambiguous situations, whether a given statement will be considered one of fact or mere puffing depends upon whether the statement becomes part of the basis of the bargain. Although the phrase *basis of the bargain* is hard to define precisely, it is reasonable to say that a given statement becomes part of the basis of the bargain if a contract to purchase is, to a large extent, induced by that statement. In the example of the enthusiastic publisher, the publisher's statement would probably not have been a determining factor in making the sale and therefore was not a warranty, but mere opinion.

ILLEGAL CONTRACTS AND LITERARY PROFITS LAWS

If either the consideration or the subject matter of the contract is illegal, the contract itself is illegal. The law generally treats an illegal contract as void, meaning that it is not binding on either party and neither will be permitted to enforce the agreement against the other. For example, if a writer and publisher sign a book contract to publish a book of images that violate child pornography laws, the contract would be void because it is illegal to possess or distribute such images. The publisher could not sue the writer if the manuscript was not prepared, nor could the writer sue to force the publisher to publish the book after the manuscript was delivered.

It is not illegal for a publisher and a convicted criminal to enter into a publishing agreement for a written account of the crime. However, many states impose restrictions on such contracts, patterned after New York's Son of Sam law. These laws are known generally as *literary profits laws* and have been found unconstitutional in New York, California, Massachusetts, and Nevada. However, many states still have laws modeled on the New York law. Depending on the language of the particular laws, some courts have found similar laws constitutional. Under the law as originally enacted, a copy of the contract had to be submitted to a special board, as well as the monies owed to the criminal under the contract. The money was then placed in an escrow account for the benefit of any victims of the crime. The escrow account was maintained for five years, during which time the victims had to obtain a money judgment against the criminal in a civil lawsuit. New York has subsequently amended its law in an attempt to avoid a ruling that it is unconstitutional.

Under the federal law, the attorney general can take legal action requiring the forfeiture of money owed to a criminal for the literary or dramatic depiction of federal crimes that injured third parties. To be compensated, a victim must win a judgment in a United States district court within five years of the criminal's conviction. Any money left in the escrow account at the end of five years must typically remain in a special crime victims fund. Some state laws allow the criminal to claim any money remaining in the escrow account at the end of the five-year period.

IN PLAIN ENGLISH

A publisher who desires to publish a book written by an author who anticipates entering into a contract with a criminal to write his or her story would be well-advised to consult a lawyer prior to doing so.

UNCONSCIONABILITY

The law generally gives the parties involved in a contract complete freedom to contract. Thus, contractual terms that are unfair, unjust, or even ludicrous will generally be enforced if they are legal. This freedom is not without limits—the parties are not free to make a contract that is unconscionable. *Unconscionability* is an elusive concept, but the courts have certain guidelines in ruling on it. A given contract is likely to be considered unconscionable if it is grossly unfair and the parties lack equal bargaining power.

New authors are typically in a weaker bargaining position than publishers and therefore are more likely to win an allegation of unconscionability—especially where the writer has simply signed the publisher's form contract. If the form contract is extremely one-sided in favor of the publisher, and if the writer was given the choice of signing the contract unchanged or not contracting at all, the courts may find that the agreement was unconscionable. If that happens, the court may either treat the contract as void or strike the unconscionable clauses and enforce the remainder. Unconscionability is generally set up as a defense by the party who is sued for breach of contract, but beware: this defense is rarely successful.

REMEDIES

The principle underlying all remedies for breach of contract is to satisfy the aggrieved party's expectations. That is, the courts will attempt to place the aggrieved party in the same position that the party would have enjoyed had the contract been fully performed. Courts and legislatures have devised a number of remedies to provide aggrieved parties with the benefit of their bargains. Generally, this will take the form of monetary damages. However, when monetary damages fail to restore the aggrieved party to the position the party would have enjoyed under the contract, the court may order *specific performance*.

Specific performance means the breaching party is ordered to perform as he or she promised. This remedy is generally reserved for cases in which the contract involves unique services or goods. In publishing, a court might specifically enforce a writer-publisher contract by compelling the writer to deliver the manuscript to the publisher, but only if the manuscript has been completed. A court would not likely compel a writer to create a manuscript or complete an unfinished manuscript as a means of satisfying the aggrieved publisher, since the Thirteenth Amendment of the US Constitution prohibits one from being forced to perform labor against one's will. Thus, for breach of a contract for services to be performed in the future, monetary damages are generally awarded.

The question of a publisher's obligation to publish a work for which it has contracted is more perplexing. In *Zilg v. Prentice-Hall, Inc.*, a case brought by an author against a publisher, a court found that a publisher had breached its contract and awarded the author damages when, in response to criticism and complaint by the DuPont family, which the book targeted, it shrank the book's advertising budget, reduced the number of copies printed, and shortened its print run. Expert witnesses testified about the royalties the author would have likely received if the contract had not been breached, and the court concluded that the author had proved that he would have made additional book sales if the publisher had published more copies.

Similarly, in *Chodos v. West Publishing Company*, a publisher was found to have breached its contract with an author when it decided not to publish a book it had contracted with the author to write, not because it was deficient in form or content, but because the publisher believed that it would not be successful. The court believed that *because of the wording of the written contract* and under the factual circumstances, the author was entitled to be compensated under the legal theory of *quantum meruit* for the time and effort that went into writing the book, but not for a guess as to the royalties he might have received, since such damages were too speculative and therefore not recoverable. The term *quantum meruit* is a legal term meaning that there is an implied contract.

Cases brought by authors have resolved the other way, as well. In *Kirschten v. Research Insts. of America, Inc.*, an author's numerous claims against a publisher were ruled to be unfounded based on the written agreement entered into by the parties. The court summarized the case as involving "the anger of a proud, talented author who was unable to have a work published that met her own strict standards and, unfortunately, has sought to remedy the problem in court, suing on a contract that as written does not provide her with the niceties she would like." In *Brabec v. Delmar Thompson Learning*, the court again relied on the language of a publishing contract to determine whether a publisher breached its duties to the author of a textbook on community nursing. The contract provided that the author had to tender a manuscript that was "acceptable for publication," a determination that was to be made "in its sole judgment." The author's claim that the publisher's decision not to publish her book was due to the fault of the publisher's editors was rejected by the court; since no express contractual language required the publisher to edit the book, it was up to her to deliver a satisfactory manuscript.

As is well illustrated by the foregoing case examples, the language of a publishing contract is critically important. Great care should be taken in drafting or reviewing such contracts. For these reasons, it is extremely important for you to work with an experienced publishing lawyer.

CHAPTER 11

Publisher-Author Contracts

Publishers should develop a standard form contract that they use on a regular basis. The standard form contract will contain tried-and-true provisions and form the foundation for negotiations with authors. The publisher should understand this basic contract and review it with an attorney.

In the past, many writers would simply sign a publisher's form contract as written, rather than bargain for more favorable terms. Over time, the trend has changed from one of acquiescence to one in which at least some negotiation is commonplace. In order to protect their interests, writers may demand that certain contract clauses be deleted or included, and contract negotiations often involve a lively give-and-take in which the demands of both writers and publishers are at least partially met.

This chapter considers the clauses typically included in book contracts and the demands likely to be made by the respective parties as to how these clauses should be written. It also points out some of the issues to be considered in magazine contracts, limited edition contracts, and music contracts, as well.

ADVANCES

An advance against royalties may be the first money received by a writer and is, in effect, typically a partial payment of anticipated royalties before they are earned. Publishers generally determine the amount of the advance based on the number of copies of the book they think will sell and the royalties that will be due the writer. Frequently, the advance is based on the anticipated royalties to be earned in the first year after the book is released. The publishing contract will govern whether the advance will be delivered to the writer as a lump sum after signing the contract or will be paid in installments triggered by various events—for example, the publishing contract would state that a portion of the advance will be paid when the parties sign the contract, another portion when the writer delivers the manuscript, and the rest upon publication.

The publishing contract will also determine whether or not the advance is refundable to the publisher. If an advance is refundable, the writer will have to return that portion that exceeds the royalties due to the writer from actual sales. For example, if the writer received a $7,000 advance, but sales of the book warranted only $3,000 in royalties, the writer would have to return the $4,000 that was not earned. When the advance is refundable, it is important that both parties agree to a specific period within which the royalties are to be matched against the advance. A nonrefundable advance (sometimes called a guarantee) need not be returned by the writer, even if it is never earned out. Most advances are nonrefundable.

Some authors feel that the advance clause is the most important clause in the contract because it provides immediate cash. In the long run, such a view can be shortsighted, since ultimately the income derived from the work will depend on other issues, such as royalty rates, subsidiary rights, and out-of-print provisions. On the other hand, many publishers never recoup their advance through sales, so there may be something to be said for large advances. Some small publishers may not be in a position to provide a writer with a large advance or any advance at all. They may attract authors by offering concessions in other areas of the contract—for example, a larger royalty rate or more subsidiary rights.

Signing Fees

Advances should be distinguished from signing fees, which may only be available to well-established writers who have proven sales records. Signing fees, unlike advances, are never refundable and are unrelated to royalties. They do not have to be earned out by sales. A signing fee is merely a payment made to a writer for purposes of attracting that writer and consummating the publishing contract.

ROYALTIES

Royalties begin to accrue once the book starts to sell. If an advance has been given, royalties will be applied against the advance, and no money will be paid to the writer until the royalties exceed the amount of the advance, referred to as an earn-out. Royalty amounts, the payment schedule, and royalty statements all must be addressed in the publishing contract. Royalties are customarily paid semiannually and are typically accompanied by a royalty statement. The royalty statement is an itemized account showing the number of copies printed, bound, sold, or given away by the publisher; the author's royalty rate; and, generally, the reserves for returns.

One aspect to consider when drafting a royalty clause is whether the royalties will be based on the list price (also known as the suggested retail price) or the net receipts (which may often be the wholesale price). Books are typically sold at a discount, often over 50 percent and sometimes up to 75 percent, off the publisher's list price. Therefore, at any given royalty rate, payment on a net-receipts basis will be about half of what the payment would be on a list-price basis or even lower depending on the discount. In the past, payment on a list-price basis was preferred because it simplified tracking royalty payments. Today, computers have no difficulty tracking any kind of royalty payments, and therefore this is no longer an issue.

Publishers should typically include a clause in the contract stating that no royalties will be paid on copies distributed for review or advertising, on copies furnished gratuitously to the writer or as samples, or for copies destroyed while in inventory or during shipment. Moreover, the publisher should consider stipulating that no royalties will be paid on books returned from bookstores. Thus, if the royalty rate is 10 percent of the list price, 8,000 copies are shipped to retailers, and 2,000 copies are returned, the writer would be entitled to royalties on only 6,000 copies, rather than on the full 8,000.

The publisher should consider adding a provision reducing the royalty rate for copies sold at a substantial discount (also known as a deep discount). Traditionally, a clause of this type was intended to reflect the lower return from special sales outside of regular trade channels or the sales of remainder copies. Remaindering refers to the sale by the publisher of the publisher's inventory of a title after the initial distribution has been completed and there is no intention by the publisher to continue selling the title. Thus, a royalty rate of 10 percent might be reduced to 5 percent for copies sold to bulk purchasers at special discounts or to wholesalers for specialized markets at larger-than-normal discounts. Similarly, the royalty rate might be reduced for all export, remainder, and premium sales.

At times, the royalty rate reduction may be determined by a particular formula. For example, the publisher might specify that the stated royalty will be reduced by one-fourth of the difference between a 50 percent discount and whatever discount is granted. A discount of 60 percent would, in this case, reduce the author's royalty rate by 2.5 percent. Of course, the writer may demand that some limitations be placed on this type of clause to ensure that, in every case, at least some royalties will be forthcoming. Publishers should be aware of this issue and they should be prepared to deal with it when it arises.

Deep-discount clauses are subject to abuse, since many publishers will sell a large portion of their inventory in the normal course of business at discounts greater than the one set forth in the contract. Since industry custom seems to be heading in the direction of increased deep discounting, writers may try to modify reduced-royalty clauses by insisting that they not apply to the ordinary sales of books to the trade. As an alternative, the publisher may offer to minimize the effect of the clause by changing the discount rate or having reductions in royalties apply on an escalating scale.

Reserves

Reserves are another significant issue. Most publishers offer booksellers the right to return unsold inventory for a refund. The customary practice is for the contract to withhold a certain percentage of royalties to cover the anticipated returns. Although the practice is commercially reasonable, it can be abused should the publisher withhold amounts that significantly exceed the actual expected returns or withhold the reserve for an excessive time. Since the percentage of returns varies considerably depending on the book, most book contracts entitle the publisher to establish a reasonable reserve. Providing the publisher with some flexibility to establish the size of the reserve is reasonable, although writers may attempt to put some limits on the publisher's discretion. For example, the publisher should be able to better estimate the anticipated returns of a book over time and therefore should be willing to agree to limit the reserve to 20 percent or less after four standard six-month accounting cycles (unless the book is remaindered or the actual returns during the preceding cycle exceeded 20 percent). Likewise, it is typical to limit the length of time that royalties can be withheld as reserves, because most returns can be expected within one or two accounting cycles after delivery to booksellers. In general, writers may negotiate for language in the contract providing that the publisher may withhold the royalties for no more than one or two accounting cycles.

Royalty Statements

Another common complaint by authors is that royalty statements are indecipherable or erroneous and that publishers have understated sales. A way to help prevent this or at least provide some cure is to include an auditing clause in the author-publisher contract. This type of clause provides that the writer, at the writer's expense, may examine the publisher's books and records upon giving reasonable advance notice. Bear in mind, though, that the cost of such examination may be quite high. Therefore, many authors request that the auditing clause provide that if any discrepancy exceeds 5 percent of the amount received by the writer, the publisher will pay all expenses attributable to the examination. If any discrepancy is less than 5 percent, the writer will bear the cost. Publishers should try to increase the percentage that will trigger the auditing cost shifting, since calculation errors could result in very costly expenses.

FORMAT AND CONTENT OF THE MANUSCRIPT

Most book contracts require the writer to submit a digital text file in a specific format. Contracts will also address other issues, such as the delivery date, schedules for returning proofs, and who has responsibility for preparing the preface, endnotes, and index, if any. Publishers usually assume the burden of preparing book covers and layouts and typically retain the sole discretion regarding their design. The contract may offer to give the writer the right to approve them or simply review and comment on them. Most often, the publishing contract will allow publishers to retain the discretion to change book titles.

A typical book contract will contain a clause in which the writer promises to deliver a manuscript that is satisfactory in form and content or one that is in all regards acceptable. Failure to produce a satisfactory manuscript can have several consequences. First, the publisher will not be required to pay further installments of the advance. Second, depending on the terms of the contract, the writer will either have to repay whatever portion of the advance has already been received or make such repayment if the book is later sold to another publishing house. Third, the writer will have to revise the manuscript in a limited amount of time if the contract so provides or if the publisher is willing to consider a revised version.

Whenever a manuscript is rejected as unacceptable, the meaning of the term "satisfactory or acceptable" becomes crucial in determining the rights of the writer and the publisher. Unfortunately, contracts almost never provide a standard for what is acceptable and what is not. While the publisher's decision will generally be subjective rather than objective, courts have imposed an obligation of good faith on publishers. Generally, publishers are allowed to reject manuscripts when they have good-faith concerns regarding the quality of the material. However, publishers are not free to reject manuscripts because their appraisal of the market has changed or because they have altered their publishing objectives. A particularly messy case involving a rejected manuscript was filed by Random House against the actress Joan Collins in 1995. The actress had negotiated a two-book contract with the publisher in 1991 for a $4 million advance to be paid in installments. Random House rejected the manuscripts and sued to recover the $1.2 million it had already paid. As befits a matter involving a glamorous celebrity, an established publishing house, and substantial commercial stakes, the media buzz surrounding the case was replete with speculation, rumors, and accusations.

Collins's editor at Random House stated that the manuscripts were rejected because they were primitive, jumbled, and disjointed. However, there was speculation in the press that Collins had lost her market appeal after her television series *Dynasty* was canceled and that Random House wanted to back out of the deal. Collins conceded that the manuscripts needed some work but asserted that Random House refused to provide the editorial assistance that she had expected. There was also speculation that she may have dumped the manuscript on Random House in the belief that the publisher valued Collins's celebrity status more than the content of the manuscripts and would rework them as necessary. Collins counterclaimed against Random House for the remainder of the $4 million she contended she was owed under the contract.

The case went to trial, and the jury ruled that the actress could keep the advance already paid and was entitled to recover another $1.3 million for the first manuscript. It also ruled that the actress was not entitled to any recovery regarding the second manuscript because it merely rehashed the first. The decision is generally regarded as a victory for writers, since it is believed to have made publishers more wary about rejecting manuscripts.

Publisher's Duty to Edit

While the standard manuscript acceptance clause does not explicitly impose a duty on the part of the publisher to edit manuscripts, some courts have ruled that the obligation to act in good faith imposes a limited duty on the part of the publisher to edit. This implied obligation stresses the need for communication between authors and publishers, particularly when specific faults are found. This includes the obligation to provide appropriate editorial work.

Although publishers have some duty to edit, they are not obligated to expend whatever effort it takes to salvage an inferior manuscript. The duty to edit does not extend to an obligation to provide *skillful* editing. Further, the extent of the publisher's duty to edit will depend on the specific language of the contract between the publisher and writer and may be limited to when the writer requests editorial assistance.

Standards of Acceptability

Rather than depend on any implied duty to comment or edit, a publisher should discuss standards of acceptability with the writer and include criteria for judging the finished product in the contract. The Authors Guild, an advocacy organization for authors and dramatists, suggests a clause providing that the manuscript submitted must be "in style and content, professionally competent and fit for publication."

Another suggestion is to reference the proposal submitted by the author, along with language specifying that the manuscript will be deemed acceptable if it conforms to the proposal. In addition, many writers request a clause that requires the publisher to specify in written detail why the manuscript is not satisfactory and provide the author with a period of time (e.g., sixty days) to submit a revised manuscript. Publishers customarily reject these attempts by writers and instead make it clear that the manuscript must be acceptable to the publisher. A midground is to have an arrangement whereby the author is given an opportunity to correct any defects, but the ultimate decision as to whether a manuscript is acceptable should remain the absolute right of the publisher.

It is also important for publishers to establish a method for fact-checking a manuscript, since inaccuracies can result in liability for both the author and the publisher.

Timeliness

Finally, writers often request that the contract specify the period of time that the publisher has in which to state that it has accepted or rejected the manuscript. One reason for this is that production can get stalled if a manuscript gets placed in a pile and is allowed to languish there. This situation is not unheard of when the acquiring editor leaves the publisher and the manuscript is assigned to an editor with little personal interest in the book. The other reason is that many contracts specify that acceptance of the manuscript is the event that triggers the publisher's obligation to pay a portion of the advance. By specifying a reasonable period for evaluation of the manuscript, writers attempt to ensure they get paid in a timely fashion. Busy publishers should establish internal guidelines for accepting manuscripts in order to continue the relationship they have with their authors.

ALTERATIONS

The writer generally agrees to pay the costs of making author's alterations or corrections on galley or page proofs that exceed a certain percentage of the manuscript. This clause is designed to discourage authors from rewriting the book after it has been edited. Many authors attempt to try to modify such a clause by requiring the publisher to absorb the cost of changes made for the purpose of updating material when a significant event has occurred. It is often common to request that the writer not be responsible for changes that merely correct the publisher's errors. Today, this issue is not as significant as it was years ago, when manuscripts were actually manually typeset. In fact, the cost of making the changes can be minimal, though, it is something publishers should consider.

PUBLICATION

The *publication clause* requires the publisher to publish the manuscript within a given time after accepting it. These clauses are important because some books will lose their commercial viability if not published in a reasonable amount of time. In addition, books that were acquired by editors who have since left the publisher may get stalled at the publisher for lack of attention. Without a publication clause, the writer will be left without the leverage needed to prompt publication or to reacquire the rights to license the work to another publisher (while keeping the advance). Publishers should be aware of this fact when negotiating the contract.

REVISIONS

The *revisions clause* generally provides that if the publisher decides that it wants to publish a revised version of the book (e.g., a second edition), the writer must be given the first option to make such a revision. This situation is generally relevant only to nonfiction works. If the writer is unable or unwilling to undertake the job, the publisher is then free to contract with someone else to do it. When the writer chooses to revise the book, the contract may provide that the royalty scheme for the revised edition remain the same or revert to the base percentage. The base percentage is the lowest percentage paid when royalties are determined on a sliding scale based on volume of sales. Some contracts provide that the author's royalty rate is to revert to the base percentage if the revision involves a substantial resetting.

To understand how this might work, assume that a writer agrees to revise the first edition and that the revision costs exceed the stated 50 percent. Further, assume that royalty rates on the first edition were 10 percent for the first 5,000 copies sold and 15 percent thereafter, and that 7,000 copies of the first edition were sold. If the contract calls for the royalty rate to revert to the base percentage, the royalty on the revised edition will start at 10 percent, even though the writer is receiving 15 percent on the prior edition.

If the publisher contracts with someone other than the writer to undertake and complete the revision, the publisher may compensate that party either with a flat fee or with royalties. The revision clause generally provides that the money paid to the reviser is to be deducted from any sums accruing to the original writer. In order to protect royalty interests, the writer may demand that no revisions of the original edition be made until a certain period of time has elapsed from the date of first release, usually one to three years. In addition, the writer may demand a phasing-out provision, whereby the author's royalties may be reduced only by a stated percentage and no more upon each revision. Thus, the author's royalties might be reduced by one-fourth upon the first revision, one-half upon the second, three-fourths upon the third, and be eliminated upon the fourth.

COPYRIGHT

The *copyright clause* establishes which party, the writer or the publisher, is to own the copyright in the published work. The norm in trade book contracts is for the writer to retain the copyright. Some publishers of nonfiction and scholarly texts ask that the copyright be assigned to them. This is justified because such works are frequently updated, and if the publisher retains the copyright, it can arrange for supplements or revisions even after the writer is no longer able to update the work.

However, this issue can be addressed in ways other than transferring the copyright. Most publishers will agree to allow the copyright to remain in the writer's name.

In trade book contracts, the writer will generally grant the publisher a license to exercise certain rights included in the copyright, such as the right to exploit the subsidiary rights. Some writers will grant the publisher the copyright under the condition that the copyright reverts to the writer at some specified time or after some specified event (for example, when the book goes out of print). Since a copyright is divisible, the rights within it may be divided between the writer and publisher. Thus, the writer may grant the publisher the right to publish and sell the work in book form but retain the movie rights for him- or herself.

The copyright clause usually requires the writer to inform the publisher if any previously copyrighted material (whether by the writer or someone else) has been incorporated into the manuscript. If it has, the writer should be required to get written permission to use the material from the original publisher or copyright owner and to submit that written permission to the publisher. Often, there will be a nominal fee for reproducing material from another publication. As a general rule, the writer pays these fees. However, depending on the nature of the book and the parties involved, this could be negotiated.

Whether the writer or publisher retains copyright ownership, the publisher should print the proper copyright notice on the completed book, register the copyright with the Copyright Office, and take any other actions necessary to protect the copyright. Sometimes a publisher will include a provision that the writer must agree to transfer ownership of the copyright in the event that the publisher wants to sue a party that has infringed the copyright of the work. Such provisions are appropriate so the publisher can zealously protect the copyright.

SUBSIDIARY RIGHTS

While the main focus of many writers is to see that their books are published and sold, in many cases, a substantial portion of the income from a given work will be earned from exploitation from the subsidiary rights. Subsidiary rights are defined as the rights of exploitation in markets not included in the primary grant of the right to publish and sell. For example, film rights would be subsidiary rights in a book contract, while book rights would be subsidiary rights in a film contract. Subsidiary rights in a publishing contract could include

- film rights
- television rights
- foreign rights
- translation rights
- book clubs
- paperback reprints
- excerpts in magazines
- newspaper syndication
- audiobooks
- abridgements and condensations
- anthologies
- dramatizations
- rights to alternative forms, such as electronic publishing
- the right to develop the characters.

Subsidiary rights may be divided between the writer and publisher in any number of ways. However, the writer (particularly if the writer has an agent) often retains motion picture, television, dramatic, foreign, and translation rights, with the book club and paperback rights held by the publisher. The ability to develop a character has become very important, since it can be very valuable. Characters such as Superman, Batman, Harry Potter, and Han Solo have taken on a life of their own. The ability to own the rights to these characters is extremely important. Whichever party owns those rights will enjoy extraordinary economic rewards from merchandising. The income from the sale of these rights is often split fifty-fifty, though, of course, this is negotiable. Since the definition of subsidiary rights can vary from contract to contract, the publisher should review the definitions to make sure they are precise and not overly broad.

Recently, authors have been arguing for—and winning—a larger percentage of subsidiary rights and more control over the way subsidiary rights are exercised. For example, the writer may demand that no license of subsidiary rights be granted by the publisher without the author's consent. A publisher faced with a clause such as this may balance it with a provision in which it is agreed that the author's consent will not be unreasonably withheld. But the writer may require that, if the publisher does not dispose of the subsidiary rights within a stated time (for example, one year), all rights will revert to the writer. This too is negotiable, and some publishers make it clear that they should be permitted to retain the rights so long as they are actively attempting to negotiate acceptable arrangements.

Publishers are resisting the trend of subsidiary rights reverting to the author, because a substantial percentage of the publisher's profits often comes from the sale and exploitation of subsidiary rights. In fact, in today's world with ebooks, audiobooks, and digital media, subsidiary rights may be the most important feature of the contract. For this reason, publishers should be careful to negotiate appropriate arrangements for these rights.

Residual Clause

Since subsidiary rights can mean money for authors as well as publishers, both parties should make clear in their contract which subsidiary rights belong to which party. Failure to do so may not only result in substantial financial losses, but may also cause the contract to be declared void for vagueness. To prevent this, a residual clause may be included in which one party is given all subsidiary rights not otherwise expressly granted to the other party. The residual clause recognizes that advances in technology are constantly broadening the uses of literary property and states which party will receive the benefits of subsidiary rights in new technology. If a residual clause is not included, the party in whose name the book has been copyrighted will automatically receive all additional subsidiary rights.

WARRANTY AND INDEMNITY

Warranty and indemnity clauses require writers to warrant that their work is neither unlawful nor obscene, and that it does not defame anyone or invade their privacy. These clauses also require the writer to indemnify or reimburse the publisher for any expenses incurred by the publisher in defending claims covered by the warranty. Publishers insist on these clauses because they are at the mercy of the writer with regard to issues such as defamation. Unless writers assume the risk of paying the litigation expenses if they write defamatory material or infringe a copyright, publishers fear that many writers will have insufficient incentive to refrain from such activities.

Warranty clauses are typically characterized by language stating that the work has not been previously published and does not plagiarize other writing. Such clauses are fairly comfortable from the authors' perspective, because they have control over whether the works have been previously published and which materials have been incorporated. In other words, absent deliberate misconduct on their part, the only significant risk faced by writers under these clauses is that another person may have published a work without the writer's authorization. The warranty clauses pertaining to defamation and infringement of privacy rights are more problematic, because the laws covering these issues can vary among the states. In these cases, it is more likely that a writer could violate a person's rights without intending to do so.

Although publishers should not agree to delete a warranty and indemnity clause altogether, writers may attempt to reduce the scope and effect of the clause. First, writers may try to limit the scope of the warranty. One reasonable request is to add a provision that the clause does not apply to claims that arise from the publisher's changes or additions to the original manuscript. In addition, the scope may be limited by modifying the warranty with the phrase *to the best of the author's knowledge*. Publishers should resist this request, since a *best of knowledge* clause will significantly undermine the warranty.

Second, writers may try to limit the effect by reducing the amount they might owe the publisher and the degree to which the publisher may withhold royalties from the writer to cover the indemnity. One way to limit the effect is to agree to indemnify the publisher if the lawsuit is settled prior to a final judgment, but only if such settlement is made with the writer's consent. This gives the writer the ability to control an overgenerous publisher during settlement negotiations. Here too, the publisher should use its best efforts to retain control in a situation like this, since the publisher is at risk because of the author's activities, and the publisher would only be involved in the litigation because of the author's work. It would be appropriate to have an experienced publishing law attorney review clauses such as this before agreeing to them.

In addition, the writer might demand that indemnification will never exceed 50 percent of the damages. In other words, the cases of the claim or lawsuit are to be divided equally between writer and publisher. Finally, if the clause allows the publisher to begin withholding royalties when a suit is filed, the writer might demand that the amount of royalties withheld not exceed a reasonable estimate of the prospective damages. Once again, publishers should be careful when presented with these demands. Experienced publishing lawyers can assist in evaluating the likely risk exposure and whether a more appropriate arrangement can be prepared.

COVENANTS NOT TO COMPETE

Most publishing agreements have clauses in which the writer agrees not to publish or authorize the publication of a work that might diminish the sales of existing works or the licensing of the rights granted under the contract without the publisher's permission. Courts tend to narrowly construe provisions in contracts that limit competition but will generally enforce provisions that are reasonable in time, place, and scope.

IN PLAIN ENGLISH

Publishers will rarely agree to delete noncompete clauses but are generally willing to modify them.

Publishers should pay particular attention to how a competing work is described. Phrases such as *similar* or *related* should be deleted, since they can be interpreted broadly. For example, a writer whose first book is *Ten Steps to Better Bowling* might be precluded from writing other books about bowling if the clause prohibits related books. A better competing book provision would use a phrase such as *reasonably likely to injure sales of the book*. This would allow the writer to license other books about bowling without the publisher's permission, provided they are sufficiently different that they would not encroach on sales of the other work.

In addition, authors often request the right to exempt scholarly or magazine articles from the restriction, since these activities would likely enhance the writer's reputation and may even help sales of the book.

TERMINATION AND REVERSION

All good things must come to an end, and the contract should address the writer's rights once the book goes out of print. It is important that the contract provide that all rights revert to the writer when the work goes out of print, because the author may want to publish the material again and therefore needs the right to do so. Since the publisher no longer needs the rights, and since the book is no longer being sold, a reversion clause may be appropriate. Because authors and publishers may not agree on when a work has gone out of print, the phrase should be clearly defined in the contract. The work should be considered to be *out of print* when the publisher is no longer putting forth sufficient effort to make the book commercially viable. The most specific way to effect this intent is to require a minimum number of sales within an accounting period for the book to be considered in print.

Another practical way is to specify that a book will be out of print when copies of the book are no longer available through normal trade channels. An issue may arise when a publisher, for all practical purposes, stops distributing the book but retains a minimal means of selling copies. The availability of technologies such as print-on-demand and electronic versions make this technologically feasible for publishers.

Contracts may also provide for termination if the publisher becomes bankrupt or insolvent. In theory, such clauses would protect the writer from having the rights sold during a bankruptcy proceeding, but they are unenforceable under the US Bankruptcy Code. Nonetheless, it is common to find such clauses in publishing agreements.

Regardless of how the contract is terminated, the termination clause generally requires that the writer be notified of such termination and be given the option to purchase the remaining copies of the book (and sometimes the electronic files, plates, films, or other media, as well). If the writer does not exercise this option, the publisher may sell the remaining copies at any price to any other party. If the remaining copies are sold by the publisher for a reduced price, the writer may receive a reduced royalty or none at all. Moreover, the contract may require the publisher to destroy the electronic files, plates, film, or other media if the writer does not purchase them.

If the publisher had sold licenses to others for use of the subsidiary rights, the reversion rights of the writer will usually be subject to the third party's license. In other words, even if the publisher's rights revert to the author, the third party will still have a valid license as granted by the publisher, providing the publisher was authorized to create the license in the first place. The writer may get around this by demanding at the outset that any license granted by the publisher will be subject to the author's reversionary rights. In this way, the writer ensures that all rights will revert. Publishers should not agree to do this because it significantly impairs the value of the subsidiary rights.

OPTION CLAUSE

The publisher may include a clause in the contract that gives the publisher the opportunity to review the writer's next book-length work and make an offer before the writer submits it to other publishers for review. The rationale is that the publisher will have played a role in developing a writer's career and should have the *right of first refusal* on the author's later works.

Writers generally do not want an option clause because it restricts their flexibility. In any case, writers who agree to such clauses may try to place limits on them. For example, the writer may demand that the publisher accept or reject the subsequent works within thirty to sixty days after they have been submitted and that the publisher agree to make its decision based on an outline and sample chapters instead of a completed manuscript. Similarly, the clause may be limited to the next work and not bind the author thereafter.

It is not uncommon for publishers to have the option provision state that, even if the publisher rejects the writer's next work, the option clause remains in effect until the writer places the book with another publisher. This is intended to preclude authors from evading the option clause by submitting an unpublishable work. In addition, the typical option clause states that the terms for the next work will be negotiated in good faith, but if an agreement is not reached, the writer cannot enter into an agreement with another publisher unless the terms are equal or better.

MULTIPLE-BOOK CONTRACTS

Publishers may attempt to hold successful authors by negotiating an agreement for multiple books. These contracts differ from those that contain option clauses. An option clause grants the publisher the first right to publish any subsequent book by the author but does not obligate the writer to create another work. A multiple-book contract, on the other hand, obligates the writer to write two or more books for that publisher. The problems that can arise from this kind of contract are substantial.

What happens, for example, if the writer fails to comply with the contract? The publisher may be able to sue for breach of contract. While a court will not order a person to perform a personal-service contract—such as writing a book—against one's will, it may award damages to the party whose economic expectations were dashed. In addition, the publisher may be able to obtain a court order prohibiting the writer from providing material to other publishers.

The amount of damages awarded the publisher would ordinarily be difficult to calculate in a case like this, since it would require speculation on the probable success of an unwritten book. For this reason, publishers will generally include a clause in the contract providing that the publisher can recover a specified amount, known as *liquidated damages*, in the event the writer fails to perform this part of the multiple-book contract.

AUTHOR'S MANUSCRIPT

In many contracts, the publisher will disclaim any liability that may arise from the loss or destruction of materials submitted by the writer. Moreover, the publisher may demand the right to destroy the author's manuscript after publication if it is not properly claimed within a given period of time. The publisher may require the writer to retain a copy of the manuscript, illustrations, and any other materials submitted to the publisher. In most instances, writers retain copies of their works in either paper or electronic form, so the damages associated with a lost manuscript are minimal. However, if the publisher will be taking possession of rare documents, illustrations, and related material of personal and possibly financial value, the writer will likely demand that the publisher be held liable if the work is destroyed while in the publisher's control. The writer may also demand that the material be returned within a stated time following publication.

IN PLAIN ENGLISH

Publishers should avoid the issue of lost or damaged material altogether by not accepting submission of valuable originals.

ARBITRATION

Arbitration is simply an arrangement for taking a dispute to an agreed-upon third party for resolution rather than going through the formalities and expense of courtroom litigation. Some book contracts may provide for *binding arbitration*, in which case the parties agree that the decision of the arbitrator shall be conclusive and that the parties will not attempt to have this decision examined by a court. If the word *arbitration* is used alone, it is presumed to be nonbinding.

Some states require that disputes that involve less than a specified amount of money—for example, $50,000—are subject to arbitration. However, this form of arbitration is nonbinding, and either party may have the matter retried before a judge or jury. A contract may provide for nonbinding arbitration. In this event, a party not pleased with the result has the right to appeal the matter.

The identity of the arbitrator is important, since a contractual provision that selects a friend of the publisher or writer will likely predetermine the outcome of any controversy. For this reason, an independent, nonpartisan arbitrator should be selected. It is common to state that arbitration will be held under the rules of the American Arbitration Association, which has procedures for selecting arbitrators. Unless the contract states how the arbitration will be initiated, commencing an arbitration can be difficult if the other party is not cooperative. In extreme cases, a party will need to petition a court to appoint an arbitrator.

Although binding arbitration may save time and money, be aware that the resulting decision cannot be appealed and the process will not contain many of the procedural safeguards that are a part of the judicial process. Arbitration clauses should be included thoughtfully, as they may decrease the publisher's negotiating leverage in the event a dispute arises. For example, if a disagreement arises and there is no arbitration clause, the publisher's ability to absorb litigation costs may be much greater than the individual author's. Thus, the publisher can take a harder line in negotiation. With an arbitration clause, the publisher cannot hold the economic threat of a lawsuit over the writer's head.

It should be noted that the rules of the American Arbitration Association do not provide for any pretrial discovery, unless the contract provides for the American Arbitration Association's Commercial Rules to be used. It is a good idea to modify any arbitration clause to include a provision in which both parties agree to have pretrial discovery similar to what would have been available if the case were tried in state or federal court rather than before an arbitrator. Here too, working with an experienced publishing lawyer is important.

AUTHORSHIP CREDIT, FREE COPIES, AND WRITER PURCHASES

The writer may demand that credit for authorship be published in a particular manner and may dictate the relative size and location of the name not only of the writer, but of a coauthor, illustrator, or a subsequent reviser other than the writer. In addition, most publishing contracts provide that the writer is to receive a certain number of free copies of the published work. Some contracts will allow authors to buy any number of books for a discounted price, but publishers should be careful in setting the price to avoid having the writer become a competitor. One method publishers have used to prevent this kind of competition is stating in the contract that free or discounted books are not to be sold by the author, or that if they are to be resold, the price must be no lower than what the publisher is charging. In other cases, the publisher may see that the writer is the best salesperson for the book and will encourage the writer to buy books for resale.

AGENCY CLAUSE

If the writer has an agent, the publishing agreement will most likely provide that the publisher make payments that are owed to the writer directly to the agent, and that such payments will satisfy the publisher's obligation to pay the writer. The intent of these clauses is to ensure that agents are compensated for their services. They are generally inserted because agents require their clients to agree to this method of payment.

Ethical agents will hold the money in a trust account until the check clears, then transfer the client's portion to the client. In the event that an agent does not pay in a timely manner, the writer will need to proceed against the agent and not the publisher. Some publishers will agree to cut separate checks to the writer and agent, but most will not because of the administrative burden. In any case, it is always better to deal with an ethical agency.

SPECIALTY CONTRACTS

If you are a magazine publisher, then clauses that would be important for you to consider would involve whether the author you are dealing with will allow you to publish the work more than once, whether the contract is for a series of articles, and whether you would be permitted the right to use those articles for other purposes, e.g. combining a number of them into a book or selling the rights to a book publisher. You should also obtain the right to publish the material both electronically and in paper form. If you contract with an author for an article, and then decide not to publish that piece, it is typical to pay the author a "kill fee," and that fee should be in the contract.

Publishers of limited edition works such as fine prints or collectors books must also comply with laws enacted in many states that impose restrictions on publishers in that industry. For example, the publisher must truly state the number of limited editions in the series, and serious consequences are imposed for violating these rules.

Music publishers will need to address the mechanical right, i.e., the right to produce the musical composition. They will also need to work out appropriate arrangements with the established clearing houses such as ASCAP, Fox, BMI, and CCI. These are very specialized areas, and it is essential for publishers in these industries to work with experienced attorneys.

BOILERPLATE PROVISIONS

The publishing agreement may include any or all of the following wrap-up provisions:

- *Merger (also known as Integration).* A merger clause will state that "the contract is intended to be the complete and final agreement of the parties," or words to this effect. This statement is designed to prevent any outside deals from becoming part of the contract. It makes it clear that the written document embodies all prior understandings, negotiations, and promises. A clause such as this will probably help to prevent future misunderstandings.
- *Modification.* Another phrase likely to be found in a contract is "No modification or waiver of the contract is valid

or enforceable unless signed by the parties." This statement will protect both parties from an alleged oral change, which can be casually spoken and easily forgotten.

- *Choice of Law.* This clause determines which state's law will be applied to interpret the contract if the parties are located in different states. Publishers generally prefer to apply their own state's laws to interpret the contract. This is something that publishers are unlikely to give up.

- *Venue.* This clause specifies the place (or venue) where any litigation involving the contract must occur. It would be disadvantageous for an author to agree to a court battle in a location far from his or her home, but it would also be unlikely for a publisher to agree to a venue far from the center of their operations.

- *Attorney Fees.* This clause will generally provide that, if it becomes necessary to enforce the contract through legal means (by lawsuit or arbitration), the party who wins the case will be entitled to recover attorney fees from the other party, in addition to any other monetary award. Be aware that some jurisdictions require that fees at both the trial level and the appellate level be specified if the parties want attorney fees to be awarded following an appeal.

The fact that the contract provides that the winning party be entitled to recover attorney fees does not necessarily mean that the prevailing party will be reimbursed for the entire legal bill. The courts have traditionally held that the amount awarded will be reasonable attorney fees. Some jurisdictions also require specificity when dealing with expenses, such as the identification of deposition costs, paralegal fees, or the like, or they will not be awarded to the prevailing party. It is not uncommon for a court to award an amount less than the actual bill. An attorney's fees and costs clause tends to discourage parties from breaching the contract, since the breaching party runs the risk of paying most of the prevailing party's expenses.

- *Waiver of Breach.* The contract might also contain a clause specifying that "a waiver of a breach of the contract shall not be deemed to waive any future breaches." This provision allows a party to agree to less than strict compliance with the contract on one occasion, without giving up the right to strictly enforce the contract later.

- *Severability.* This kind of clause provides that, if for some reason any part of a contract is not enforceable, the balance of the contract still be enforced and oftentimes states that if there is any way to read the contract to make a suspect clause enforceable, the clause should be read in that way.

Starting with a thoughtful standard form contract can make negotiations with an author efficient and effective. A publisher should know how each provision can be modified and the acceptable terms that can be offered to an author and what circumstances warrant compromise. Once a deal has been negotiated, the final draft of the contract should be reviewed by the legal team of both parties before execution. The contract should be kept on file as a valuable legal document and referred to whenever a question arises. A well-formed contract can resolve issues before they become full-blown disputes and salvage relationships that would otherwise end up in court. An experienced attorney and dedication to crafting a thorough document are a publishing company's best tools for having a healthy and long relationship with its authors.

CHAPTER 12

The Internet

The growth of the Internet has radically changed the environment in which publishers acquire, produce, and distribute books. Although the Internet has caused a profound cultural change, for the most part, online publications are governed by the same substantive legal principles that apply to print media. Nonetheless, there are some issues that publishers should take care to address.

An example of one of these issues is whether an agreement permitting one-time print publication of a work also gave the publisher the right to post that piece on its website. Publishers contended that under one-time publication rights, they were legally entitled to publish the piece in several editions of the same issue. For example, a newspaper could publish the article in both the morning and evening editions of a daily newspaper. They further contended that making the editions available on their websites gave them the right to publish the freelance articles on the Internet without additional compensation to the writers. Writers contended that websites constituted a different publication that was not encompassed by one-time rights, and therefore they were entitled to additional compensation. This issue was resolved in favor of the writers, but the lesson to publishers is that they must be mindful of how new technology may affect the rights they have acquired.

INCREASED MAGNITUDE FOR PROBLEMS

Publishers are no doubt aware that the ability to disseminate information widely and swiftly over the Internet has increased the magnitude of the consequences associated with legal issues. For example, the elements of a defamation claim are the same irrespective of whether a defamatory statement is published in a book or online. The greater accessibility of the Internet, however, makes it more likely that a potential claimant will discover the defamation and that the damage to the claimant's reputation will be greater. Similarly, the elements of a copyright infringement claim are identical, irrespective of the media in which publication occurs. Material that is published online can be readily copied by downloading and is, therefore, easier to infringe than material published in print form. The overall effect is that publishers need to be even more cognizant of the laws that affect them.

In addition, many form contracts that were entered into before the Internet era do not deal with it. Contracts not addressing electronic publishing or *new media* do not give the publisher the right to post material online or publish the work electronically. Many publishers have requested amendments to pre-existing arrangements to include these rights. If you have older contracts or you are unsure if your existing contracts will allow you to publish in new media or formats that may be developed, you should seek the guidance of an experienced publishing attorney for help evaluating and redrafting your contracts.

OPPORTUNITIES

The Internet also presents publishers with a host of opportunities. Most publishers have used this relatively inexpensive means of communicating as a vehicle for marketing the works they publish. It is vital that publishers monitor not only what they say online, but also the reblogs, reposts, and retweets of others. In some circumstances, an individual or entity that republishes defamatory content is liable for the harm to the same extent as the original publisher.

The law of agency also applies to the digital realm. This means that the publisher may be responsible for the online statements of its employees. A publisher should be careful who has the authority to speak on its behalf and ensure there are strong policies behind what can be tweeted, posted, or snapped using official accounts. Unofficially, social media policies can also be put in place to guide employees on how to avoid appearing to speak on behalf of the company and how to use the Internet in smart and safe ways.

The bookselling market has also changed significantly as a result of the Internet. Statistics about book sales vary a great deal depending on the source; there is also conflicting information on the percent of the market captured by ebooks, but it is indisputable that online sales have bypassed brick-and-mortar bookstore sales. Although Amazon has opened some physical bookstores and is planning on opening more, the importance to booksellers of online book sales should not be underestimated.

Websites

Websites can be inexpensive to create and maintain and provide publishers with a means of providing information to large numbers of people at little expense. Many publishers have found that software has made it feasible for their authors to create their own websites without outside assistance. Some writers have been successful at creating websites that provide useful information about topics covered in their books, while also making their books available for sale. This benefits publishers by generating more sales and greater visibility. Some authors remain hesitant to create their own websites and may need assistance or encouragement from publishers.

Publishers and writers also use their own websites for purposes of announcing upcoming publications, awards, personal appearances, book signings, and the like. Further, most publishers have websites identifying their catalog, upcoming events, new titles, and other relevant information. Having a website is becoming increasingly crucial and a good way to advance the publisher's offerings.

Hosting a website, however, has increasingly complex legal obligations, particularly for publishers who wish to host reader forums or other means of publishing user-generated content. If you intend to host user-generated content, it is important to speak to an experienced attorney to ensure you are complying with safe harbor requirements that will insulate you from liability for the defamatory words or infringing content that users may upload to your site.

Research

The Internet provides enhanced opportunities to access information and to disseminate material. For example, some kinds of fact-checking or research that once required expensive and time-consuming travel can now be done from computers located anywhere in the world. Much of the business of publishing depends on obtaining information. The Internet can also provide publishers with important information about the publishing industry that was previously available primarily only to industry insiders. The Internet, when used creatively, can be an incredible source of information about the publishing industry.

USING THE WEB TO EVALUATE WRITERS, AGENTS, AND EDITORIAL SERVICES

Anyone reading many of the other chapters of this book probably realizes that the publishing world has a dark side, where scam artists prey on the naive hopes and expectations of new publishers. In the past, it has not always been easy to distinguish between legitimate and disreputable writers, editors, and agents because of the lack of available information about them. Prior to the Internet, the only source of information available to most publishers was in the form of directories that listed distributors, publishers, and agents. Unfortunately, many of these directories include listings from entities that are far more interested in taking money from publishers than in making money for them. Fortunately, the emergence of the Internet has greatly increased the kind of information that publishers can use to navigate the often turbid waters of the publishing industry.

Much information about the shady denizens who inhabit the publishing world can be found on websites that track this information. Likewise, the availability of listservs, Internet forums, blogs, and social media allows publishers to communicate with one another about dishonest entities and improper business practices. Publishers who are new to the business are highly encouraged to subscribe to these forums. Monitoring the normal course of discussions will provide a lot of good information about publishing and other publishers' experiences, even though some judgment will be needed to discern the inevitable misinformation. Moreover, the forums provide excellent opportunities to ask questions. For example, publishers can get information about specific distributors, agents, and editors that would be difficult to get by other means.

The Internet can also be used to gather background information about distributors, independent of the personal experiences of other publishers. For example, one of the most important factors about a prospective distributor to most publishers will likely be whether they pay their bills on time and have established the ability to distribute books to the trade. In addition, their financial stability based on their track record in dealing with other publishers is also important. The reason is that commercial success for a trade book will almost always depend on the book being stocked by booksellers. If a distributor does not have a system that adequately puts its inventory into the trade market, it is unlikely to be able to distribute very many trade books and to pay its bills.

Traditionally, it was difficult for publishers to assess the quality of the distribution efforts by distributors. In some respects, this is still difficult, since many kinds of books, such as textbooks and professional titles, are not distributed through conventional retail channels. Fortunately, for the majority of publishers who are looking for trade distribution, the Internet has made it easier to assess whether a distributor has a serious trade presence and a good reputation. While it has always been feasible to visit local booksellers and see what titles they were stocking and ask who distributes those books, it is impractical for most people to visit bookstores throughout the country and check on their wares. However, retailers' websites allow customers to check to see if individual titles are stocked in particular stores. With that information, you can check with the publishers identified and find out their experience with the distributors they are working with. This makes it possible to determine how well a distributor distributes its titles to the conventional booksellers.

When one is doing Internet research regarding bookseller inventories, it is important to distinguish books that are physically stocked in stores from those that are available through special order. Although a retailer's website may claim that its books are available for purchase, books that are mostly available by special order are unlikely to sell well.

A good place to start the evaluation is to look at the websites of the major online booksellers. The major online retailers, such as Amazon and barnesandnoble.com, allow publishers to list their books free of charge. Since books can be listed with very little effort, there is no excuse for a publisher not to list its books or to list them in a substandard manner. A good listing for a book at an online retailer's site should provide substantive information about the book's content, size, and format. If a publisher does not list its books on the major websites or does not provide good descriptive information, this is a strong sign that the publisher is not serious about trade distribution.

Another aspect to examine is the shipping time. For example, most books offered through Amazon.com ship within twenty-four hours of an order being placed, but occasionally, the shipping time may be extended to two to three days if the inventory has sold out (a good sign). Shipping times that exceed more than a few days may indicate that the distributor is not set up to do effective trade distribution.

In researching distributors, in addition to the matters discussed above, there are a myriad of other things to consider. There are different kinds of distributors and services to evaluate. Good information about factors to examine when selecting, and dealing with, a distributor can be found online. For example, does a proposed distributor follow a traditional model, not charging for the majority of its services, or is it a hybrid distributor, offering to provide services for a fee? Has the distributor experienced problems with making payments so that other publishers have expressed concern? If you enter into a relationship with a distributor, you need to know if you will be charged for storage of digital files, marketing, or promotion. Will a specific number of copies of your books be printed, or will printing be done only on demand? Many of these questions can be answered based on information readily available online. Use the Internet as a resource to investigate your options and to help you make the best choices under the circumstances specific to you and your needs.

The Internet has expanded opportunities for publishers to advertise at a relatively low cost. It has also expanded the ability of publishers to obtain essential information about the people and businesses dealt with, as well. In fact, the Internet has enabled small publishers to effectively compete with their larger competitors in the publishing industry. The World Wide Web has truly made the publishing business global and provided opportunities that are expanding on a daily basis.

CYBERSECURITY

As more and more data are stored in the cloud, cybersecurity becomes a larger problem with almost overwhelming consequences. Cybersecurity laws govern data storage, computer crime, and data disposal laws. These laws are passed on the federal and state level, revised and redrafted, adjudicated and appealed on a constant basis. Publishers will undoubtedly encounter information that is governed by these laws, and much of that is beyond the scope of this chapter. If your publishing website markets to children or if you store personally identifying information, financial information, or health information for employees, customers, or authors, we strongly recommended that you discuss your cybersecurity requirements and risks with a cybersecurity specialist or experienced attorney. In the event of a data breach, it is vital that you immediately contact an attorney to ensure you comply with all of the notice requirements and resolve your legal obligations.

Each publisher, especially those with a public website, should develop a privacy policy that complies with state and federal privacy laws and honor that policy. Publishers should assign an employee to the role of cybersecurity specialist or hire someone specifically for that role. This person should take responsibility to learn and comply with the applicable laws. As an employer, a publisher should develop an acceptable use policy for computers and accounts. Publishers should insist on physical workplace security to protect paper documents as well as digital assets. Password and encryption policies can help publishers protect data, especially in the event of employee turnover. Develop an incident response plan and consider purchasing a data breach insurance policy. Train your employees on your policies and best practices to increase effectiveness and compliance. If your publishing house does not have the resources to have a data security specialist on staff, consider developing a plan and having it reviewed by an IT professional and a lawyer to help shore up any weaknesses.

The Internet has created a cultural shift and brought information to our fingertips. The law has attempted to keep up with all of these radical changes in most ways by simply applying the same principles that exist in the physical world. In the instances where that has not worked, the law is still in a state of flux. Publishers are well-advised to seek the advice of an experienced attorney to fully embrace novel technology and adapt quickly to the ever-changing legal landscape.

CHAPTER 13

Books in the Digital Age

With the availability and sophistication of technology, the definition of traditional publishing has expanded to include stories told, not only in print, but in digital formats of all varieties. As the technology blurred the lines of what is or is not a book, other formats previously relegated to different silos and channels of distribution have merged. A "traditional publisher" now may have print, ebook, graphic novel, and emerging technology teams that all peacefully coexist under one roof. This presents publishers with unusual legal challenges and opportunities that we will discuss in this chapter.

EBOOKS AND THE RISE OF INDEPENDENT PUBLISHING

The growth of the Internet and electronic technologies has expanded the opportunities for publishers to distribute their work without having to go through conventional trade channels or dedicate resources to printed media. With the availability of handheld devices and digital content, ebook sales increased rapidly throughout the 2000s and into the 2010s. Amazon, Apple, Barnes and Noble, Google, and Kobo developed direct-to-consumer ebook channels that spanned the globe. This new market opened retail channels to independent publishers that were previously closed to them. New publishing houses with inventive business models suddenly found themselves on equal footing with behemoth publishing houses like Penguin Random House and HarperCollins. By 2011, the *New York Times* began featuring a best-seller list for ebooks.[1] In August 2012, Smashwords,

---

1   Julie Bosman, "*Times* Will Rank E-Book Best Sellers," *New York Times* (November 10, 2010), http://www.nytimes.com/2010/11/11/books/11list.html.

an independent ebook distributor, had four of its authors featured on the list in one week.[2]

After a wild increase in revenue through 2014, the ebook market began to stabilize. Print sales increased 3.3 percent in both 2015 and 2016. As of this publication, ebooks make up 49 percent of adult fiction sales, 24 percent of adult nonfiction, 12 percent of juvenile fiction, and 6 percent of juvenile nonfiction for traditional publishers. Independent ebook sales continue to rise with ebook sales from independent, self-published, and small publishers making up 59 percent of US ebook sales, with independent authors capturing over a third of all ebook sales worldwide.[3]

PUBLISHING CONTRACTS AND EMERGING TECHNOLOGY

Until Amazon released the Kindle in 2007, ebooks were an oddity—only a few niche markets saw digital sales, and those were insignificant. Consequently, publisher contracts said nothing about ebooks or digital rights. In 2001, Rosetta Books contracted with several authors to produce ebooks of physical books that Random House had previously published. Random House asserted that pre-ebook author contracts granting them rights to the author's work "in book form" included ebooks. Random House sued Rosetta Books and lost—the court holding that the language of the contract itself established that digital content is separate and distinct from the work "in book form." This decision shocked the industry. Virtually every publisher revised the contracts they would use in the future and attempted to amend their existing contracts as well in order to deal with this very significant issue.

Publishers should be aware of definitions and clauses that deal with digital or electronic rights and phrases that may have consequences for emerging technologies, such as "other versions created in a technology now known or later developed." Further, publishers should carefully consider royalties

---

2   Stephanie Chandler, "How Books by Self-Published Authors Can Land on the *New York Times* Bestsellers List," *Nonfiction Authors Association* (May 17, 2016), https://nonfictionauthorsassociation.com/how-books-by-self-published-authors -can-land-on-the-new-york-times-bestsellers-list/.

3   "February 2017 Big, Bad, Wide & International Report: Covering Amazon, Apple, B&N, and Kobo eBook Sales in the US, UK, Canada, Australia, and New Zealand," *Author Earnings* (February 2017), available at http://authorearnings.com /report/february-2017/.

for ebook rights. Print royalties take into account the overhead required for printing, storing, and distributing physical books. Ebook royalties must still take into account the overhead for editing, developing, designing, marketing, and electronically storing the files. However, without the physical overhead, authors may be eager to negotiate higher royalty rates for digital content.

Under traditional publishing contracts, there is often a clause wherein the rights to the work revert automatically once the book is out of print. In traditional contracts, this was easy to define: whenever the publisher decided not to invest in further print runs or stopped marketing or selling the book, the rights reverted to the author. Now, with print on demand and ebooks, a book may never go "out of print" in the traditional sense. Contracts should therefore be drafted with a trigger for reversion that makes sense with digital technology or explicitly defines what going *out of print* means. If the author and publisher intend for a reversion of rights to occur when no further print runs of a certain size are ordered, this should be explicitly stated in the contract.

DISTRIBUTION IN THE DIGITAL AGE

Publishers who distribute their work directly to online channels should read the agreements they enter with online ebook retailers carefully and consult an experienced attorney to discuss the ramifications of entering these agreements. Online retailer agreements often contain "most favored nation" clauses. These clauses essentially mean that if an ebook is sold for less money anywhere, the retailer reserves the right to automatically drop the price of the book in their store, as well. Thus, if a publisher decides to give a book away for free on a website or through social media, the online retailer would be within its rights to drop the price to $0.00. Further, retailer agreements frequently contain difficult-to-understand royalty structures that incentivize publishers to sell books at a certain level. This functions to keep book prices artificially low.

PROTECTING CONTENT IN THE DIGITAL AGE

While the Internet allows publishers to reach a wider audience, it comes with unique challenges, not the least of which is piracy. Publishers and authors alike have wrangled with what to do about the ease with which content can be misappropriated and spread in violation of copyright law. The Copyright

Act supports a publisher's attempt at self-help by protecting digital rights management, or DRM, of ebooks. DRM encrypts the ebook files to restrict copying, distributing, and sharing ebooks.

Online retail ebook stores and ebook distributors often provide digital rights management on the books they sell at no cost to the publisher. DRM is also available for individual titles from companies like Adobe; however, it is generally cost-prohibitive for small publishers to purchase DRM for individual titles.

The Digital Millennium Copyright Act makes it illegal for users to purposefully circumvent, or break, DRM. There are some exceptions for libraries and persons with print disabilities that change on a yearly basis as per the recommendations of the Librarian of Congress. DRM also comes under fire from proponents of the free exchange of information. In an industry that relies on the sale of content to thrive, publishers must be cautious when determining whether a title should be distributed without DRM protection. Keep in mind, however, that distributing a title without DRM does not mean the reader is free to copy or distribute that work. A digital work, even one without DRM, is still protected by the Copyright Act. If you believe your work has been infringed, it is important to discuss your options with an experienced attorney who can help you determine which legal action would be the most appropriate to protect your work.

INTERNET-INSPIRED ALTERNATIVE LICENSING SCHEMES

Some well-known authors including Cory Doctorow[4] and Peter Watts[5] are proponents of alternative licensing schemes such as Creative Commons. Creative Commons (CC) licenses are appealing to some publishers that have observed authors flourish in the remix culture of sharing that thrives on the Internet. Most CC licenses allow others to copy, modify, and share the work without the author's permission—the only requirement being that the author be identified in every copy.[6] While this license may be useful in some circumstances, it is important for publishers to recognize that it is difficult,

---

4 "Case Studies/Cory Doctorow," *Creative Commons*, accessed May 25, 2018, https://wiki.creativecommons.org/wiki/Case_Studies/Cory_Doctorow.

5 Peter Watts, "The Backlist," *Rifters* (accessed May 25, 2018), http://www.rifters.com /real/shorts.htm.

6 For more, see Creative Commons at https://creativecommons.org/.

if not impossible, to revoke this kind of license. Publishers should be aware when seeking to acquire an author's book that has been previously distributed under a CC license that the work will be tainted by that license and it may be much more difficult to sell a book that can be acquired elsewhere legally, for free.

SELLING STORIES

Another opportunity for publishers in the digital era is to sell digital versions of stories that incorporate interactive features more suitable to an application than to a standard ebook. When they deal with these channels of distribution, it is vital that publishers be aware that the traditional publishing rules may not apply. Distribution agreements with app stores often require periodic updates. A traditional publisher that is accustomed to pushing updates only when a new edition is written may find their content suppressed by the app store for failure to comply with the update requirements. It is important for any publisher wishing to enter a new channel of distribution to discuss the agreement with an experienced attorney and fully understand all of its aspects and requirements.

RENTING, BORROWING, AND LENDING DIGITAL CONTENT

Innovative publishers have attempted new retail schemes, subscription models, and licensing and sharing experiments in an effort to balance economic realities with consumer expectations in a digital world. For example, publisher O'Reilly Media engenders goodwill with readers and incentivizes them to purchase directly from its site by specifically authorizing lending, donation, and resale of its ebooks.[7]

Innovative parties trying to monopolize on a digital secondary market while still complying with the spirit of copyright law have used technology to develop apps and methods for transferring "used" digital products among

---

7   O'Reilly Media, Inc., "The shop.oreilly.com Ebook Advantage," accessed on December 20, 2014, http://shop.oreilly.com/category/ebooks.do. ("Unlike most other retailers, ebooks from shop.oreilly.com are not restricted. You can freely loan, re-sell or donate them, read them without being tracked, or move them to a new device without re-purchasing all of them.")

consumers. In 2009, Amazon Digital Services filed a patent[8] that enabled a system for transferring digital goods among users. The system charges a transactional fee and limits how many times a particular file can be resold, simulating the physical product's wear and tear.[9]

ReDigi Inc. attempted to go beyond the traditional "copy and delete" method that Amazon's patents employ.[10] In 2011, ReDigi launched a service that allowed users to upload legitimately purchased music, use and stream the music from the cloud, and then sell the music through an instantaneous event that both transferred the file to the new owner and removed it from the original owner's data storage.[11] Copyright holders would receive a royalty payment as part of the transaction.[12] In 2013, the court found that ReDigi's process violated copyright. The court analogized ReDigi's methods to allowing users to resell cassette recordings of vinyl records in a bygone era.

In 2013, Apple filed its own patent for a used, digital, retail market.[13] Apple's system uses data embedded in the digital content.[14] Rather than making a copy of the original owner's file, Apple's system would simply alter the

---

8 Secondary market for digital objects, U.S. Patent No. 8,364,595 (filed May 5, 2009) (issued Jan. 29, 2013).

9 Todd Bishop, "Amazon Wins Broad Patent on Reselling and Lending 'used' Digital Goods," *GeekWire* (February 4, 2013), http://www.geekwire.com/2013/amazon -wins-patent-reselling-lending-used-digital-goods.

10 ReDigi Inc., "ReDigi Issues Statement on Amazon's Patent for the Resale of 'Used' Digital Goods," *PR Newswire* (February 6, 2013), https://www.prnewswire.com/ news-releases/redigi-issues-statement-on-amazons-patent-for-the-resale-of -used-digital-goods-190036661.html. (Responding to Amazon's patent for a used retail system, ReDigi replied that it did not employ a similar "'copy and delete' mechanism, in which a user sells a 'copy' of a digital good to another user while both the buyer and seller simultaneously own the copy (even if only for an instant in time), and then supposedly/subsequently the seller's copy is 'deleted.'").

11 ReDigi, Inc., "ReDigi, Inc. Awarded Significant U.S. Patent," *PR Newswire* (January 29, 2014), http:// newsroom.redigi.com/redigi-inc-awarded-significant-u-s-patent.

12 Bruce Houghton, "Is Selling Used MP3s Legal? ReDigi Responds," *Hypebot* (February 22, 2011), http://www.hypebot.com/hypebot/2011/02/mp3-reseller-redigi -responds-to-legality-questions.html.

13 Jacqui Cheng, "Apple Follows Amazon with Patent for Resale of e-Books, Music," *Ars Technica* (March 8, 2013), http://arstechnica.com/apple/2013/03/apple-follows -amazon-with-patent-for-resale-of-e-books-music/.

14 Managing Access to Digital Content Items, U.S. Patent Application No. 20130060616 at [60] (filed Sep. 6, 2011).

embedded data to allow access by a different user. Apple's patent also describes a method of payment based on how much the original owner has used the file. This system would simulate the lower price a reseller can expect from a used physical copy. Like ReDigi's method, Apple allows for the copyright holder to receive remuneration.[15] It is important to understand that a patent remains in effect for twenty years from the date the application was filed and, therefore, this process will remain active for some time.

New opportunities to distribute books that align with trends in reader expectations may have broad, unanticipated legal consequences to the rights in a copyrighted work. It is important that publishers who wish to take advantage of new technologies for distribution discuss the opportunities and potential risks with an experienced attorney.

STORAGE AND BACKUP AGREEMENTS

Survival of artistic work has historical interest for documentarians and scholarly research, but beyond this historic interest, work may receive renewed commercial or critical interest that publishers cannot anticipate and may be the catalyst for new content or technological exploitation publishers cannot yet implement. Alexander Stille spoke of the importance of preservation:

> Homer and Virgil survived intact because of their enduring popularity and the multiple copies that were made at different times. But many of the works that we regard as fixtures of our culture (including Plato) were lost for centuries and are known to us only because of a copy or two that turned up in medieval monasteries or in the collections of Arab scholars. Some works of undoubted greatness did not survive at all: Sophocles is known to have written some 120 plays, of which we possess only nine.[16]

Archivists understand this principle and seek to disseminate information in as many locations, conditions, and formats as possible to ensure at least some copy will survive. The preservation of a digital file is often left to the

---

15 Ibid., at [87].

16 Alexander Stille, "Are We Losing Our Memory? or The Museum of Obsolete Technology," in *The Future of the Past* (New York: Picador, 2002), 308.

publisher. It is vital that the publisher thus maintain a digital archive or use a distributor or online storage service to perform this task.

Digital preservation operates under the same rules as physical preservation. The more diverse environments a file can reside in, the more likely it is to survive. Digital media are quite perishable—archival quality CDs may last forty-five years in the correct conditions before catastrophic error degrades the data—but keeping the correct conditions and backing up data require effort and money. Privacy, piracy, power outages, and the intentional theft by hackers must all be considered by the prudent publisher. Insurance, liability, indemnification, termination, backup, and communication in the event of a breach should be addressed in any contract regarding digital media storage. Publishers should work with an experienced attorney before entering a digital storage agreement.

CHAPTER 14

Distribution and Sales

In order for a publisher to succeed, it must distribute the books it publishes, and those books must wind up in the hands of consumers. The timeline for priming the market and arranging for effective distribution is well established.

First, it's customary to arrange for some book reviews before the book is actually published. In fact, traditionally, a publisher will provide a copy of the final manuscript to a number of potential reviewers at the same time that manuscript is sent to the printer. The review of the book will then appear at about the same time as the book itself is available for purchase. Many publishers try to get copies of the reviews early so that quotes from those reviews can appear on the cover of the book.

It is also common for publishers or their authors to arrange for blurbs about the book to be written by prominent people. The blurbs appear on the cover of the book and are used for advertising purposes, as well. Publishers will also arrange for signings, author interviews, and the like so that the book and publicity about it will all be available at about the same time.

By "priming the pump," the publisher can be sure to maximize visibility of the author and the book at the best time for sales. One concern that should be considered is the legal issues that may arise when a manuscript is made available before the book is published. In a notorious case, *Harper & Row v. Nation Enterprises*, the manuscript for President Ford's book covering his pardon of President Nixon was made available before the book was actually released. President Ford had a contract for first distribution rights with *Time* magazine. When *The Nation* received the manuscript for review purposes, it published an article containing numerous quotes and describing the significant events in the book. Since *The Nation* published its article first, *Time* canceled its contract with President Ford, claiming that it could no longer enjoy the first serialization rights it had contracted for.

Publishers should be careful when providing prepublication manuscripts for review, and it would be appropriate to restrict their use or establish appropriate guidelines in order to avoid situations like the one that befell President Ford.

Next, the publisher must arrange for distribution. Some publishers work with distributors. The distributors have retailers to which they distribute. Other publishers distribute themselves through their own websites or their own distribution channels such as book clubs. Some publishers merely make their books available to Amazon and do very little more. It depends on the publisher and the arrangements they have made. The publishers also make arrangements for the writer to go on talk shows, to be available for book signings once the book is available, and go on tours. All of this helps provide demand for the books.

WORKING WITH DISTRIBUTORS

As noted above, publishers employ a variety of methods for making the books they publish available. Many publishers establish arrangements with book distributors. These distributors then make the books available to retailers, book clubs, and the like. The vast majority of distributors are legitimate and do an excellent job—however, there have been some problems with distributors that have experienced financial problems. A number of large distributors wound up in financial difficulty, and, as a result, many publishers were not paid for the books they published.

It is standard in the publishing industry that when a book is to be sold, the purchaser may return that book without restriction and receive back the money paid for that book. This means that a book is not actually irrevocably sold when it is first placed in the hands of a purchaser. It is for this reason that publishers customarily retain some portion of the royalties to be paid authors as a reserve for returns. It also means that publishers cannot consider books to be sold immediately after they are shipped; rather, there must be a "reasonable time" before the publisher will actually consider that book to be sold.

The comic book industry does not have a similar rule, and as a result, it is more difficult for comic book sellers to arrange for the purchase of comic books.

Publishers should contractually establish a fund for possible returns in the author-publisher contract, and they should also take steps to protect themselves from the possibility of having a book distributor or bookstore wind up in bankruptcy. The method by which a publisher can have some protection is to file a form in the appropriate state office.

Article 9 of the Uniform Commercial Code, adopted in some form in all fifty states, provides that if a party files a UCC-1 form with the appropriate state agency where the recipient of the book is located, then that party will be secured for the value of the items identified in the form in the event the recipient of the property winds up in bankruptcy. There are a number of exceptions to this rule and a number of strict requirements for complying with the UCC, so a publisher should work with an experienced publishing lawyer in order to take advantage of this very important protection.

INTERNATIONAL STANDARD BOOK NUMBERS (ISBNs)

When bookstores, department stores, and other retailers desire a particular book, there is a vehicle available to help them find out who has published that book. The vehicle is the International Standard Book Number (ISBN).

The ISBN was created to have a complete and uniform system for identifying publications of all kinds. It is administered in the United States by the R.R. Bowker Company. The number is an order fulfillment tool and is also useful for cataloging. It commonly appears in major bibliographies and is used by retailers for order purposes as well as by libraries for cataloging. All publishers should apply to the R.R. Bowker Company for a publisher identifier number. The publisher will receive a computer sheet containing unassigned numbers that should be assigned by the publisher to each title to be published. The book titles must be entered on the Advanced Book Information sheet, which must be returned to R.R. Bowker. Here too, the publisher should communicate online. There is a charge for purchasing a single ISBN, but the price for purchasing numerous ISBNs decreases significantly as the number of ISBNs increases.

Each ISBN consists of thirteen digits (if assigned after January 1, 2007) or ten digits (if assigned before 2007). The ISBN is divided into five parts. The first part consists of three numbers administered by GS1. These numbers conform the ISBN to bar code standards for purposes of ordering the books by companies using bar code standards. The second part generally identifies the location of the publishing country and/or language. Part three is the identification number of the particular publisher. Part four is the number assigned to the specific title by the publisher, and, finally, part five is a computer check digit that aids in determining whether the number is correct. Whenever the number is used, it should be preceded by the letters ISBN.

On hardcover books, the complete ISBN should be printed on the copyright page, in the lower right-hand corner of the back cover, and the back jacket. Where appropriate, it should also appear on the upper edge of the left-hand jacket flap. Paperback books should have the ISBN printed on the copyright page and on the lower right-hand corner of the back cover. For publishers involved in serial publications such as periodicals and yearbooks, the International Standard Serial Number (ISSN) is available. This number identifies the serial and title, while the ISBN identifies a particular book within the series. The numbers are assigned by the Library of Congress National Series Data Program.

CHAPTER 15

Publishing as a Business

The same legal system that governs billion-dollar industries governs the publisher. This does not need to be a bad thing, since publishers can learn to use some of these laws to their advantage. Few publishers realize the importance of selecting the legal form their business should adopt, even though it affects their working relationships, taxes, ability to borrow, and exposure to liability. It only makes sense to structure the business to address these concerns.

Each business has an organizational form best suited to it, whether it be a sole proprietorship, partnership, corporation, limited liability company, or one of the hybrid business forms. When considering which form to use to conduct business, publishers should go about it in two steps. First, there are the considerations of taxes and liability. Once the appropriate form is determined, the organizational details, such as partnership agreements and corporate documents, must be drafted. These documents define the structure of the business and the rules for day-to-day operations. Since each business is unique, these documents must be tailored to the individual business.

This chapter describes the features of the various kinds of business organizations, including their advantages and disadvantages. There are many intricacies involved in setting up a business. Publishers are advised to consult a business attorney before deciding to adopt any particular structure. The information that follows is intended to increase your understanding of the choices and facilitate communication with your lawyer.

SOLE PROPRIETORSHIP

The term *sole proprietorship* may be unfamiliar to many publishers, although it is the form of business by which some operate. It is an unincorporated business owned by one person. As a form of business, it is elegant in its simplicity.

All it requires is a little money and a lot of work. The legal requirements associated with operating as a sole proprietor are few and simple. In some localities, you may be required to procure a business license, although professionals, such as publishers, are often not required to have them. If you wish to operate using an assumed or fictitious business name (e.g., The Uncle Bob Publishing Company), the name must be registered with the jurisdiction in which you are doing business. In most states, this will be through a state agency. However, in some states, registration is handled by the county. With these details taken care of, you are in business.

There are risks involved in operating your business as a sole proprietor. If you recognize any of these dangers as a real threat, you should give some consideration to doing business under another form of organization. Sole proprietors are personally liable for the debts and other liabilities that may be incurred by the business. In other words, their personal assets may be at stake should the liabilities of the business exceed its assets. For example, if someone prevails in a defamation case against a publisher who is a sole proprietor, all the property owned by the publisher would be at risk in order to satisfy the judgment, not just the publisher's business assets. An unexpected lawsuit, as well as economic difficulties, can drive a small business into bankruptcy. For sole proprietors, this will mean a personal bankruptcy.

Publishers can obtain insurance that covers some risks, but insurance is not readily available for all the risks faced by publishers. For example, it is difficult for publishers to obtain insurance against defamation. In any case, insurance policies have policy limits, deductibles, and premiums and are not a cure-all.

Sole proprietors are taxed on all profits of the business and may deduct the losses. The options for managing tax liabilities are more limited for sole proprietorships than for corporations and LLCs. In some cases, a publisher can reduce its tax burden by establishing a formal business entity.

PARTNERSHIPS AND OTHER COLLABORATIONS

When a publisher agrees to work on a manuscript with another publisher, or when a publisher and an illustrator agree to produce an illustrated manuscript, a partnership is formed. A partnership is defined by most state laws as an association of two or more persons to conduct, as co-owners, a business for profit. No formalities are required. In fact, some people have been held to be partners even though they never intended to form a partnership. This is important because each partner is subject to unlimited personal liability for the debts incurred by the partnership. Also, each partner is liable for the negligence of the other partner and the partnership's employees, when a negligent act occurs in the course of business. In effect, each partner is considered an employee of the partnership.

The economic advantages of doing business as a partnership are the pooling of capital, collaboration, easier access to credit because of the collective credit rating, and a potentially more efficient allocation of labor and resources. A major disadvantage is that each partner is fully and personally liable for all the debts of the partnership, even if not personally involved in incurring those debts.

A partnership does not possess any special tax advantages over a sole proprietorship. As a partner, you will pay tax on your share of the profits, whether they are distributed to you or not. You may also claim your share of deductions and credits. The partnership must file an annual information return known as a K-1 form with the IRS, against which the IRS can check the individual returns filed by the partners.

The most common situation in which publishers do business as partnerships is when they collaborate to publish a book or magazine. As stated previously, no formalities are required to create a partnership. If the publishers do not have a formal agreement defining the terms of the partnership, such as control or the distribution of profits, state law will determine the terms and legal obligations of each party. State laws are based on the fundamental characteristics of the typical partnership as it has existed throughout the ages and therefore tend to express what most partners would reasonably expect. The most important aspects of state partnership laws are as follows:

- no one can actually become a member of a partnership without the unanimous consent of all partners;
- all members have an equal vote in the management of the partnership, regardless of the size of their interest in it;
- all partners share equally in the profits and losses of the partnership, no matter how much capital they have contributed;
- a simple majority vote is required for decisions in the ordinary course of business, and a unanimous vote is required to change the fundamental character of the business; and

- a partnership is terminable at will by any partner. A partner can withdraw from the partnership at any time. This withdrawal will cause the dissolution of the partnership.

State laws also contain provisions that allow partners to make their own agreements regarding the management structure and division of profits that best suit the needs of the individual partners. It is recommended that publishers working in partnership take the time to consider defining the structure of the partnership before it commences. When drafting a partnership agreement, the parties should consider the following aspects.

The Name of the Partnership

Many partnerships simply use the surnames of the major partners as the partnership name. The choice in that case is nothing more than the order of names, which depends on various factors, from prestige to the way the names sound. If a name other than the partners' is used, it will be necessary to file the proposed business name with the appropriate governmental agency. Care should be taken to choose a name that is distinctive and not already in use. If the name is not distinctive, others can copy it; if the name is already in use, you could be liable for trade name infringement. It would also be a good idea to determine whether the name has been registered as a trademark both on the Federal Registry and the State Registry in the state in which the publisher is conducting business.

A Description of the Business

In describing the business, partners should agree on the basic scope of the project (e.g., the partnership shall be for one book or all written work to be published), its requirements with regard to capital and labor, the parties' individual contributions of capital and labor, and perhaps some plans regarding future growth.

Partnership Capital

After determining how much capital to contribute, the partners must decide when it will be contributed, how to value the property contributed, and whether there is to be a right to contribute more or to withdraw any at a later date.

Duration of the Partnership

Sometimes partnerships are organized for a fixed period of time or are automatically dissolved on certain conditions, such as the publication of a book.

Distribution of Profits

Partners can make whatever arrangement they want for distribution. Although a partner does not ordinarily receive a salary, it is possible to give an active partner a guaranteed salary in addition to a share of the profits. Since the partnership's profits can be determined only at the close of a business year, usually no distribution is made until that time. However, it is possible to allow the partners a monthly draw of money against their final share of profits. In some cases, it may be necessary to allow limited expense accounts for some partners.

Not all of the profits of the partnership need to be distributed at year's end. Some can be retained for expansion, an arrangement that can be provided for in the partnership agreement. It is important to note that whether the profits are distributed or not, each partner must pay tax on his or her share of the distributable profit. The federal tax code refers directly to the partnership agreement to determine what that share is. This underscores the importance of a formal partnership agreement.

Management

The division of power in the partnership can be established in many ways. All partners can be given an equal voice, or some can be given more authority than others. A few partners might be allowed to manage the business entirely, while the remaining partners are given a vote only on specifically designated issues. Besides voting, three other areas of management should be covered.

First is the question of who can sign checks, place orders, or enter into contracts on behalf of the partnership. Under state partnership laws, any partner may do these things so long as they are in the usual course of business. Such a broad delegation of authority can lead to confusion, so it might be best to delegate more narrowly in the written agreement.

Second, it is a good idea to determine a regular date for partnership meetings. This way, partners can plan their schedules to ensure their attendance at meetings. Not only does this allow for more productive meetings, it can protect the other partners from charges that they were trying to exclude a particular partner from important decisions.

Third, some consideration should be given to the possibility of a disagreement among the partners that leads to a deadlock. One way to avoid this possibility is to distribute the voting power in a way that makes a deadlock impossible.

In a two-person partnership, this would mean that one partner would be in absolute control. This situation might be unacceptable to the other partner. If instead the power is divided evenly among an even number of partners, as is often the case, the agreement should stipulate a neutral party or arbitrator who could resolve any dispute and thereby avoid dissolution of the partnership.

Prohibited Acts

By law, each partner owes the partnership certain duties by virtue of being an employee or agent of the partnership. First is the duty of *diligence*. This means the partner must exercise reasonable care in acting as a partner. Second is a duty of *obedience*. The partner must obey the rules of the partnership and, more important, must not exceed the authority the other partners have vested in him or her. Finally, there is a duty of *loyalty*. A partner may not, without approval of the other partners, compete with the partnership in another business. A partner may not seize upon a business opportunity that would be of value to the partnership without first telling the partnership about it and allowing the partnership to pursue it. A list of acts prohibited to any partner should be made a part of the partnership agreement, elaborating and expanding on these fundamental duties.

Dissolution and Liquidation

A partnership is automatically dissolved upon the death, withdrawal, bankruptcy, or expulsion of a partner. Dissolution identifies the legal end of the partnership but need not affect its economic life if the partnership agreement provided for the continuation of the business after dissolution. Nonetheless, dissolution will affect the business. The partner who withdraws, declares bankruptcy, or is expelled, or the estate of a deceased partner, will be entitled to a return of the proportionate share of capital that the departing partner contributed.

Details such as how this capital will be returned should be decided before dissolution, because at the time of dissolution, it may be impossible to negotiate. One method of handling this situation is to provide for a return of the capital in cash over a period of time. Some provision should be made so the remaining partners will know how much of a departing partner's interest they may purchase.

After a partner leaves, the partnership may need to be reorganized and recapitalized. Again, provision for this should be worked out in advance, if possible. Finally, since it is always possible that the partners will eventually want to liquidate the partnership, it should be decided in advance who will liquidate the assets, which assets will be distributed, and which property will be returned to its original contributors.

UNINTENDED PARTNERS

Unintended partnerships can occur when publishers collaborate on a work, but their relationship is not described formally. In situations such as when a publisher informally co-ventures with another publisher or when a small publisher works with a single author, it is important for the parties to spell out in detail the arrangements between them, or they are at risk of being treated as a partnership under state law. In such cases, a person could legally be held to be a partner and thus entitled to half of the income of the partnership, even though his or her contribution was minimal. Such situations can be avoided by hiring parties as contractors or specifying that their compensation will be a percentage of the proceeds. Whichever arrangement is chosen, it is important to have a clearly drafted written agreement that specifies that the other person's contribution is in a capacity other than as a partner.

THE LIMITED PARTNERSHIP

The limited partnership is a hybrid containing elements of both partnerships and corporations. A limited partnership may be formed when one or more parties wish to invest in a business and share in its profits but do not wish to participate in the control of the partnership. In effect, the limited partner is very much like an investor who buys a few shares of stock. Because of the limited partner's passive role, the law limits that party's liability only to the amount invested.

In order to establish a limited partnership, it is necessary to have one or more general partners who run the business and one or more limited partners who play a passive role. A general partner will have the same potential liability, duties, and authority as a member of a regular (general) partnership. To form a limited partnership, a certificate must be filed with the proper state agency. If the certificate is not filed or is improperly filed, the limited partner could be treated as a general partner. The limited partner must refrain from trying to influence the day-to-day operation of the partnership. Otherwise, the limited partner might be found to be actively participating in the business and thereby held to be a general partner with unlimited personal liability.

Limited partnership may be appropriate for publishers who need economic backing and wish to reward their sponsors with a share of the profits from the sale of the work without exposing them to personal liability. A limited partnership can be used to attract investment when credit is hard to get or is too expensive. In return for investing, the limited partner will generally receive a designated share of the profits. This way to fund your business can be attractive, since the limited partner receives nothing if there are no profits except potential tax write-offs, whereas if you had borrowed money from a creditor, that person could sue if you failed to repay.

Another use of the limited partnership is to facilitate reorganization of a general partnership after the death or retirement of a general partner. A partnership, remember, can be terminated when any partner requests it. Although the original partnership is technically dissolved when one partner retires, it is not uncommon for the remaining partners to agree to buy out the retiring partner's share and keep the business going. A practical problem arises, however, if a large cash source is not available, in which case the partners might be forced to liquidate some or all of the partnership's assets to return the retiring partner's capital contribution. Rather than withdrawing, if the retiring partner simply becomes a limited partner, he or she can continue to share in profits, which are at least in some part the fruits of that partner's past labor. This can be done while removing personal assets from the risk of partnership liabilities, yet not forcing the other partners to immediately come up with return of capital.

THE CORPORATION

Many people assume that corporations are large companies with many employees and an impersonal demeanor. This misconception is in large part due to people lambasting the uncaring and profit-minded entities that they describe as *corporations* or the even more perfidious *multinational corporation.* In reality, a corporation is an entity created by law that is set up for the purpose of doing business. There is nothing inherent in the nature of a corporation itself that requires it to be large or impersonal, and many states allow incorporation by a single individual.

There are advantages and disadvantages to incorporating. When it appears advantageous to incorporate, many publishers are surprised to learn that it can be done easily and at modest expense.

A good way to understand a corporation is to compare it to a partnership. Perhaps the most important difference is that, like limited partners, the owners of the corporation, commonly known as shareholders or stockholders, are not personally liable for the debts and liabilities of the corporation. They stand to lose only their investment if the corporation becomes insolvent. But, unlike a limited partner, a shareholder is allowed to participate in the control of the corporation through the shareholders' voting privileges.

For the small corporation, however, limited liability may be something of an illusion in many situations, because creditors will often demand that the owners personally cosign for any credit extended. In addition, individuals remain responsible for their wrongful acts. Thus, a publisher who is personally responsible for an infringing or defamatory publication may still be personally liable, even if incorporated. Nevertheless, the *corporate liability shield* does protect a publisher when a contract is breached and the other contracting party has agreed to look only to the corporation for responsibility. For example, publishing contracts frequently require authors to make certain guarantees and statements of fact. If the author will contract with the publisher's corporation, rather than with the publisher as an individual, then the corporation alone will be liable if there is a breach. Similarly, if a publishing company is responsible for copyright infringement or for publishing a defamatory work, then the company would be liable, but the owner of that company would not.

The corporate shield also offers protection when an employee of the publisher has committed a wrongful act while working for the publisher's corporation. If, for example, a research assistant runs over a pedestrian while driving to the library to pick up some books for the publisher, the assistant and the corporation may be liable, but the publisher who owns the corporation will probably not be.

Another difference between corporations and partnerships is the *continuity of existence.* There are many events that can cause the dissolution of a partnership that will not have the same effect on a corporation. It is common to create a corporation with perpetual existence. Unlike partners, shareholders cannot decide to withdraw and demand a return of capital from the corporation. All they can do is sell their stock. A corporation may, therefore, have both legal and economic continuity. But the continuity can also be a tremendous disadvantage to shareholders or their heirs if they want to sell their stock but cannot find anyone who wants to buy it. Agreements can be made, however, that guarantee a return of capital should the shareholder die or wish to withdraw.

Other differences between corporations and partnerships are the free *transferability of ownership* and the structure of management and control. In a partnership, no one can become a partner without the unanimous consent of the other partners unless otherwise agreed. In a corporation, however, shareholders can generally sell their shares, or a portion of them, to whomever they wish. If the shareholders do not want a corporation to be open to outside ownership, transferability may be restricted. Partners generally have equal say in the governance of a partnership, but common shareholders are given a vote in proportion to their ownership in the corporation. A voting shareholder uses the vote to elect a board of directors and to create rules under which the corporation will operate.

The basic rules of the corporation are stated in the *articles of incorporation*, which are filed with the appropriate state agency. These serve as a sort of constitution and can be amended by shareholder vote. More detailed operational *bylaws* should also be adopted. Both shareholders and directors may have the power to create or amend bylaws. This varies from state to state and may be determined by the shareholders themselves. The board of directors then makes operational decisions for the corporation and might delegate daily control to a president.

A shareholder, even one who owns all the stock, may not act contrary to a decision of the board of directors. If the board has exceeded the powers granted to it by the articles or bylaws, any shareholder may use the courts to fight the decision. But if the board is acting within its powers, the shareholders have no recourse except to remove the board or any board member. In a few progressive states, a small corporation may entirely forego having a board of directors. In such cases, the corporation is authorized to allow the shareholders to vote on business decisions just as in a partnership.

Corporations have more legal ways available of raising capital than partnerships. Partnerships are restricted to borrowing money, taking on additional partners, or requesting additional capital from existing partners. However, all the partners must generally be in agreement for any of these actions. A corporation, on the other hand, may issue more stock, and this stock can be of many different varieties, for example, recallable at a set price or convertible into another kind of stock.

A method that corporations frequently use to attract new investors is to issue *preferred stock*. This means that the stock has some form of *preference*. This can be dividend preference, liquidation preference, or both. *A dividend preference* is the corporation's agreement to pay the preferred shareholder some predetermined amount before it pays any dividends to other shareholders. *Liquidation preference* means that if the corporation should go bankrupt or liquidate, the preferred shareholders will be paid out of the proceeds of liquidation before the common shareholders are paid, though after the corporation's creditors are paid. In most cases, the issuance of new stock merely requires approval by a majority of the existing shareholders. In addition, corporations can borrow money on a short-term basis by issuing notes or for a longer period by issuing debentures or bonds. In fact, a corporation's ability to raise additional capital is limited only by its lawyer's creativity and the economics of the marketplace.

Taxation

The last distinction between a partnership and a corporation is the manner in which a corporation is taxed. Under both state and federal laws, the profits of the corporation are taxed to the corporation before they are paid out as dividends. Then, because the dividends constitute income to the shareholders, they are taxed again as personal income. This double taxation constitutes the major disadvantage of a corporation. There are, however, several means of avoiding double taxation. First, a corporation can plan its business so as not to show very much profit. This can be done by drawing off what would be profit in payments to shareholders for a variety of services. For example, a shareholder can be paid a salary, rent for property leased to the corporation, or interest on a loan made to the corporation. All of these are legal deductions from the corporate income.

The corporation is entitled to larger deductions than sole proprietorships or partnerships for various retirement benefits provided its employees. For example, within certain limits, a corporation can deduct all of its payments made to an employee retirement plan, and the employees are not subject to personal income tax on the employer's contribution to the plan.

The corporation can also reinvest its profits for reasonable business expansion. This undistributed money is not taxed as income to the shareholders, as it would be to the owners in a partnership. Reinvestment has at least two advantages. First, the business can be built up with money that has been taxed only at the corporate level. Second, the owners can delay the liquidation and distribution of corporate assets until they are in lower tax brackets, thereby possibly lowering their personal tax liabilities.

S Corporations

In addition to the standard corporation, Congress has created a hybrid form that allows the owners of a small corporation to avoid the double taxation problem. This form of organization is called an *S corporation* (small business corporation), which is taxed differently from a *C corporation* (the regular corporation discussed above), but it is otherwise like a regular business corporation. The corporation owners must make an election in their corporate documents and through the IRS (IRS form 2553), and if that is properly accomplished, the corporation will not be subject to federal income tax (although they must file tax returns)—instead, the owners will be responsible for any taxes on income and will be able to deduct losses, take deductions, and so forth, like a partnership. This can be particularly advantageous in the early years of a corporation, because the owners of an S corporation can deduct the losses of the corporation from their personal income, whereas they cannot in a standard or so-called C corporation. They can have this favorable tax situation while simultaneously enjoying the corporation's limited liability status.

To qualify as an S corporation, the corporation must have fewer than 100 shareholders, all of whom must be individuals (with some limited exceptions); no shareholder may be a nonresident alien; and there can be only be one class of stock. There are both benefits and detriments to this form of business organization, and there are many rules and regulations that apply that are beyond the scope of this book. A good accountant can help you make a determination if an S corporation is a good choice for you based on all your circumstances.

THE LIMITED LIABILITY COMPANY

Doing business as a *limited liability company* (LLC) has become a very popular way to organize a small business and to limit the liability of the business owners. The LLC business form combines the limited liability features of the corporate form with tax advantages available to the sole proprietor or partnership. A publisher conducting business through an LLC can shield personal assets from the risk of the business for all situations, except the individual's own wrongful acts. This liability shield is the same as that offered by the corporate form. Although it is a newer business form than partnerships or corporations, it is becoming more and more often the first choice for many businesses and is available for use even if there is a single owner. It is not a corporation, and certain rules relating to corporations do not need to be followed, allowing more flexibility in its formation and management. Much less paperwork is required than for a corporation.

A one-owner limited liability company is taxed as a sole proprietor, and companies with more than one owner can be taxed as partnerships, or C corporations. A limited liability company may also be taxed as an S corporation if it first elects to be taxed as a corporation and then elects to be taxed as an S corporation. The correct boxes need to be checked and the right forms must be filed so that the company will be entitled to the sort of taxation model preferred. The LLC can have as many members as it wants, and there is no residency or citizenship requirement. In fact, members do not need to be individuals but can be another LLC or other business entities, as well.

LLCs do not have the same restrictions imposed on S corporations regarding the number and types of owners. Corporations, LLCs, sole proprietors, and partnerships can own interests in LLCs. LLCs may also have more than one class of voting ownership. There is, however, a restriction imposed on the transferability of ownership interests in the LLC. Due to this restriction, this business form may not be as desirable for larger businesses as is the corporation or limited partnership form. The LLC form can be particularly useful because of its flexibility. Virtually any internal structure for an LLC can be provided for in the LLC's *operating agreement*.

THE LIMITED LIABILITY PARTNERSHIP

For businesses that have been conducted in the partnership form and desire a liability shield, the limited liability partnership (LLP) is available. This business form parallels the LLC in most respects, though it is created by converting a partnership into an LLP. Generally, the partnership agreement is then replaced by an operating agreement, which may follow the same general pattern as the original partnership agreement.

BENEFIT CORPORATIONS

Fairly recently, a new sort of business model is being used by socially conscious groups. Known as *benefit corporations*, they are established with more than profit in mind. The first state to authorize such corporations was Maryland in 2010, and they are now permitted in more than half of the states. It is a for-profit business form, the purpose of which also takes into consideration social goals and the impact of its decisions on its shareholders, society, and the environment. In some states, reports must be filed that discuss the success of its performance in these areas. This is a new and developing business form. There are significant variations between states that allow it as a choice. A good business lawyer will be able to tell you whether this company form is available in your state, the requirements for forming one, and what the reporting requirements are, if any.

PRECAUTIONS FOR MINORITY OWNERS

Dissolving any business entity is not only painful because of certain tax penalties, but it is almost always impossible without the consent of the majority of the owners. If you are involved in the formation of a business entity and will be a minority owner, you must realize that the majority owners will have ultimate and absolute control—unless minority owners take certain precautions from the start. There are numerous horror stories relating to what some majority owners have done to unprotected minority owners. Avoiding these problems is no more difficult than drafting an agreement among owners at the outset and before problems arise. Corporations, LLCs, and LLPs have bylaws or operating agreements that can be structured to provide for minority protection. You should always retain your own attorney to represent you during the business entity's formation rather than relying on the entity's lawyer.

FORMALITIES

The benefits of the corporate form, as well as those of LLCs, LLPs, limited partnerships, etc., derive from the state's recognition that the business is a legal entity separate from its owners. To enjoy these benefits, a corporation must act like a corporation, and the other forms of business entities must act as such entities. Courts consider observance of formalities to be an important factor in deciding whether the business has, in fact, been operating as a separate legal entity. If the business is not properly operating as a separate entity, creditors or other claimants against the business are much more likely to be able to *pierce the veil* and hold the owner personally responsible for liabilities. An experienced business attorney can advise about basic formalities that will help preserve the business form and its protection.

CONSULTING AN ATTORNEY

It is important to determine which business form will be most advantageous. This can best be done by consulting with an experienced business lawyer. An attorney's services should be used to help comply with state business organization laws and other formalities, and to ensure that agreements are enforceable and adequately protect individual interests.

CHAPTER 16

Keeping Taxes Low

Since publishers have to pay taxes like everyone else, it is in their best interest to understand how to minimize their tax liabilities. The main way to do this is to understand what expenses can be taken as *business deductions* and how to keep track of these expenses.

Although many of the incentives offered to businesses to encourage investment do not apply to small publishers, even they can benefit in some cases from certain provisions of the Internal Revenue Code to reduce their tax liability. However, publishers should also be aware that many taxpayers have abused the opportunities to take deductions for legitimate business expenses by claiming that expenses for vacations, entertainment, and hobbies were incurred as part of their businesses. The abusive use of sham deductions has long caused the IRS to view such deductions with a fair degree of skepticism. While publishers are encouraged to claim the deductions to which they are lawfully entitled, they should also be careful to understand what can be properly claimed and know how to document their expenses.

QUALIFYING FOR BUSINESS DEDUCTIONS

Publishers may deduct their business expenses and thereby significantly reduce their taxable income. To deduct them, the publisher must have incurred the expenses with the motive to make a profit. They also must be *ordinary and necessary* expenses to carry on a business. An ordinary expense is one that is common and accepted in a particular field of trade, business, or profession. A necessary expense is one that is helpful and appropriate for that business. An expense does not have to be required to be considered necessary. Deductions are not allowed for personal, living, and family expenses, such as the cost of the first telephone line in a residence.

People who publish as hobbyists are not entitled to trade or business deductions, except against income earned specifically from a given project. For example, if an avid hunter spends $2,500 on an elk hunting trip in eastern Oregon, and later earns $250 by publishing a pamphlet on the trip, he will be able to deduct $250 of the expenses if he is a hobbyist. However, if a publisher incurs the same expenses to develop a book on which he intends to earn more than $2,500, the expenses would likely be deductible even though the IRS might take a hard look at it. Even if the specific trip did not result in a profit, the publisher is still allowed to deduct the expenses of the trip from the gross income derived from other publishing projects, whereas the hobbyist would not be.

The tax laws presume that a publisher is engaged in a business as opposed to a hobby if a net profit results during three out of the five consecutive tax years. In other words, if the publisher meets this standard, the IRS will not question that the publisher is engaged in a business (though it may still question individual deductions). Publishers who do not meet this standard will have to prove the expenses were incurred with a *profit motive* in order to claim them as business expenses. To prove this, the publisher is not required to show that a profit was actually made, but only that he, she, or it *intended* to make a profit. In determining whether a profit motive existed, the IRS and courts will look to the following nine factors when evaluating an activity:

1. the manner in which the taxpayer carries on the activity (e.g., effective business routines and bookkeeping procedures);
2. the expertise of the taxpayer or the taxpayer's advisors (e.g., study in an area, awards, prior publication, critical recognition, membership in professional organizations);
3. the time and effort expended in carrying on the activity (e.g., at least several hours a day devoted to publishing, preferably on a regular basis);
4. expectations that business assets will increase in value (a factor that is of little relevance to the publisher);
5. the success of the taxpayer in similar or related activities (i.e., past publishing successes, either financial or critical, even if prior to the relevant five-year period);
6. history of income or losses with respect to the activity (e.g., increases in receipts from year to year unless losses vastly exceed receipts over a long period of time);

7. the amount of profits earned, if any;

8. financial status of the taxpayer (wealth derived from other sources sufficient to support a hobby would weigh against the profit motive); and

9. elements of personal pleasure or recreation (e.g., if significant traveling is involved and little publishing produced, the IRS and tax court may be suspicious of profit motive).

No single factor will determine the results. However, claims that publishing was done as a business will be subject to close scrutiny by the IRS if the expenses appear to have been motivated by personal enjoyment instead of profit. Examples of the kinds of expenses that suggest an insincere profit motive are *research trips* to see concerts or experience a cruise, and the purchase of household entertainment equipment, such as televisions and video equipment, for *review.* This does not mean that such expenses cannot be considered legitimate business expenses or that publishers cannot incur business expenses for items they enjoy personally. However, one cannot convert a personal trip into a business trip merely by publishing it and trying to sell the work.

Nonetheless, many expenses that superficially appear to be personal in nature may be deductible—*if* the publisher can prove they were incurred with an actual and honest intent to make a profit. This is illustrated in a tax court opinion involving several deductions taken by a writer, including payments to prostitutes and the travel expenses incurred to visit brothels in another state. The writer was a retired federal employee whose career had entailed writing budget justifications and procedures for an agency. He began writing fiction about two years before his retirement in the hopes of making writing a second career. In order to authenticate the story and develop characters for his manuscript, the writer traveled several times from Virginia to Nevada, where he visited legal brothels and acted as a customer for prostitutes. He kept a journal that recorded extensive information about the brothels and prostitutes.

After completing the manuscript, the writer paid a subsidy publisher $4,375 to publish the novel *Searchlight, Nevada.* He continued his research at Nevada brothels and prepared another manuscript, which apparently was never published. The subsidy publisher filed for bankruptcy without paying the writer. However, the writer did submit a proof of claim for about $18,000 to the bankruptcy court. Although the writer earned no income from writing during 1994 and 1995, he deducted $37,800 as business expenses. When the IRS objected, the writer petitioned the tax court to allow the deductions.

The court noted that the writer's record-keeping, level of effort, promotional activities, and extensive search to find a new publisher after the rights to *Searchlight, Nevada* were returned to him indicated that he had an actual and honest intent to make a profit. It allowed the writer to deduct his home office expenses, the payment to the subsidy publisher, and much of his travel expenses. However, the court disallowed the $9,100 in expenses he incurred in visiting the prostitutes, on the grounds that the expenses were too inherently personal to qualify as business expenses. While this case involved a writer, the same conclusion would be reached if the person in question were a publisher.

There are some strategies available to help publishers show the IRS that they are a legitimate business. The following are some ideas that can help you:

- Keep a good set of accounting records, including the use of a separate business bank account.
- If there are any assets that are used for both personal and business use (such as an automobile, computer, or photo equipment), keep a log of the personal and business use of each.
- Have a business credit card that is never used for personal expenses.
- Get business insurance.
- Properly register your business with any applicable state or local agencies.
- Secure your business name (if any) with the applicable state authorities.
- If you have a home office, consider setting up a separate telephone line just for business use.
- Keep records that show that you have periodically reviewed the profitability of the business and which ideas were implemented to improve the financial performance of the enterprise.

The above recommendations are pertinent to smaller publishers; nevertheless, larger publishers should follow the same rules, particularly where the publishing house is owned and controlled by an individual or a family group.

THE HOME OFFICE DEDUCTION

Tax law changes have made taking a home office deduction much more attractive than it has been in the past. Publishers who works out of their homes from time to time should consider the benefits of taking a home office deduction carefully, even if they have been told in the past that they would be better served not to take the deduction. The home office deduction allows various home expenses to be deducted against the net business income. Expenses that fall into this category include, but are not limited to,

- mortgage interest;
- real estate taxes;
- home repairs/maintenance;
- rent;
- utilities;
- insurance;
- security system; and
- depreciation.

The expenses for a home office are broken down into two categories—indirect expenses and direct expenses. Indirect expenses are those that benefit both the business and the personal use portions of the home. The business portion of the expense is taken as a percentage of the total spent. The business use percentage is determined by dividing the square footage of business use of the home by the total square footage. Direct expenses are those that were made to improve only the business use portion of the home. These amounts are allowed in full.

In order for an area of your home to be considered for business use, it must be used regularly and exclusively. *Regularly* means that the space is consistently used for business purposes only—occasional use does not qualify. *Exclusively* means that the area is used only for the business purpose (there is an exception for the storage of inventory). Generally, an area is used for business if it meets the above tests and is

- the principal place of business (this includes administrative use);
- a place to meet clients or customers; and
- used for business purposes.

A separate structure from the taxpayer's personal residence (such as a detached garage converted into a publishing warehouse or office) that is used for business purposes qualifies, as well.

IN PLAIN ENGLISH

A home office will generally qualify as a business use for administrative work if the area is used exclusively and regularly and there is no other location available for the taxpayer to conduct these activities.

Determining the Deduction

There are now (beginning in tax year 2013) two ways to calculate the deduction for business use of a home: the regular method and a simplified method. The simplified method makes the calculation and record-keeping requirements easier. The taxpayer can choose either method for any taxable year. Once you have chosen one method for a particular year, you cannot change to the other method for that year. If you use the simplified method one year and change to the regular method in a subsequent year, there are rules about how you must calculate the depreciation deduction. The depreciation rules for the regular method of calculation are beyond the scope of this book. It is wise to consult a good accountant to be sure that you do this properly. For both methods, you can deduct a portion of the residence for home office use *only if* that portion is used *exclusively* and on a *regular basis* for business purposes. Under the simplified method of calculation:

- determine the square footage of the home that is used for business (not to exceed 300 feet);
- apply the currently approved standard per square foot amount to determine the deduction;
- home-related itemized deductions are to be claimed in full on Schedule A;
- there is no depreciation deduction;
- there is no recapture of depreciation on the sale of the home;
- the deduction cannot exceed the gross income from the business use of the home less the business expenses;
- any amount in excess of the gross income limitation may not be carried over to subsequent years; and

- any loss carryover from the use of the regular method of computation in prior years may not be claimed.

Under the regular method of calculation:

- determine the percentage of the home used for business;
- the actual expenses must be determined and good records maintained;
- home-related itemized deductions must be apportioned between Schedule A and the business Schedule—Schedule C or Schedule F;
- a depreciation deduction for the portion of the home used for business may be taken;
- the depreciation is recaptured on any gain from the sale of the home;
- the deduction cannot exceed the gross income from the business use of the home less the business expense;
- any amount in excess of the gross income limitation may be carried over in subsequent years; and
- any loss carryover from using the regular method in prior years may be claimed if the gross income test is met in the current year.

An allocable portion of mortgage interest and property taxes can be deducted against the business income. These would be deductible as personal itemized deductions anyway. The advantage of deducting them against the business, in the regular method, is that the business profit subject to self-employment taxes is reduced. A taxpayer who lives in a rented house and otherwise qualifies for the home office deduction may deduct a portion of the rent that would not otherwise be tax-deductible. The primary tax advantage for both renters and owners comes from a deduction for an allocable portion of repairs and utility bills and, for owners using the regular method of computation, depreciation. Otherwise, these would not be deductible at all.

OTHER BUSINESS EXPENSES

As mentioned earlier, deductible business expenses for a publisher include all the ordinary and necessary expenditures involved in publishing as a business. Most of the expenses that publishers incur are classified as current expenses, which are items with a useful life of less than one year. Examples include office supplies, postage, the cost of reference books, and telephone bills. These expenses are fully deductible in the year incurred.

Some business expenses, however, cannot be fully deducted in the year they were incurred but must instead be depreciated. These kinds of costs are called *capital expenditures.* Examples include equipment and furniture. Instead, the taxpayer must *depreciate*, or allocate, the cost of the item over the estimated useful life of the item. This is sometimes referred to as *capitalizing the cost.* Although the actual useful life of office equipment varies, fixed periods have been established in the Internal Revenue Code over which depreciation may be deducted. In addition, Section 179 of the Internal Revenue Code allows businesses to deduct all the expense of tangible personal property in the year they are placed in service, up to a certain limit (e.g., $500,000 in 2016). This means that a publisher can claim a deduction for all the equipment and furniture purchased during a tax year if the expenditures do not exceed the limit.

There is also what is called a "safe harbor," which would permit certain taxpayers, without audited financial statements, to avoid capitalization of items. The criteria for this safe harbor are technical and beyond the scope of this book. You should discuss this issue with your accountant or tax preparer.

In some cases, it may be difficult to decide whether an expense is a capital expenditure or a current expense. Repairs to machinery are one example. If you spend $200 to repair a computer, this expense may or may not constitute a capital expenditure. The general test is whether the amount spent restoring the machine adds to the value or substantially prolongs the useful life of the machine. Since the cost of replacing short-lived parts of a machine to keep it in efficient working condition does not substantially add to the useful life of a machine, such a cost would be a current cost and would be deductible. A major upgrade that significantly extended the useful life of the computer, on the other hand, would be a capital expenditure that must be depreciated.

Expenditures for professional services, such as commissions paid to agents and fees paid to accountants and attorneys, are generally deductible as current expenses. The same is true of salaries paid to typists, editors, designers, and others whose services are necessary for the publishing business. If you need to hire help, it might be a good idea to hire people on an individual project basis as *independent contractors* rather than as regular employees.

This avoids liability for Social Security, disability, and withholding tax payments. When hiring, you should specify the job-by-job basis of the assignments, detail when each project is to be completed, and if possible, allow the person you are hiring to choose where to work (since this might emphasize the person's independence). Further, the IRS is getting stricter in requiring W-9 forms and 1099 forms to be filed. There are penalties for failure to properly file them. The IRS applies a twenty-factor test, which focuses on who has control over the work being done, to determine whether a worker is an employee or an independent contractor. It is recommended that a publisher, as an employer of either an employee or an independent contractor, consult with a qualified accounting professional to be certain that the employment relationship is properly structured at its inception. There are also state laws that must be complied with when characterizing a person as an employee or independent contractor. This area is very technical, and if the characterization is improper, there can be significant liability.

Travel

Publishers can also deduct expenses for travel provided they can show that the travel expenses were incurred for a business purpose. On a business trip, whether within the United States or abroad, ordinary and necessary expenses may be deductible if the travel is solely for business purposes. Transportation and lodging costs are fully deductible, except when traveling by ocean liner, cruise ship, or other form of luxury water transportation, for which the deductions are subject to a daily limit. Only 50 percent of the costs of meals consumed while on a business trip are deductible, unless they are fully reimbursed by the employer and are adequately documented.

In situations where the trip was primarily for business but was extended for personal activities, the business-related travel expenses can be deducted. These expenses include the travel costs of getting to and from the business destination and any business-related expenses at that destination. If the trip is primarily for personal reasons, such as a vacation, the transportation cost is a nondeductible personal expense, even if some incidental business is done on the trip. However, expenses incurred at the destination that are directly related to your business may be deducted. For example, if you travel to attend a friend's wedding and take a writer to lunch while in town, the trip would be a personal expense, but the costs directly associated with the writer lunch would be deductible as a business entertainment expense.

When any part of your business travel is outside the United States, some of the deductions for the cost of getting to and from your destination may be limited. For tax purposes, the United States includes the fifty states and the District of Columbia. If the trip is entirely for business, then all expenses may be deducted. If someone travels outside the United States primarily for business but spends some of their time on other activities, he or she generally can only deduct the business portion of the cost of getting to and from the destination. However, in certain cases, the trip will be considered entirely for business even if some personal aspects are involved.

One situation applies to employees who are reimbursed or paid a travel expense allowance, are not related to their employer, and are not managing executives. Another applies to trips in which the time spent outside of the United States is for a week or less. In such cases, the entire cost of transportation getting to and from the business destination is deductible, as are the other costs associated with days on which business was done. Related to this situation are trips in which the taxpayer is outside the United States for more than a week and spends less than 25 percent of the total time on nonbusiness activities. Finally, there is a catch-all exception, where the trip is considered entirely for business if the taxpayer can establish that a personal vacation was not a major consideration, even if they had substantial control over arranging the trip.

If you are claiming one of these exceptions, you should be careful to have supporting documentation. If you cannot take advantage of one of the exceptions, then you must allocate expenses for the trip abroad according to the percentage of the trip devoted to business versus vacation.

Business Day

Whether inside or outside of the United States, the definition of what constitutes a business day can be very helpful to the taxpayer in determining a trip's deductibility. Travel days, including the day of departure and the day of return, count as business days if business activities occurred on such days. If travel is outside the United States, the same rules apply if the foreign trip is for more than seven days. Any day that the taxpayer spends on business counts as a business day, even if only a part of the day is spent on business. A day in which business is canceled through no fault of the taxpayer counts as a business day. Saturdays, Sundays, and holidays count as business days, even though no business is conducted, provided that business is conducted on the

Friday before and the Monday after the weekend, or on one day on either side of the holiday.

This is a very technical area of the tax law, and mischaracterization can result in serious problems. It is therefore important for you to consult with your accountant regarding the proper characterization of travel expenses.

Entertainment

Entertainment expenses incurred for the purpose of developing an existing business used to be deductible in the amount of 50 percent of the actual cost. However, starting in 2018, only meals are allowed as entertainment expenses. Keep in mind that you must be especially careful about recording these expenses. You should record the amount, date, place, business purpose, substance of the discussion, the participants in the discussion, and the business relationship of the parties who are being fed. Keep receipts for any expenses. You should also keep in mind that the tax code disallows deductibility for expenses that are lavish or extravagant. The IRS has not precisely defined what constitutes *lavish and extravagant* but advises taxpayers that an expense is not considered lavish or extravagant if it is *reasonable* considering the facts and circumstances of it. The IRS also has stated that expenses will not be disallowed just because they exceed a certain dollar amount or take place at deluxe restaurants, hotels, nightclubs, or resorts.

Conventions and Seminars

The IRS tends to review very carefully any deductions for attendance at conventions and business seminars that may serve as a pretext for a vacation, whether inside the United States or abroad. In order to deduct the business expense, the taxpayer must be able to show, with documentation, that the reason for attending the meeting was to promote production of income. Normally, for a spouse's expenses to be deductible, the spouse's presence must be required or the spouse must be attending as a bona fide employee of the publisher's business.

You cannot deduct expenses for attending a convention, seminar, or similar meeting held outside of the North American area unless the meeting is directly related to your business. Furthermore, to qualify, you must be able to show that it was as reasonable to hold the meeting outside the North American area as within it. If the meeting meets these requirements, you must also satisfy the rules for deducting expenses for business trips in general.

Deductions for conventions and seminars on cruise ships are even more restricted. No more than $2,000 may be deducted per year, and the ship must be a United States flagship (registered in the US). In addition, all ports of call must be within the United States or its possessions. You must provide documentation with your tax return that provides the total days of the trip, the number of hours each day that you devoted to scheduled business activities, and a program of the scheduled business activities of the meeting. You must also attach a written statement signed by an officer of the organization sponsoring the meeting that includes the schedule of the business activities and the number of hours you attended those activities.

Documentation

Maintaining documentation and an expense diary is probably the best means of ensuring that your deductions will withstand scrutiny from the IRS. When you are traveling, keep the following in mind.

With respect to travel expenses:

- keep proof of the costs;
- record the time of departure;
- record the number of days spent on business; and
- list the places visited and the business purposes of your activities.

With respect to the transportation costs:

- keep copies of all receipts;
- if traveling by car, keep track of mileage; and
- log all other expenses in your diary.

Similarly, keep receipts for all items and make sure to record all less expensive items in a logbook for meals, tips, and lodging.

CHARITABLE DEDUCTIONS

The law regarding charitable deductions by creative people of their own work is not very advantageous. Individuals who donate items they have created may only deduct the cost of materials used to create those works. This provision has had unfortunate effects on libraries and museums, which, since the law's passage in 1969, have experienced enormous decreases in charitable contributions from publishers, artists, and craftspeople. The Museum of Modern Art, for example, received fifty-two paintings and sculptures from artists from 1967 to 1969, but between 1972 and 1975, only one work was donated.

Although several modifications of the law have been proposed, Congress continues to resist change in the area of tax treatment regarding individuals' donations of their own work. However, some states have been more responsive. For example, Oregon and Kansas allow creators to deduct the fair market value of their creations donated to qualified charities, and California treats creative property as a capital asset.

Publishers donating books may enjoy greater benefits. Here too, it is important to discuss the donation with your accountant before it is made in order to determine whether it would qualify for the charitable donation deduction. In addition, it is also important to determine the tax status of the recipient, since greater benefits are available for qualified charities that use the item to fulfill their charitable purposes.

DEFERRING AND SPREADING INCOME

Another way to reduce tax liability is to *defer* the income to future tax years or to *spread* it to more than one person. One way the publisher can spread income is to receive payments in installments. Care must be taken with the mechanics of these kinds of arrangements. If a publisher arranges to accept compensation in the form of a negotiable note due at some future date as payment for the sale of books, the IRS will consider that the compensation is essentially equivalent to cash. Therefore, it is required that proceeds be reported as income realized when the note is received and not when the note is paid off. However, if the agreement provides for payments to be made in installments received in successive tax years, the income is taxed only as the payments are received.

For example, suppose a publisher sells a number of books for $3,000. Ordinarily, the entire $3,000 would be taxable income in the year it was received. However, if it is paid with four payments of $750, received annually over four years, the income will be taxed as the installments are received. In either case, the amount of income is $3,000, but under the installment method, the amount is spread out over four years, and the publisher may be able to take advantage of being taxed in a lower tax bracket than if the full $3,000 were received in the year the books were sold.

IN PLAIN ENGLISH

Publishers can agree in a sales contract that payments for a book will not exceed a certain amount in any one year, with excess payments to be carried over and paid to the publisher in the future.

Negative factors associated with tax deferral include the uncertain effects of inflation, the risk that the distributor or retailer may go broke before you are fully paid, and the possibility that income tax rates will rise. The publisher should consider these risks carefully before entering into a contract for deferred payments, because it might be quite difficult to change the arrangement if the need arises later.

Shifting Income

Another strategy for publishers in high tax brackets is to divert some of their income directly to members of their immediate family who are in lower tax brackets by hiring them as employees. Putting dependent children on the payroll can result in tax savings for publishers, because their salaries can be deducted as a business expense. The child can earn up to the amount of the standard deduction and the personal exemption without incurring tax liability, unless they are claimed as dependents on the publisher's tax return. If they are claimed on the return, the child may not claim the personal exemption. In addition, the following must be true:

- the salary must be reasonable in relation to the child's age and the work performed;
- the work performed must be a necessary service to the business; and
- the work must actually be performed by the child.

Family Partnerships

A second method of transferring income to members of your family is the creation of a family partnership. Each partner is entitled to receive an equal share of the overall income, unless the partnership agreement provides

otherwise. The income is taxed once as individual income to each partner. Thus, the publisher with a family partnership can break up and divert
income to the family members, where it will be taxed to them according to
their respective tax brackets. The income received by children may be taxed
at a significantly lower rate, resulting in more net income reaching the family than if it had all been received by the publisher, who is presumably in
a higher tax bracket than the children. But a publisher must be vigilant to
avoid the *kiddie tax* that applies to a child's unearned income, such as income
received from income-producing or investment types of property—the kiddie tax brackets now are correlated to the trust income tax rates. This affects
children under the age of nineteen, or between nineteen and twenty-three
who are full-time students and whose earned income does not exceed half of
the annual expenses for their support. You should work with an experienced
accountant regarding the kiddie tax, since the laws have been revised.

Although the IRS allows family partnerships, it may subject them to close
scrutiny to ensure that the partnership is not a sham. Unless the partnership
capital is a substantial income-producing factor, and unless partners are reasonably compensated for services performed on the partnership's behalf, the
IRS may deny the shift in income. The IRS would be relying on the section of
the code that deals with distribution of partners' shares and family partnerships. This section provides that a person owning a capital interest in a family
partnership will be considered a partner for tax purposes, even if he or she
receives the capital interest as a gift. However, the gift must be genuine, and
it cannot be revocable.

Incorporating

In the past, some families had incorporated in order to take advantage of the
then–more favorable corporate tax rates. If the IRS questioned the motiva-
tion for such an incorporation, the courts examined the intent of the family
members, and if the sole purpose of incorporating was tax avoidance, the
scheme was disallowed. There is rarely a substantial tax benefit to be derived
by incorporating a business, but there may be other reasons for incorporating, such as limiting personal liability. If the publisher employs a spouse and
children, salaries paid to them will be considered business deductions, thus
reducing the publisher's taxable income. When the spouse and children are
made owners of the corporation by being provided with shares of stock in it,
then all of the benefits discussed in the previous section on partnership will

be available. The unearned income received from the corporation by a child to which the kiddie tax applies follows the same rule as unearned income from a family partnership.

NOTE

The scope of this chapter and the information contained in it are not intended to offer tax advice specific to your circumstances. Its purpose is to point out issues and areas of concern or opportunity to enable you to obtain further information. It is highly recommended that you locate, and retain, a good tax accountant to give you advice pertinent to your particular situation.

CHAPTER 17

The Publisher's Estate

Awareness of estate planning issues can be especially important to publishers because of their unique situation. Proper planning ensures that the ownership of a publisher's assets after his or her death will end up in safe and knowledgeable hands. A publisher may wish to deal very specifically with the disposition of various intangibles such as copyrights, trademarks, patents, trade secrets, and even passwords and social media accounts, websites, and email accounts or issues. A carefully drafted estate plan affords the opportunity to direct distribution of these rights and control how the assets are used. For example, a publisher who wants to donate certain assets to a library or university, but only if certain conditions are adhered to, can specify these conditions in the legal documents that constitute an estate plan.

In addition to giving the publisher significant posthumous control over assets, an estate plan can greatly reduce the overall amount of estate tax paid at death. Because valuations of assets for estate tax purposes are not precise, estate taxes may turn out to be significantly higher than might have been anticipated. Thus, it is very important for publishers to reduce their taxable estate as much as possible.

An estate plan may be either will-based or trust-based. Each type has advantages, but both are legitimate forms of estate planning. Estate laws and probate procedures vary throughout the United States, and a plan that works well for one person in one state may be inappropriate in other situations. Proper estate planning requires a knowledgeable lawyer and sometimes the assistance of other professionals, such as life insurance agents, accountants, and bank trust officers, depending on the nature and size of the estate.

THE WILL

A *will* is a legal instrument by which a person directs the distribution of property in his or her estate upon death. The maker of the will is called the *testator*. Gifts given by a will are referred to as *bequests* or *devises*, generally based on which state you live in. Certain formalities are required by state law to create a valid will. Most states require that the instrument be in writing and signed by the testator in the presence of two or more witnesses. In these states, the witnesses affirm by their signatures that the testator declared the will to be genuine and signed it in their presence. Some of these and other states permit unwitnessed wills, known as *holographic wills*, if they are entirely handwritten and signed by the testator.

When carefully prepared, wills not only address how the assets of the estate will be distributed, but also foster better management of the assets. Those persons responsible for administering the estate of a decedent are known as *executors* in some states and *personal representatives* in others. It may be a good idea for publishers to appoint joint executors so that one has publishing or writing experience and the other has financial expertise. In this way, the financial decisions can have the benefit of at least two perspectives. If joint executors are used, it will be necessary to make some provision in the will for resolving any deadlock between the two. For example, a neutral third party might be appointed as an arbitrator who is directed to resolve any impasses after hearing both sides. It is also advisable to define the scope of the executor's power by detailed instructions. A lawyer's help will be necessary to set forth all of these important considerations in legally enforceable, unambiguous terms.

It is essential to avoid careless language that might be subject to attack by survivors unhappy with the will's provisions. A lawyer's help is also crucial to avoid making bequests that are not legally enforceable because they are contrary to public policy.

IN PLAIN ENGLISH

A will is a unique document in two respects. First, if properly drafted, it is *ambulatory*, meaning it can accommodate change, such as applying to property acquired after the will is made. Second, it is *revocable*, meaning it can be changed or canceled before death.

Revocation

A will is *revocable*, meaning that the testator has the power to change or cancel it before death. Even if a testator makes a legally enforceable agreement not to revoke the will, he or she will still have the power to revoke it, although liability for breach of contract could result. Generally, courts do not consider a will to have been revoked unless it can be clearly shown that the testator either

- performed a physical act of revocation, such as burning or tearing up a will, with the intent to revoke it; or
- executed a valid superseding will that revokes the earlier one.

Most state statutes also provide for automatic revocation of a will in whole or in part if the testator subsequently divorces.

To change a will, the testator may execute a supplement, known as a *codicil*, which has the same formal requirements as those for creating a will. To the extent that the codicil contradicts the will, those contradicted parts of the will are revoked. A testator may also execute a completely new will that takes the place of the old one.

Distributions

Before the property in a will can be distributed, all outstanding debts and taxes must be paid. When the property owned by the testator at death is insufficient to satisfy all the bequests in the will after all debts and taxes have been paid, some or all of the bequests must be reduced or even eliminated entirely. The process of reducing or eliminating bequests is known as *abatement*. The priorities for reduction are set according to the category of each bequest.

The legally significant categories of gifts are generally as follows:

- specific bequests or devises, meaning gifts of a particular kind or uniquely identifiable items (*I give to X all the furniture in my home*);
- demonstrative bequests or devises, meaning gifts that are to be paid out of a specified source, unless that source contains insufficient funds, in which case the gifts will be paid out of the general assets (*I give to Y $1,000 to be paid from my shares of stock in ABC Corporation*);

- general bequests, meaning gifts payable out of the general assets of an estate (*I give Z $1,000*); and
- residuary bequests or devises, meaning gifts of whatever is left in the estate after all other gifts and expenses are satisfied (*I give the rest, residue, and remainder of my estate to Z*).

Intestate property, or property not disposed of by the will, is usually the first to be taken to satisfy claims against the estate. (If the will contains a valid *residuary clause*, there will be no such property.) If this property is not sufficient, residuary bequests will be used. If more money is needed, general bequests will be used, and last, specific and demonstrative bequests will be taken together in proportion to their value.

If the testator acquires more property in the time between the execution of the will and death, the disposition of such property will also be governed by the will. If the will contains a valid residuary clause, the property will go to the residuary beneficiaries of the will. If there is no such clause, the property will pass outside the will to the persons specified in the state's law of intestate succession.

Intestate Distributions

When a person dies without leaving a valid will, this is known as dying *intestate*. When a person dies intestate, his or her property is distributed according to the state law of intestate succession, which specifies who is entitled to which parts of the estate. These rules vary from state to state. An intestate's surviving spouse will always receive a share, generally at least one-third of the estate, most often more. An intestate's surviving children likewise may get a share, in some states depending on whether the children were children of the surviving spouse or a former spouse. If some of the children do not survive the intestate, the grandchildren of the intestate may be entitled to a share by representation. *Representation* allows surviving children to stand in the shoes of a deceased parent in order to inherit from a grandparent who dies intestate.

If there are no direct descendants surviving, the intestate's surviving spouse may take the entire estate or may share it with the intestate's parents. If there is neither a surviving spouse nor any surviving direct descendants of the intestate, the estate may be distributed to the intestate's parents, or if the parents are not surviving, to the intestate's brothers and sisters. If there are no surviving persons in any of these categories, the estate may go to surviving grandparents and their direct descendants. In this way, the family tree is constantly expanded in search of surviving relatives. If none of the persons specified in the law of intestate succession survive the decedent, the intestate's property ultimately goes to the state. This is known as *escheat*.

Distributions to a Spouse Left Out of the Will

State law will often provide a testator's surviving spouse with certain benefits from the estate even if the spouse is left out of the testator's will. Historically, these benefits were known as *dower*, in the case of a surviving wife, or *curtesy*, in the case of a surviving husband. In place of the old dower and curtesy, modern statutes give the surviving spouse the right to elect against the will and receive a certain share, such as one-fourth of the estate. This is generally called the spouse's *elective share*.

Here again, state laws vary. For example, in some states, the surviving spouse's elective share is one-third. The historical concepts of dower and curtesy are, in large part, a result of the law's traditional recognition of an absolute duty on the part of a husband to provide for his wife. Modern laws are based on the notion that most property in a marriage should be shared, because the financial success of either partner is due to the efforts of both.

DISTRIBUTING PROPERTY OUTSIDE THE WILL

Another aspect of estate planning is distributing property outside the will. This can be done by making gifts to individuals (known as *inter vivos gifts*) or by placing the property in *trust* prior to death. Thought should also be given to other methods of transferring property before or after death, such as joint bank accounts that go to the survivor on the death of one of the account owners, or POD (payable on death) or TOD (transfer on death) designations that may be permitted for bank accounts or investment accounts, or through beneficiary elections available for things like retirement accounts. Married people should hold title to real property as *tenants by the entirety*, so that the property passes to the surviving spouse on death without the necessity for probate. Some states, by statute, now allow a TOD deed for real estate. Title to vehicles may be held by "x or y," instead of by either individually, or by "x and y," so that the surviving party may hold or dispose of the property without the need for probate or the signature of the other party. Be cognizant of the fact, however, that in having joint bank accounts during the life of both parties, or owning vehicles by two parties, while they both live, the "or" designation makes either party able to spend, sell, or otherwise deal with the property without the consent of the other party while both are alive.

The main advantage to distributing property outside of the will is that the property escapes the delays and expense of *probate*, the court procedure by which a will is validated and administered.

Gifts

In order to qualify as an inter vivos gift for tax purposes, a gift must be *complete and final*. Control is an important issue. For example, if a publisher retains the right to revoke a gift, the gift may be found to be testamentary (occurring on death) in nature, even if the right to revoke was never exercised. The gift must also be *delivered*. An actual, physical delivery is best, but a symbolic delivery may suffice if there is strong evidence of intent to make an irrevocable gift. An example of symbolic delivery is when the donor puts something in a safe and gives the intended recipient the only key.

There used to be significant tax advantages to making inter vivos gifts, rather than gifts by will, but since the estate and gift tax rates are now unified, few tax advantages remain. One remaining advantage to making an inter vivos gift is that if the gift appreciates in value between the time the gift is made and the death of the giver, the appreciated value will not be taxed. If the gift were made by will, the added value would be taxable, since the gift would be valued as of the date of death (or six months after). This value difference can represent significant tax savings for publishers who have recently realized fame and whose companies are rapidly gaining value.

The other advantage to making an inter vivos gift is the yearly exclusion from gift taxes. The general rule is that any gift is taxable, but fortunately, there are many exclusions from the general rule. The major exceptions are tuition or medical expenses paid for someone else and gifts to a spouse, political organization, or charity. There is also an annual exclusion amount that applies on a per recipient basis. In 2017, the yearly exclusion was $14,000 per recipient. For example, if $18,000 worth of gifts were given to an individual in 2016, only $4,000 worth of gifts would actually have been taxable to the donor (who is responsible for the gift tax). Married couples can combine their gifts and claim twice the yearly exclusion per recipient.

Gift Tax Returns

Gift tax returns must be filed by the donor for any year in which gifts made to any one donee exceed the exclusion amount. It is not mandatory to file returns when a gift to any one donee amounts to less than the exclusion amount. However, if the valuation of the gift may become an issue with the IRS, then it is a good idea to file a return anyway. Filing the return starts the three-year statute of limitations running. Once the statute of limitations period has expired, the IRS will be barred from filing suit for unpaid taxes or tax deficiencies due to higher government valuations of the gifts. If a taxpayer omits gifts that should have been included on the return amounting to more than 25 percent of the total amount of gifts stated in the return, the statute of limitations is extended to six years. There is no statute of limitations for fraudulent returns filed with the intent to evade tax or for no return filed.

Trusts

Another common way to transfer property outside the will is to place the property in a trust that is created prior to death. A trust is simply a legal arrangement by which one person holds certain property for the benefit of another. The person holding the property is the trustee; those who benefit are the beneficiaries.

To create a valid trust, the publisher must identify the trust property, make a declaration of intent to create the trust, transfer property to the trust (this is often a step that is missed and can create a multitude of problems), and name identifiable beneficiaries. Failure to name a trustee will not defeat the trust, since if no trustee is named, a court will appoint one.

The publisher may name him- or herself as trustee, in which case segregation of the trust property satisfies the delivery requirement. Trusts can be created by will, in which case they are termed *testamentary trusts,* but these trust properties will be probated along with the rest of the will. To avoid probate, the publisher must create a valid inter vivos or living trust.

Generally, in order to qualify as an inter vivos trust, a valid interest in property must be transferred before the death of the creator of the trust, who is known as the *settlor.* For example, if the settlor fails to name a beneficiary for the trust property or make delivery of the property to the trustee before death, the trust will likely be termed testamentary. So designated, the trust will be deemed invalid, unless the formalities required for creating a will were complied with.

A trust will not be termed testamentary simply because the settlor retained significant control over the trust, such as the power to revoke or modify the trust. For example, if a person makes a deposit in a savings account in his or her own name as trustee for another, but reserves the power to withdraw the money or revoke the trust, the beneficiary will still be able to enforce the trust provisions and claim the money in the account upon the death of the depositor (provided that the depositor has not revoked the trust). Many states allow the same type of arrangement in authorizing joint bank accounts with rights of survivorship as valid will substitutes. Property transferred under one of these arrangements is passed outside the will and need not go through probate.

However, even though such an arrangement escapes probate, since the settlor retains significant control, the trust property will likely be counted as part of the gross estate for tax purposes. In addition, if the deceased settlor created a revocable trust for the purpose of decreasing the statutory share of a surviving spouse, the trust will be declared illusory in some states. The surviving spouse is then granted the legal share not only from the probate estate, but from the revocable trust.

Advantages of Using a Trust

The use of trusts to prepare a trust-based plan will, in certain situations, have significant advantages over a traditional will-based plan. For example, the careful drafting of trusts can allow the publisher's estate to avoid probate, which in some states is a lengthy and expensive process. Similarly, the execution of an estate through a trust-based plan can ensure a level of privacy not possible in probate court. Although these kinds of provisions provide some control over the estate, publishers are cautioned that trusts cannot adequately substitute for a will if used haphazardly. Professional assistance is strongly recommended, and it is important not to miss the step of legally transferring the property to be included in the trust to the trust.

Life Insurance Trusts

Life insurance trusts can also be used for paying estate taxes. The proceeds of a life insurance trust will not be taxed if the life insurance trust is irrevocable and the trustee is someone other than the estate executor. Even when the trust is irrevocable and the trustee is a third party, the proceeds are taxed to the extent they are used to pay taxes to benefit the estate. The advantage to this arrangement, then, is not so much tax avoidance as guaranteed liquidity. This advantage is especially important for publishers and other creative people, since otherwise survivors can be forced to sell assets for much less than their real value in order to pay estate taxes.

ESTATE TAXES

The Economic Growth and Tax Relief Reconciliation Act of 2001 significantly revised the law regarding federal estate and gift taxes. It imposes a schedule in which the amount of estates excluded from paying taxes is set at $5.49 million for 2017. The changes in the tax laws are complicated and have only enhanced the need for competent counsel in such matters. A number of states also have inheritance or estate taxes.

While the increase in the exclusion amounts will reduce the concerns about estate taxes for many publishers, it is still useful to understand how estate taxes are assessed and the relationship between estate and gift taxes. It is also important to understand how issues, such as valuation of assets, can lead to higher-than-necessary tax burdens.

The Gross Estate

The first step in evaluating an estate for tax purposes is to determine the *gross estate*. The gross estate includes all property in which the deceased had an ownership interest at the time of death and before the will is administered. The key element in determining ownership is control. Thus, the gross estate will include all property over which the deceased retained significant control at the time of death. Examples would include life insurance proceeds, annuities, jointly held interests, and revocable transfers.

Under current tax laws, the executor of an estate may elect to value the property in the estate either as of the date of death or the date six months after death. The estate property must be valued in its entirety at the time chosen. If the executor elects to value the estate six months after death and certain pieces of property are distributed or sold before then, that property will be valued as of the actual date of distribution or sale.

Fair market value is defined as the price at which property would change hands between a willing buyer and a willing seller, when both buyer and seller have reasonable knowledge of all relevant facts. Such a determination is often very difficult to make, especially when books are involved.

Disagreements with the IRS on Value

Although the initial determination of fair market value is generally made by the executor when the estate tax return is filed, the Internal Revenue Service (IRS) may disagree with the executor's valuation and assign assets a much higher fair market value. For example, in 1979, the IRS claimed that writer Jacqueline Susann's diary had an estate tax value of $3.8 million as a literary property. The diary, which neither Susann nor her executor had considered particularly valuable, had been destroyed by the executor pursuant to Susann's directions.

When the IRS and the executor (or whoever represents the estate) disagree on a valuation, the matter will be litigated. The majority of these cases are settled out of court. Thus, there is very little case law dealing with the valuation of artistic or literary properties for estate tax purposes. The *Estate of David Smith* case is most often cited as an example of this type of valuation. While the decedent in this case was a sculptor and the controversy was over valuation of his creations, the same types of problems would arise in the attempt to value assets in a publisher's estate.

When David Smith died, there were 425 works in his estate. The market for his sculptures was limited, since most pieces were large and abstract, but prior to Smith's death, each of the 425 pieces had been photographed and marked with an estimated sales price. When the executors of the estate figured fair market value of the pieces, they first reduced the figure representing the sum of all the estimated prices ($4,284,000) by 75 percent to account for the devaluing effect that the sudden availability of so many sculptures had on the limited market. They then reduced that figure by one-third to account for the gallery's commission, as set out in the agency contract between the deceased and the gallery that had the exclusive right to sell his work. Thus, the executors' final figure representing fair market value on the tax return was $714,000. The IRS determined fair market value for the sculptures by simply adding up the one-at-a-time prices in Smith's gallery contract, claiming that the simultaneous availability factor would have no adverse impact on the market value. The IRS, thus, set the total valuation at the $4,284,000 figure and sued the estate for the tax deficiency.

When the case went to court, the court allowed a 50 percent reduction for sudden availability but refused to deduct the gallery's commission, holding that the measure of value is the amount received—not retained from a sale. Thus, the court's final figure was $2,700,000—a compromise between the executors' listed value of $714,000 and the IRS figure of over $4 million. Notwithstanding the reduction, the estate tax was devastating for the estate.

Mauldin v. Commissioner is another case in which the IRS claimed a tax deficiency based on disagreement over the value of artistic assets. At question was a series of cartoons and an original manuscript and sketches donated to the Smithsonian. Mauldin used experts provided by the Smithsonian to arrive at this valuation of the works. The interesting part of this case is that the court ruled that when one government agency (the Smithsonian) makes an appraisal in order to induce a charitable donation, another government agency (the IRS) should not challenge or disregard the appraisal after the contribution has been made.

In addition to valuing actual drawings or manuscripts, the executor of a publisher's estate will need to make some effort to value copyrights and other intangible assets owned by or licensed to the decedent or to the decedent's corporation. There is no hard-and-fast rule for valuing copyrights. The method most widely used is the *sinking fund method*, which uses a formula known as *Hoskins's formula*. Hoskins's formula basically involves determining the present value of future earnings from the copyrighted material. Needless to say, there may be much disagreement about this figure.

As mentioned earlier, when an executor and the IRS disagree as to valuation, the court will decide the matter. In most cases, the burden will be on the taxpayer to prove the value of the copyright. Thus, expert testimony and evidence of the sale of the same or similar properties will be helpful, as in cases involving original manuscripts and drawings. In general, courts are reluctant to accept valuation by formula as determinative.

It is extremely difficult to determine a fair market value for a manuscript or the literary rights connected to a manuscript. The cases demonstrate that there is no guarantee that court evaluations will necessarily be fair, and since a publisher or the business owned by the publisher will likely have these assets, this is an important issue to consider. Even a compromise approach by the court can result in artificially high valuations, which inflate a publisher's gross estate and can lead to higher taxes. An estate may therefore face real hardship in paying administration and tax costs when estate assets are not easily convertible to cash.

The Net Estate

The next major step in figuring the taxable estate is to evaluate the *net estate*. Typical deductions from the gross estate include funeral expenses, certain estate administration expenses, debts and enforceable claims against the estate, mortgages and liens, and—perhaps most significant—the marital deduction and the charitable deduction.

The *marital deduction* allows the total value of any interest in property that passes from the decedent to the surviving spouse to be subtracted from the value of the gross estate. The government will eventually collect the tax on this property when that spouse dies, but only to the extent such interest is included in the spouse's gross estate. This deduction may occur even in the absence of a will making a gift to the surviving spouse, since state law generally provides that the spouse is entitled to at least one-third of the overall estate, regardless of the provisions of the will.

The *charitable deduction* is the tax deduction allowed when property is transferred from an estate to a recognized charity. The charitable deduction is especially significant to the publisher. Although the income tax benefits from donating copyrights and manuscripts are negligible, the estate tax benefits may be substantial. In effect, the fair market value of donated works is excluded from the taxable estate. Although leaving the work in the estate will pass some value to those inheriting at a high rate of taxation, that value will be considerably less than the tax-free value of the work donated to a charitable institution. Since the definition of charity for tax purposes is quite technical, it is advisable to insert a clause in the will providing that, if the institution specified to receive the donation does not qualify for the charitable deduction, the bequest will go to a substitute qualified institution at the choice of the executor.

Once deductions are figured, the taxable estate is taxed at the rate specified by the Unified Estate and Gift Tax Schedule. The unified tax imposes the same rate of tax on gifts made by will as on gifts made during life. It is a progressive tax, meaning the percentage paid in taxes increases with the amount of property involved. Whether the estate tax will eventually be repealed altogether, be fixed at an intermediate amount, or revert to a former form will depend on future congressional action.

Paying Estate Taxes

Generally, estate taxes must be paid when the estate tax return is filed within nine months of the date of death, although arrangements may be made to spread payments out over a number of years, if necessary. It is not uncommon for executors to be forced to sell properties for less than full value in order to pay taxes. This situation can be avoided by publishers obtaining insurance policies, the proceeds of which can be payable into a trust.

PROFESSIONAL ESTATE PLANNING

All publishers should give some thought to estate planning and make the effort to address these issues adequately. Without a soundly prepared plan, there is simply no way to control the disposition of property. Posthumous control is especially important in the case of manuscripts, copyrights, and so forth, and their attendant legal rights.

Sound estate planning may include transfers outside of the will, since these types of arrangements escape the delays and expenses of probate. It makes more sense to consult with an experienced professional to develop a comprehensive plan than to rely on form documents. The generally modest added expense associated with professional estate planning will most likely be recouped when the plan is finally executed.

CHAPTER 18

Agency Issues, Avoiding, and Resolving

Publishers are responsible for the acts and omissions of their employees and may be responsible for many of the wrongful acts of their independent contractors, as well. The law in this area is well established.

AUTHORITY

The publisher as principal will be liable to third parties for its agent's breach of contract only if the agent was acting within the scope of the agent's authority. Employees are agents of their employers. The law recognizes three different types of agency authority—actual, apparent, and inherent.

Actual authority is what the publisher intentionally confers upon the agent either by written or oral agreement. This authority may vary considerably. At one extreme, the agreement might include a power of attorney that grants the agent absolute authority to contract on behalf of the publisher. This is not the customary relationship between agent and publisher. Generally, the publisher gives the agent the authority to negotiate contracts but reserves the right to accept or refuse the contract. Sometimes, the publisher may limit the agent's authority to negotiate contracts for specific works or certain rights only, such as movie or serial rights. The agent's authority may also be confined to a particular geographical area, such as North America.

The agent's actual authority to act on behalf of the publisher need not always be expressed explicitly—sometimes it may be implied from circumstances. Implied actual authority is what the publisher as principal intentionally or inadvertently allows the agent to believe he or she possesses. If, for example, the agreement with the agent expressly limits the agent's authority to negotiation with North American writers, but the publisher has customarily allowed the agent to negotiate worldwide, then the agent probably does have implied actual authority to negotiate with any writer in the world. In this example, the agent may also have apparent authority to act.

Apparent authority is authority the publisher has not actually granted to the agent, but that the publisher indicates to a third party has been granted to the agent. Thus, if the publisher leads a particular writer to believe that the agent is authorized to negotiate on the publisher's behalf, even if that writer is outside the scope of the agency contract, the publisher will be responsible for the agent's negotiations with that particular writer. It should be emphasized that apparent authority exists only in dealings with the third party to whom the agent's authority has been stated. A fourth party cannot allege the agent's apparent authority because of hearing about it from the third party.

Finally, an agent may have *inherent authority* to act. This type of authority encompasses all acts and duties that are customarily permitted to an agent while carrying out an agreed-upon responsibility. The scope of an agent's inherent authority depends upon whether a person is a *general agent* or a *special agent*. The distinction between these two types of agents is based on the agent's status, especially in regard to the duration of the agent's relationship with the publisher.

A general agent is authorized to act in a series of transactions involving continuous service. A special agent, on the other hand, is authorized to act in a single transaction only, or possibly in a short series of transactions not involving continuous service. The general agent is usually considered to have inherent authority to act on behalf of the principal in all matters connected with the job the agent has been hired to do. The special agent's inherent authority, on the other hand, is limited to specific acts dictated by the principal's instructions or necessarily implied from the act to be done. Agents who are retained for a single project would be considered special agents. The agent's inherent authority, therefore, would probably not extend beyond those acts actually or apparently authorized. Should the agent be in the continuous employment of the publisher—and therefore a general agent—the inherent authority will encompass all acts customarily associated with the publisher's agents.

Ratification

Ratification is an important concept when dealing with the acts of an agent. The term describes affirmation or confirmation by a principal of a previously unauthorized act by an agent. By ratifying, the principal affirms the unauthorized act and is legally bound by it as if it had been initially authorized. Thus, although the publisher will be liable for any of the agent's acts for which the agent has actual, apparent, or inherent authority, the principal will not be liable for unauthorized acts unless they are ratified.

Ratification may be express or implied from any act, words, or course of conduct that tend to show the principal's intent to ratify. Even silence may constitute ratification. If, for example, a publisher has full knowledge of a contract executed without authority by an agent and accepts the benefits of the contract, the publisher may have ratified the act and therefore is bound to the contract.

Disclosure

The agent alone will be liable to a third party for breach of contract if the agent did not have authority or if the act was not ratified. Where the act was authorized or ratified, the agent, as well as the publisher, may be liable depending upon whether the publisher (and thus the agency relationship) was fully disclosed, partially disclosed, or not disclosed. If the agency relationship was *fully disclosed*, generally the publisher alone will be a party to the contract and is thus liable for its breach. As a general rule, the agent will be liable, as well, if the publisher was partially disclosed or undisclosed. The publisher is *partially disclosed* if the agent reveals that he or she is acting as an agent but does not say on whose behalf, or if the publisher is named but there is no indication of an agency relationship. The publisher is *undisclosed* when the agent does not name the publisher or indicate the agency relationship but instead appears to the third party to be acting alone. If both the agent and publisher are liable for the same breach, the third party cannot sue them both but must instead elect to sue one or the other.

Employment

The liability of a publisher for an agent's torts is determined, in part, by the nature of the agent's employment; that is, by whether the agent is legally considered to be an independent contractor or a servant. The term *servant*, in the legal sense, means an employee over whom an employer has more control than the employer has over an independent contractor. If the publisher retains only the right to control or approve the end result of the agent's activities and leaves the means to the agent's discretion, the agent is probably an independent contractor. If the publisher retains the right of control and approval over most of someone's activities and decisions, the law will probably regard that person as a servant, whether or not the publisher actually exercises the right of control or approval. Literary agents are almost always independent contractors, though other people hired by the publisher (such as secretaries and research assistants) would more likely be considered servants. Many publishers work with freelance editors, book designers, and illustrators. These individuals can be employed by the publisher, though it is more customary for them to be independent contractors.

The publisher is liable for the servant's torts that were within the scope of employment. For example, if a fact-checker provides the publisher with inaccurate information that defames another, the publisher will likely be liable—even though the publisher did not know that the information was false. The publisher will generally not be liable for the torts of an independent contractor, but there are exceptions. First, the principal will be liable for any torts of the independent contractor that involve nondelegable duties. These are duties that are so important to the public welfare that the principal is legally responsible for their proper performance even if that performance is delegated to an independent contractor. For example, a publisher would be liable for not paying payroll withholding taxes even if the publisher delegated responsibility to its accountant to see that taxes were paid. Similarly, a publisher that publishes a defamatory book will be liable even if a private detective was hired to check out the accuracy of the facts.

Fraud and deceit are other circumstances in which the publisher will be liable for the acts of an agent if the publisher has authorized the agent to make misrepresentations to a third party. Likewise, a publisher could be liable for not exercising due care in hiring or retaining an agent. For example, if the publisher continues to employ an agent known to respond violently, the publisher may be liable to others hurt by the agent. The other circumstance in which principals can be liable for the acts of an agent—ultrahazardous activities, such as the use of explosives—rarely concerns the publisher.

TERMINATION OF AGENCY

The authority of the agent to act on behalf of the publisher ends with the termination of the relationship. By law, the relationship automatically terminates

- upon the death or loss of capacity of either the agent or the publisher;
- when the goal of the agency becomes impossible to achieve;
- once the purpose of the relationship has been fulfilled; or
- when the time period for which the agency was created has lapsed.

The agency can generally be terminated voluntarily if the publisher revokes or if the agent renounces the agency relationship. With the exception noted in the paragraph below, the parties are free to revoke or renounce at any time, regardless of whether the agency is governed by a contract, since the agency relationship is consensual. However, if a contract is involved, termination of the agency may result in liability for its breach. If, for example, the contract calls for the agency to last for one year, either party is free to terminate prior to that time—but not without incurring liability for damages.

The only exception to the rule of voluntary termination is an agency relationship that involves *a power coupled with an interest*. In this situation, neither party may terminate prior to the expiration of the interest. A power coupled with an interest exists when the agent has a vested interest in the thing or property involved in the agreement. For example, a literary agent might have a power coupled with an interest if the agent has contracted with the writer for partial ownership of a work. The agent's power to negotiate or execute contracts for that work would be coupled with an ownership interest, and the agent's power would be irrevocable. When an agent is compensated simply for acting as an agent, as is the case when an agent receives a commission for negotiating a writer-publisher contract, there is no power coupled with an interest, since the agent does not have an interest in the publishing contract itself. A mere interest in the proceeds from the sale is not sufficient to make the power irrevocable. The concept of a power coupled with an interest is extremely complex, and a lawyer should be consulted if an irrevocable agency is desired or involved.

IN PLAIN ENGLISH

It is not uncommon for a literary agent to have a provision in the writer-publisher contract stating that the agent will continue to be paid under the contract even though the writer has terminated the relationship. This is important to the publisher, since it must be aware of whom it should pay royalties to.

When the agency is terminated, the writer must give *actual notice* to third parties who have dealt with the agent and *reasonable notice* to third parties who have knowledge of the agency but who have not actually dealt with the agent. This is assuming the agent is a general agent, such as one who has been hired to represent the publisher on an ongoing basis. Reasonable notice means reasonable efforts to notify these third parties, whether or not the efforts succeed and the third parties actually receive notice of the termination. The publisher is not required to give notice to third parties that have neither dealt with the general agent nor know of the relationship. If the publisher is required to give notice but fails to do so, the publisher remains liable for the acts of the agent even though that agent's authority has, in fact, been terminated. The publisher is not required to give notice of termination of a special agency, a situation in which the agent has merely been hired for a single project or to accomplish a single goal. Third parties who deal with a special agent do so at their own risk.

AVOIDING AND RESOLVING DISPUTES

The costs of avoiding a dispute are always lower than those of resolving one, and in the long run, publishers are better off when they act to minimize their legal risks in appropriate ways. These risks can be reduced by avoiding actions that are likely to incur litigation, looking for warning signs of a pending dispute, and knowing how to engage professionals so disputes can be resolved in a cost-effective manner. Becoming familiar with the law will go a long way in making the business of publishing more enjoyable and profitable. In addition, recognizing the onset of problems and developing the interpersonal skills needed to work out disputes are important assets. The remainder of this chapter provides publishers with an overview of how they can minimize the occurrence of disputes and efficiently resolve those that do arise.

PRUDENCE AND COMMON SENSE

Creative entrepreneurs are often eager to become publishers and get their business operations up and running quickly. They sometimes foolishly find themselves having been taken advantage of by unscrupulous agents and editorial services. There are several reasons why individuals seeking to become publishers should avoid being victimized by shady operators. The most obvious is that being cheated costs money and deprives the publisher of resources that could otherwise be put to better use. Second, falling for a scam may mark a publisher as an amateur and diminishes the prospects of being successful.

To maintain their marketability, it is important that publishers familiarize themselves with how the publishing industry operates and learn to distinguish between appropriate business practices and unfavorable or unethical business practices. There is a lot of information about the publishing industry available from books, magazines, and the Internet. Learning about the industry will develop a degree of prudence that will likely prove invaluable to sustaining a publisher's career and reputation. There are many examples where common sense and prudence should tip publishers off to the fact that something is amiss and that they should not engage in those activities. Common ones include literary agents who charge fees to evaluate submissions, distributors who falsely claim to be traditional or legitimate, and writing contests that require the writers to purchase the anthology as a condition for being published.

References are another good way to get information. One way to find references is to ask the prospective freelancer, agent, distributor, or other party to provide them. It is, however, fairly easy to find references independently. For example, many freelancers and distributors maintain websites that provide contact information. Knowing this, you can contact the freelancers or distributors by email and ask about their experiences with retailers or publishers. Another good way to get a reference about the financial viability of a distributor is to obtain a credit report from Dun & Bradstreet's website, www. dnb.com, for a modest charge. A publisher may also contact the attorney general's office or the Better Business Bureau in the state where the business is located.

PREVENTIVE LAW

Preventive law is about understanding the rights that you have as a publisher, so you can capitalize on them, and anticipating the problems you face, so you can avoid them. The fundamental premise underlying preventive law is that the legal costs associated with avoiding disputes are much lower than those associated with resolving them. Through the appropriate use of preventive law, publishers can use their resources more efficiently.

To conduct your publishing business in accordance with preventive law principles, it is important to consider your business activities from the perspective of the opportunities and risks you face. In addition, preventive law can help you set up frameworks that enable the efficient resolution of any disputes that might arise. For example, assume that you are considering publishing a book about a well-known celebrity's not-so-well-known marital indiscretions. Such an endeavor obviously raises potential claims of defamation and invasion of privacy. There are also less obvious issues, such as how you can protect yourself from frivolous lawsuits and how the responsibility for accuracy should be distributed between the publisher and the writer. In such a case, a preventive law approach will formulate a comprehensive plan for protecting the publisher. Some of the issues that might be considered in depth are

- what aspects of the research for the book should be addressed to ensure that the research be sufficiently complete, and to show that you have the requisite absence of malice;
- how you can document your research to ensure credibility and fend off claims that you were reckless;
- how you can protect your sources from claims;
- how you and the author are going to allocate legal liability among yourselves, for example, should one of you be solely responsible for publishing a defamatory book;
- what the writer's rights are with regard to revisions made by the publisher;
- who will review the publisher's edited revisions and approve changes; and
- whether the author can be named as an additional insured under the publisher's insurance.

These are the kinds of factors that can be very significant when it comes to deterring or defending against claims, and they need to be considered long before a claim arises.

It is also important to understand that while the purpose of preventive law is to reduce legal risks, in most cases it cannot eliminate them completely. Minimizing legal risks is a prudent approach to doing business, but many publishers (and sometimes their attorneys) would be well-advised to ensure that risk elimination not become an end in itself. For example, the safest approach to handling substantive content from a legal perspective would be to avoid publishing anything that a reader could find offensive, controversial, or risqué. While such publishing may reduce the risk of lawsuits, it may also reduce the chances of publishing interesting material and unduly restrict the professional opportunities available to a publisher.

Fortunately, an overly cautious approach to publishing is neither necessary nor desirable. Thousands of pieces are published daily that express controversial opinions, say unflattering things about people, and shock the sensibilities. The reason these publishers are not sued is that they publish within the protections given by laws such as the First Amendment. Under a proper preventive law approach, the laws that protect publishers should be given the same level of consideration as those that may impose liability.

RESOLVING DISPUTES IN GENERAL

The importance of avoiding disputes cannot be overemphasized, since resolving them can be time-consuming and expensive. Nonetheless, knowing how to handle disputes appropriately can not only enable timely and cost-effective resolutions, it can help preserve working relationships and enhance the writer's reputation for professionalism. In many cases, disputes are caused either by a misunderstanding or because a party does not understand that the other party's legitimate interest in a matter has not been met. When these kinds of disputes occur, respectful communication will often lead to fast and painless resolution.

Such communications should explain the facts as they are perceived, the publisher's interest in the matter, and some options for resolution. Likewise, a willingness to listen and address the other party's concerns can go a long way in resolving many disputes. Heavy-handed threats or emotionally abusive accusations are usually counterproductive. For example, a publisher who disagrees with an editor's revision should approach the issue by asking why the revision was made and then explaining that the revision has inadvertently introduced an inaccuracy. A publisher who assumes that the editor cannot comprehend simple concepts and then resorts to insults or profanity is unlikely to resolve the issue successfully and will almost assuredly damage the working relationship.

It is sometimes helpful to attempt to resolve disputes through written communication. The advantages of written communications are that they can be carefully constructed, they document the history of the dispute and the attempts to resolve it, and they are less likely to be ignored. Sometimes oral communication works better, such as when a give-and-take discussion is needed to air the facts and the parties' concerns. The downside to oral communication (and sometimes email) is that the ability to make instant responses increases the risk that the discourse will break down into counter-productive accusations, insults, and threats.

Of course, some kinds of disputes arise because the other party is not meeting its end of the deal or is deliberately disregarding the publisher's rights. In such cases, persistence may be the publisher's best ally. By making regular requests that a particular need be addressed, publishers can often prompt a recalcitrant party to comply with its obligations.

The sheer number of legal issues that affect publishers sometimes can make it seem that there are an infinite number of ways for disputes to arise. Nonetheless, some matters occur more frequently than others. Common disputes and suggestions on how to resolve them are presented in the following sections.

Resolving Payment Disputes

You provided books to a distributor months ago and still have not received the check. This is an unfortunate situation that happens to many publishers. In many cases, the amount at issue is too small to make litigation practical, so it is important to consider options carefully. This is also a situation that can be avoided by taking a preventive law approach. For example, many distribution agreements fail to state when payment is due, and such omission can be abused by those distributors who favor leisurely payments. A simple alternative is to have the contract specify when the payment is to be made.

In the event that payment is not forthcoming, a good approach is to make a tactful inquiry to the distributor about when the payment should be expected. It is not uncommon to be told that the payment is in the mail or that your inquiry will be (or has been) forwarded to the accounting department. If the payment does not arrive during the next week, send a letter to the distributor or attempt to speak with the appropriate person in accounting. If the payment continues to be delayed, be persistent until it comes. The key in such cases is to keep reminding the distributor that it is in arrears and that you will not go away until you are paid. Further, make it clear that no additional books will be provided until the matter is appropriately worked out.

Resolving Acceptance Disputes

One of the most upsetting disputes for publishers is to have to reject a manuscript on the grounds that the quality is not satisfactory. Care should be taken not to provide harsh criticism, since this will likely be inflammatory. This is a particularly dicey area for writers and publishers. On the one hand, it is unreasonable to expect a publisher to go forward with a manuscript that is seriously flawed, since the book will likely flop in the marketplace. On the other hand, publishers should not abuse the right to reject unsatisfactory manuscripts as a pretext for dropping a work because they think the market has changed or because they want to put resources into other books.

The better publishers will provide writers with an opportunity to revise the manuscript and provide at least some guidance regarding the changes that are needed. Many writers will have negotiated such a provision into the contract. However, some publishers merely notify the writer that the manuscript is unsatisfactory, state that the contract is terminated, and ask that the writer refund any advances. It is critical for the parties to remain calm and attempt to work constructively with each other.

IN PLAIN ENGLISH

When in disputes with an author, having an agent involved can be beneficial.

The first step in resolving the dispute is to maintain a mature and professional discourse with the writer. Most editors are uncomfortable informing writers about unsatisfactory manuscripts and tend to be reluctant to provide the bad news in the first place. If the writer responds in an insulting, abusive, or otherwise unpleasant manner, many editors will stop communicating altogether, which makes resolving the problem almost impossible.

In general, the publisher should communicate why the publisher believes the manuscript is unsatisfactory and what needs to be done to address the concerns. It is critical in such situations to listen carefully and draw out as much information as possible.

The Advance

The other issue is what to do about any advance you paid the author. Many writers will simply keep the money and wait to see if the publisher sues. The risks associated with keeping an advance under such circumstances will vary according to the terms of the contract. Obtaining legal advice is prudent in these circumstances.

Resolving Requests for Unnecessary Permissions and Releases

Another frustrating kind of dispute arises when a publisher does not want to go forward with a project because one of the editors working for its company does not understand how the law applies to a particular situation. For example, an editor might condition the acceptance of an article about high-sugar cereals that describes Kellogg's Honey Smacks as a potential contributor to tooth decay and obesity in children on the writer getting a release from Kellogg's. Since corporations are generally reluctant to release others from prospective legal liability and the article takes a dim view of a Kellogg's product, it is doubtful that the company would provide such a release. Since the writer and publisher both agree that describing the product as an unidentified *highly sweetened puffed-wheat cereal* made by an unidentified company will deprive the article of its impact, the only realistic option in this situation is to convince the editor that there is no legal need to get a release from Kellogg's.

When you are dealing with a situation in which the other party misunderstands the legal aspects of a work, you have several options for dealing with the matter. In many cases, referring the editor to a general reference about legal principles may be sufficient to allay his or her concerns. If that fails, you can tactfully suggest that the editor contact either a more senior editor or a publishing attorney.

In any case, it is important to remember that the goal is to receive sufficient assurances to become comfortable with publishing the article. Avoid demeaning the editor or trivializing his or her concerns. For example, implying that the editor is ignorant about matters a reasonable professional should understand is not likely to bring him or her to your side. The key is to provide credible information that does not come across as self-serving or condescending.

GOING TO COURT

Sometimes it is impossible to resolve disputes without resorting to litigation, arbitration, or mediation. *Litigation* is the traditional process of filing a lawsuit in court and having the case tried before a judge or jury. Disputes involving small sums can sometimes be heard in small claims court, which is relatively fast and inexpensive. Otherwise, litigation can be a long and resource-consuming process. The most significant advantages to litigation are its formal procedures, which provide the opportunity to discover the other party's evidence through depositions and document production, and also provide the litigants with an opportunity to appeal adverse rulings.

Arbitration and mediation are different forms of alternative dispute resolution. *Arbitration* is similar to litigation, except that the parties try the case before a neutral party, called an arbitrator. The arbitrator is a private person hired by the parties to decide the matter. In this way, arbitration is sort of like hiring a private court. The procedures in arbitration tend to be more flexible than those in litigation, usually allowing for disputes to be resolved less expensively and faster. Arbitration decisions, however, can rarely be appealed or set aside.

Mediation differs from litigation and arbitration in that the mediator does not have the authority to decide the dispute. Instead, the mediator's role is to assist the parties in working out a resolution to the dispute. It is most often used prior to, or in conjunction with, litigation or arbitration to see if the dispute can be resolved without a hearing.

Attorneys vary in their opinions regarding the respective merits of litigation, arbitration, and mediation. Some attorneys favor litigation, because it allows for broad discovery and provides the opportunity to appeal an unfavorable decision. Others favor arbitration because of its reputation for flexibility and lower cost. Many attorneys have found mediation to be very cost-effective, but others believe it is largely ineffectual. The true merits of the means of dispute resolution will often depend on the nature of the case and what the parties desire. In a complex matter in which a great deal of money is at stake, many parties will be more comfortable with litigation because of its comprehensive procedures and protections. On the other hand, many parties will favor arbitration for matters that involve moderate sums, or those that need to be resolved promptly or privately.

CHAPTER 19

Finding an Attorney and an Accountant

Most publishers expect to seek the advice of a lawyer only occasionally, for counseling on important matters such as the decision to incorporate or the purchase of a building. If this is your concept of the attorney's role in your business, you need to reevaluate it. Most publishing businesses would operate more efficiently and more profitably in the long run if they had a relationship with a business attorney more like that between a family doctor and patient. An ongoing relationship that allows the attorney to get to know the business well enough to engage in preventive legal counseling and to assist in planning makes it possible to solve many problems before they occur.

If your publishing business is small or undercapitalized, you are no doubt anxious to keep operating costs down. You probably do not relish the idea of paying an attorney to get to know your business if you are not involved in an immediate crisis. However, it is a good bet that a visit with a competent business lawyer right now will result in the raising of issues vital to the future of your business. There is good reason why larger, successful businesses employ one or more attorneys full-time as in-house counsel. Ready access to legal advice is something you should not deny your business at any time, for any reason.

An attorney experienced in business and intellectual property law can give you important information regarding the risks unique to your business. Furthermore, a lawyer can advise you regarding your rights and obligations in your relationship with present and future employees, the rules that apply in your state regarding the hiring and firing of employees, permissible collection practices, licensing the rights of authors, and so forth. Ignorance of these issues and violation of the rules can result in financially devastating lawsuits and even criminal penalties. Since each state has its own laws covering certain business practices, state laws must be consulted on many areas covered in this book. A competent local attorney is, therefore, your best source of information on many issues that will arise in the running of your business. Many law firms have attorneys who are licensed in several jurisdictions, and others have relationships with attorneys in other locales.

IN PLAIN ENGLISH

Most legal problems cost more to solve or defend after they arise than it would have cost to prevent their occurrence in the first place. Litigation is notoriously inefficient and expensive. You do not want to sue or to be sued, if you can help it.

FINDING A LAWYER

Publishers should understand that publishing is a specialized industry and it involves legal issues that will likely be unfamiliar to most general business lawyers. Each state has its own laws covering certain business practices. A competent local business attorney may be your best source of information on many issues that will arise in running your business, such as selecting the form of organization and tax issues. To get legal advice that is specific to publishing, however, it is recommended that you consult with an attorney with expertise in publishing law.

If you do not know any attorneys, ask other publishers if they could recommend a good one. You want either a lawyer who specializes in business, or intellectual property, or a general practitioner who has many satisfied business clients. Finding the lawyer who is right for you may require that you shop around a bit. Most local and state bar associations have referral services. A good tip is to find out who is in the business law or intellectual property law section of the state or local bar association or who has served on special bar committees dealing with law reform. It may also be useful to find out if any books or articles covering the area of law with which you are concerned have been published, in either scholarly journals or continuing legal education publications, and if so, if the author is available to assist you.

It is a good idea to hire a specialist or law firm with a number of specialists rather than a general practitioner. While it is true that you may pay more per hour for the expert, you will not have to pay for the attorney's learning time. Experience is valuable. In this regard, you may wish to keep in mind that it is uncommon for a lawyer to specialize in business practice and also handle criminal matters. Thus, if you are faced with a criminal prosecution for the death of an employee, you should be searching for an experienced criminal defense lawyer.

Evaluating a Lawyer

One method by which you can attempt to evaluate an attorney in regard to representing business clients is by consulting the Martindale-Hubbell Law Directory in your local county law library or online at www.martindale.com. While this may be useful, the mere fact that an attorney's name does not appear in the database should not be given too much weight, since there is a significant charge for being included and some lawyers may have chosen not to pay for the listing. In addition, you should check Yelp, Avvo, or Google for reviews and recommendations. Many law firms have established websites. The larger firms usually include extensive information about the firm, its practice areas, and its attorneys.

After you have obtained several recommendations for attorneys, it is appropriate for you to talk with them for a short period of time to determine whether you would be comfortable working with them. Do not be afraid to ask about their background, experience, and whether they feel they can help you.

Using a Lawyer

Once you have completed the interview process, select the person who appears to best satisfy your needs. One of the first items you should discuss with your lawyer is the fee structure. You are entitled to an estimate. However, unless you enter into an agreement to the contrary with the attorney, the estimate is just that. Business lawyers generally charge by the hour, though you may be quoted a flat rate for a specific service, such as incorporation or a simple will.

Contact your lawyer whenever you believe a legal question has arisen. Your attorney should aid you in identifying which questions require legal action or advice and which require business decisions. Generally, lawyers will deal only with legal issues, though they may help you to evaluate business problems.

Some attorneys encourage clients to feel comfortable calling at the office during the day or at home in the evening. Other lawyers, however, may resent having their personal time invaded. Some, in fact, do not list their home telephone numbers. You should learn your attorney's preference early on.

The attorney-client relationship is such that you should feel comfortable when confiding in your attorney. This person will not disclose your confidential communications; in fact, a violation of this rule, depending on the circumstances, can be considered an ethical breach that could subject the attorney to professional sanctions.

If you take the time to develop a good working relationship with your attorney, it may well prove to be one of your more valuable business assets.

FINDING AN ACCOUNTANT

In addition to an attorney, most publishers will need the services of a competent accountant to aid with tax planning, the filing of periodic reports, and annual tax returns. Finding an accountant with whom your business is compatible is similar to finding an attorney. You should ask around and learn which accountants are servicing businesses similar to yours. State professional accounting associations may also provide a referral service or point you to a directory of accountants in your area. You should interview prospective accountants to determine whether you feel you can work with them and whether you feel their skills will be compatible with your business needs.

Like your attorney, your accountant can provide valuable assistance in planning for the future of your business. It is important to work with professionals you trust and with whom you are able to relate on a professional level.

Internet Resources

The following list contains websites that may be useful to publishers.

Agents

Association of Authors' Representatives (www.aar-online.org)
   This the primary professional organization for literary agents in the United States. Agents must have a record of sales and agree to abide by ethical guidelines prior to becoming members.

ISBNs

Bowker (www.myidentifiers.com)
   Distributor of ISBNs in the United States.

Book Distributors

Ingram Content Group, Inc. (IngramContent.com)
   Largest supplier of books to bookstores in the United States.

Independent Publishers Group (IPG) (ipgbook.com)
   Second largest independent book distributor in the U.S.

Baker & Taylor (baker-taylor.com and bookmasters.com/services/distribution)
   Large supplier of books to retailers, largest supplier of books to libraries in the U.S.

Consortium Book Sales (cbsd.com)
   Book distributor that works with independent book publishers.

National Book Network (nbn.books.com)
Book distributor of adult and children's books—will not partner with
publishers with fewer than two books.

Publishers Group West (pgw.com)
Largest distributor of independent titles in the U.S.

Publishers Group Canada (pgcbooks.ca)
Distributes to independent and specialty retailers in Canada.

Combined Book Services Limited (combook.co.uk)
One of the largest book distributors in the United Kingdom.

Booksellers

Amazon (www.amazon.com)
The online bookseller with the most comprehensive information about
books.

American Booksellers Association (www.bookweb.org)
The major trade organization for booksellers.

Barnes & Noble (www.barnesandnoble.com)
Another major online bookseller.

Books-a-Million (www.booksamillion.com)
Another major online bookseller.

Powell's Books (www.powells.com)
One of the preeminent independent booksellers in the United States.

Legal Sites

About the Freedom of Information Act (nsarchive.gwu.edu/nsa/foia/aboutfoia
.html)
Useful and timely information on using the Freedom of Information Act.

American Civil Liberties Union (www.aclu.org)
A major organization promoting the protection of the freedom of
expression.

Fair Use Index (www.copyright.gov/fair-use/fair-index.html)
Search judicial decisions regarding fair use to better understand the
application of fair use in various contexts.

Lumen (formerly Chilling Effects Clearinghouse) (www.lumendatabase.org)
A site devoted to the protection of free speech.

US Copyright Office (www.copyright.gov)
A well-designed government website that provides useful information about copyright law.

What is the FOIA? (www.foia.gov)
The US Government's Freedom of Information Act website.

Independent Publishing & Ebooks

Amazon Kindle Direct Publishing (kdp.amazon.com) and CreateSpace (www.createspace.com)
Barnes & Noble Press (press.barnesandnoble.com)
Book Baby (www.bookbaby.com)
The Book Designer (www.thebookdesigner.com/getting-ready-to-publish/)
Independent Book Publishers Association (www.ibpa-online.org/)
Indigo Editing and Publication Management (www.indigoediting.com)

Publisher Directories

Directories of publishers are helpful in finding leads, since many established publishers are not well known outside their specialties.

Academic Books (www.socialpsychology.org/acadpub.htm)
Audio Publishers Association (www.audiopub.org)
Children's Books Council (www.cbcbooks.org)
Colossal Directory of Children's Publishers (childrens-publishers.com/)
Computer Publishers' Directory (publishersglobal.com/directory/subject/computer-publishers)
Literary Market Place (www.literarymarketplace.com)
Military History Books (www.simonides.org/users/bibliotheca/)
Publishers' Catalogues (www.lights.ca/publisher)
University Presses (www.aaupnet.org)
Young Adult Books (publishersarchive.com/young-adult-book-publishers.php)

Publishing Industry Information

Keeping track of developments in the publishing industry is important, because professionals are expected to be knowledgeable about the major players and current conditions. The sites described below provide information about market conditions and the demand for various properties.

Association of American Publishers (www.publishers.org/)
Represents the American publishing industry's legislative, regulatory, and trade priorities regionally, nationally, and worldwide.

Publishers Marketplace (www.publishersmarketplace.com)
Provides information on agents and publishers as well as recent acquisitions by publishing houses and their acquiring editors.

Publishers Weekly (www.publishersweekly.com)
Website for the leading trade publication for the publishing and bookselling industry.

Publishing Trends (www.publishingtrends.com)
Information about changes and developments in the publishing industry, including personnel changes.

Writers' Information and Forums

The Internet has many sites and forums that offer information for publishers. Some of these sites provide excellent information about market conditions and scurrilous practitioners in the industry. Others provide fee-based services that have dubious utility. Caveat emptor.

Author Link (www.authorlink.com)
Online service for catering to writers, agents, and editors. Offers a writer's registry.

Book Market (www.bookmarket.com)
Information about book promotion, free publicity, self-publishing, e-publishing, and print-on-demand publishing.

Market List (www.marketlist.com)
Information source about potential markets for fiction.

Print-on-Demand Database (www.dehanna.com/database.html)
Online resource regarding the fee-based print-on-demand industry. Excellent summaries of fee and rights information of individual publishers.

Southern Scribe (www.southernscribe.com)
 Clearinghouse of information for writers in the South and those writing
 about the southern United States.

Writer's Net (www.writers.net)
 Forum site dedicated to various aspects of the writing business.

Writer's Weekly (www.writersweekly.com)
 Information for freelance writers with forum on which writers post
 reports of bad publishing and agent experiences.

Writers' Organizations

Participation in a writers' organization can help you keep current on trends
in writing and the legal concerns of writers with whom you work. Most organizations provide opportunities for networking with established and aspiring
writers.

American Society of Journalists and Authors (www.asja.org)
 This organization provides very useful information regarding the rights
 of nonfiction writers. Its "Contracts Watch" page monitors ongoing
 developments regarding rights practices among major American
 publishers.

Authors Guild (www.authorsguild.org)
 A major advocate of writers' legal rights and provider of contract
 information and health benefits. Membership is limited to book authors
 published by an established American publisher and freelance writers
 with at least three works published by a periodical of general circulation.

Garden Writers Association (www.gwaa.org)
 An organization of professionals who write about horticulture and
 gardening.

National Association of Science Writers (www.nasw.org)
 An organization dedicated to the needs of professional science writers.

National Writers Union (www.nwu.org)
 A labor union that represents freelance writers in all types of media.

Romance Writers of America (www.rwa.org)
A large professional association for romance writers. It provides networking, advocacy, and support services for its members.

Science Fiction and Fantasy Writers of America (www.sfwa.org)
An active organization promoting the rights and better treatment of science fiction and fantasy writers, it also presents the prestigious Nebula Awards for the best short story, novelette, novella, and novel of the year.

Society of American Travel Writers (www.satw.org)
An organization for writers, photographers, editors, journalists, film lecturers, and public relations representatives who deal with travel and tourism topics. In addition to the standard services provided by other writers' organizations, it provides information on travel destinations, facilities, and services.

Society of Children's Book Writers & Illustrators (www.scbwi.org)
An international organization that provides a variety of services to people who write, illustrate, or edit children's literature. It acts as a network for writers, illustrators, editors, publishers, agents, librarians, educators, booksellers, and others involved with the children's literature market.

Society of Environmental Journalists (www.sej.org)
An organization for working journalists in the field of environmental reporting.

Text and Academic Authors (www.taaonline.net)
Organization for textbook and academic authors oriented to the creation of educational materials.

Glossary

A

action. A lawsuit filed with a court.

administrator. The person appointed by a probate court to administer the estate of someone who has died. Also known as a personal representative or executor/executrix.

admissible. Evidence that can be properly presented in court and considered by the judge or jury.

affidavit. A notarized, written statement about facts, made under penalty of perjury.

agent. A person who is authorized to carry out activities on behalf of another, known as a principal, and to enter into agreements that bind the principal.

alternative dispute resolution (ADR). A process of settling a dispute without the necessity of a formal lawsuit or trial; includes arbitration, mediation, and settlement.

answer. The pleading by which a defendant responds to the plaintiff's allegation of facts known as a complaint.

appeal. A proceeding in which a higher court or tribunal reviews the decision of a lower court, agency, or arbitration award.

appellant. The party who has appealed a decision or judgment to a higher court or tribunal. Also known as an *appellant-petitioner*.

appellate court. A court or tribunal having jurisdiction to review the judgments of a lower court, agency, or arbitration award.

appellee. The party against whom an appeal is filed. Also known as an *appellee-respondent*.

arbitration. A mandatory or voluntary proceeding to resolve a dispute conducted outside the courts by one or more independent third parties selected by the parties to the dispute. Arbitration awards may or may not be final or appealable.

articles of incorporation. A document filed with a state in order to formally create a corporation's legal existence.

articles of organization. A document filed with a state in order to formally create a limited liability company's legal existence.

assignment. A transfer by its owner to another of an asset or right (e.g., copyright).

author. The creator of a work.

B

bad faith. Dishonesty or deceit in a transaction, such as entering into an agreement with no intention of performing according to its terms.

bailment. A relationship created when one's property is in the rightful possession of another (e.g., a manuscript sent to a publisher for evaluation). The custodian of the property (publisher) is known as a bailee, while the owner of the property (author) is a bailor.

bankruptcy. Judicial proceedings in which persons or businesses that are legally insolvent may satisfy creditors or discharge debts.

beneficiary. The person or entity designated to receive a benefit through a formal instrument, such as a will, trust, insurance policy, or the like.

bequeath. To give money to another through a will.

bequest. The money or property given through a will.

Berne Convention. Technically, the Convention for the Protection of Literary and Artistic Works. One of the oldest multinational treaties dealing with international copyright protection.

board of directors. The group charged by state law and elected by a corporation's shareholders to run the business and affairs of a corporation.

breach of contract. Failure to perform a contractual obligation.

burden of proof. The obligation of the party bringing a lawsuit to prove its case. Generally, in criminal cases, the state must prove its case beyond a reasonable doubt. In civil cases, the plaintiff must prove its case by a preponderance of evidence. In a case of fraud, proof must be by clear and convincing evidence.

bylaws. A corporation's internal rules and regulations.

C

capital gain. The profit made from the sale of a capital asset, such as real estate, stocks, and bonds.

capital loss. The loss that results from the sale of a capital asset, such as real estate, stocks, and bonds.

case law. Law based on judicial decisions.

cause of action. A lawsuit.

caveat emptor. Latin for "Let the buyer beware." The doctrine that a buyer assumes the risks of purchase.

charitable trust. A trust set up to fulfill a charitable mission.

citation. In legal reference, a means for identifying a case, administrative proceeding, rule, statute, and the like.

civil action. A noncriminal lawsuit. A lawsuit filed by a person or company to redress a wrong (tort) or to obtain a benefit (contract). Differs from a criminal action, brought by a government (local, state, or federal) for violation of a penal statute (felony, misdemeanor).

claim. An assertion of a right to money, property, or some other benefit or forbearance.

clear and convincing evidence. The standard of proof requiring that the truth of the facts asserted be highly probable.

codicil. An addition to a will.

collective work. A work, such as a periodical, anthology, or encyclopedia, in which several independent works are assembled into a collective or unitary whole.

common law. Law arising from tradition and judicial decisions rather than laws, rules, and regulations.

compilation. A work consisting of several other independent works.

complaint. The initial document filed in court by a party making a claim.

condition. A circumstance imposed or agreed to by the parties to a contract, before or after which performance or forbearance must occur.

consent. An agreement.

conservator. A person with the legal right and obligation to manage the property and financial affairs of another.

consideration. Something of value given in return for something else of equivalent value, including money, property, performance, or forbearance.

contract. A legally enforceable agreement between two or more parties.

copyright. The right to publish, distribute, reproduce, or display a work, or to exclude others from doing the same. In the United States, it is authorized by Article I, Section 8, Clause 8 of the Constitution. This is based on the original copyright law, first adopted in England in 1710 as the Statute of Anne.

corporation. A hypothetical legal person created by statute for the purpose of engaging in lawful activity. It may be for commercial purposes (a business corporation) or for charitable purposes (a nonprofit corporation).

counterclaim. A claim by a defendant in a civil case against the plaintiff.

court costs. The fees assessed by a court for use of its resources in connection with a court proceeding.

D

damages. Monetary compensation that may be recovered in the courts by any person who has suffered loss, detriment, or injury to his or her person, property, or rights through the unlawful act of, breach of contract by, or negligence of another.

declaration. A written statement about facts, made under penalty of perjury. Unlike affidavits, declarations are typically not notarized.

defamation. The act of injuring a person's reputation.

defendant. The person or entity against whom a lawsuit is brought. In domestic relations matters, often known as the respondent.

donor. A person or entity that gives money or property to another (e.g., donations to charity).

dramatic work. A work that is performed, such as a play, screenplay, script, film, or video.

due process. The regular course of administration of law through the courts or administrative bodies.

duress. Conduct that attempts to compel a person to do something he or she otherwise would not do.

duty to warn. The legal obligation to warn of a potential danger.

E

elective share. The right of a spouse under probate law to take a specified portion of an estate when the other spouse dies, regardless of what was stated in the will.

employee. A person hired by another to provide services not as part of an independent business.

enjoin. A court's action, through the issuance of an order, to require a person to perform or to abstain from a specific act.

equitable action. An action brought to restrain a wrongful act or prevent a threatened illegal action. Historically, under English common law, courts were divided into two categories: the Court of Law, which was sanctioned by the king pursuant to writs issued by the king; and the Court of Equity, established for the purpose of dealing with all other legal process, including ecclesiastical. In the United States today, law and equity have merged. Juries may consider only claims at law—claims in equity may be heard only by judges.

escheat. The process by which a deceased person's property goes to the state if no heir can be located.

estate. A person or entity's personal property, real property, and intangible property.

estate tax. A tax assessed against the taxable assets of an estate.

executor/executrix. *See administrator or personal representative.*

express warranty. An explicit promise or statement concerning the quality of goods or services.

F

fair use. An exception to copyright protection that allows people to legally use protected works, without the owner's permission, for purposes such as research, criticism, and news reporting.

federal law. Federal statutes, regulations, and rules having the force of law.

fiduciary. A person having a legal relationship of trust and confidence to another and having a duty to act primarily for the other's benefit. For example, a guardian, trustee, or executor.

forbearance. The agreement or obligation of a party not to take an action.

fraud. Intentional act designed to induce or deprive another person through deception.

G

general partner. A partner who has the right and obligation to participate in the management of a partnership and has unlimited personal liability for its debts.

good faith. Honesty in a transaction, such as entering into an agreement with every intention of performing according to its terms.

grantee. A person who receives property from another, either outright or through a trust.

grantor. The person who gives property to another, either outright or through a trust.

guardian. A person appointed by the court to be responsible for the care and management of affairs for another, generally an incompetent adult or a minor.

H

hearsay. Statement by a person who did not have firsthand knowledge of the content of the statement. Hearsay is generally inadmissible in court.

holographic will. A handwritten will.

I

implied contract. Not explicitly written or stated. Determined by deduction from known facts or from the circumstances or conduct of the parties.

implied warranty. A guarantee imposed by law even in the absence of an explicit promise.

income tax. A tax levied on income or receipts.

incompetent. Unable to make or carry out important decisions.

independent contractor. A person or business that performs services for others but is not subject to the other's direct control.

infringement. Violation of another's intellectual property right, such as a copyright, trademark, or patent.

inheritance tax. A state tax levied on an heir or beneficiary for property received under a will.

injunction. An order of the court prohibiting or compelling the performance or forbearance of a specific act.

intangible assets. Items, such as intellectual property or other rights, that do not have physical manifestation but nevertheless have value.

intellectual property. A form of creative expression that can be protected through copyright, trade dress, trademark, trade secret, patent, and the like.

inter vivos gift. A gift made during the donor's lifetime.

inter vivos trust. A trust created during the trustor's lifetime.

intestate. Dying without a will.

intestate succession. The order of distribution of the property of a person who has died without a will. This order varies from state to state.

irrevocable trust. A trust that may not be revoked by the trustor.

J

joint tenancy. A form of property ownership in which two (or more) surviving parties own undivided interests in property and the co-owner becomes the sole owner of the property after the other co-owner dies.

joint work. A work prepared by two or more authors with the intent that their contributions be merged into inseparable or interdependent parts of a unitary whole.

judgment. The final disposition of a lawsuit.

jurisdiction. A court's ability to hear a case brought before it.

just cause. A legitimate and lawful reason for taking a particular action.

L

liable. Legally responsible.

libel. A form of defamation expressed in the form of written words or graphic images.

license. A legal right or permission. In copyright, authorization to use another's work for certain purposes or under certain conditions.

lien. A claim against another person's property. Liens may be created by common law, statute, or contract. (For example, a mechanic's lien is given for payment of work performed on another's property.)

limited liability company. A hypothetical legal person created by statute for the purpose of conducting business.

limited partner. A partner who provides financial backing to a limited partnership but whose liability for partnership debts is limited to his, her, or its investment.

limited partnership. A partnership with one or more general partners and one or more limited partners.

literary work. Work consisting of text, such as books and articles.

litigant. A party in a lawsuit.

living trust. A trust created during the lifetime of the grantor. Also known as an inter vivos trust.

M

mediation. A form of alternative dispute resolution in which the parties voluntarily bring their dispute to a neutral third party who helps them to reach a voluntary settlement.

minor. A person who does not have the legal rights of an adult, generally under the age of eighteen.

N

negligence. Acting or failing to act in accordance with the standards established for a reasonable person in the particular locale.

nom de plume. Literally, "pen name." A name that is not a writer's real name. Also known as a pseudonym.

notary public. Any person commissioned by the state to perform notarial acts as defined by law.

O

obligation. The requirement to do or refrain from doing what is imposed by a law, promise, contract, or court order.

offer. An act expressing willingness to enter into a contract.

officers. The people charged with day-to-day responsibility for running a corporation, such as the president and chief financial officer.

operating agreement. A limited liability company's internal rules and regulations.

opinion. A written decision of a court that explains the rationale behind the decision.

option. A type of contract that gives the holder the right to buy or sell a specific property at a fixed price for a limited period of time.

P

partnership. An association of two or more persons who are engaged in a business for profit.

party. A person named in a contract or legal proceeding. Plaintiffs and defendants are parties to initial lawsuits; appellants and appellees are parties in appeals. (In domestic relations matters, the parties are often known as *petitioners* and *respondents*.)

performance. The taking of an action.

perjury. The criminal offense of making a false statement under oath.

personal property. Tangible physical property and intangible assets that are not land or rights in land.

personal representative. *See administrator or executor/executrix.*

plagiarism. Claiming the work of another as one's own.

plaintiff. The person who files a complaint in a civil lawsuit. In domestic relations matters, often known as the petitioner.

precedent. A previously decided case or course of conduct that guides future decisions.

preponderance of evidence. A standard of proof requiring the weight of the evidence to make a particular finding more probable than improbable.

presumption. A rule of law establishing that a particular hypothesis is true unless evidence to the contrary is presented to rebut it (e.g., a criminal defendant is presumed innocent till proven guilty).

principal. The person an agent serves and who may be legally bound by the agent.

probate court. The court with authority and obligation to supervise estate administration.

probate estate. Estate property that may be disposed of by a will.

property right. The right to use or possess a determinate thing.

publication (copyright context). Distribution of copies of a work to the public by sale or other transfer of ownership such as by gift, rental, lease, or lending. The phrase "copies of a work" includes the original work.

publication (defamation and privacy context). Communication to third parties.

R

real property. Land, buildings, and the improvements thereon.

reasonable care. The level of care an ordinary person would use under specific circumstances.

reasonable doubt. A standard of proof in which uncertainty is created in the mind of the person considering the evidence.

receiver. A person appointed by a court or government agency to manage the property of another.

registration. The record of a copyright held by the US Copyright Office.

royalty. A sum paid for the sale or use of works or other subject matter.

S

settlor. *See grantor.*

slander. A form of defamation expressed orally.

sole proprietorship. The method of conducting business by an individual who has full personal liability for all acts and contracts of the business.

specific performance. The requirement of a person (by a court) to perform specifically what he or she originally agreed to do.

standing. The legal right to sue or pursue a claim on a particular matter.

stare decisis. Latin for "to stand by decided matters." The doctrine that courts will adhere to the principles established in prior cases.

state law. Statutes, regulations, and rulings having the force of law.

statute. A law enacted by a legislature.

statute of frauds. A body of laws requiring certain transactions to be in writing before they become enforceable.

statute of limitations. Sometimes referred to as *statute of repose*, a law setting the time period within which a lawsuit must be filed. It is intended to balance the rights of the parties by providing a limited period within which rights may be enforced and wrongs redressed. After the period expires, the other party may claim the statute as a defense to the action.

stay. An order suspending a judicial proceeding.

subpoena. Latin for "under penalty." A court order compelling the attendance of a witness.

subpoena duces tecum. Latin for "under penalty you shall bring with you." A court order that requires a witness to produce certain documents or records.

substantive law. Law dealing with the rights, duties, and liabilities of people, as opposed to law that regulates procedures followed by courts and agencies.

suit in equity. *See equitable action.*

summary judgment. A court order issued in a lawsuit because there is no triable issue of fact.

T

testamentary capacity. The legal ability to make a will.

testamentary trust. A trust set up pursuant to a will.

testimony. Spoken evidence given under oath.

third-party claim. A claim filed by a defendant that brings a previously unnamed third party into an existing lawsuit.

title. Legal ownership of or to property.

tort. A civil wrong.

trademark. A word, symbol, or design used to distinguish the goods and services of one person or organization from others in the marketplace.

trust. A legal instrument used to manage property, established by one person for the benefit of him- or herself or another.

trustee. A person who manages property held in trust.

trustor. *See grantor.*

U

Universal Copyright Convention. A multinational copyright treaty.

V

venue. The particular court in which a case is to be tried. Venue should be distinguished from jurisdiction (e.g., only federal courts have jurisdiction over copyright cases), but the particular federal court in which a copyright case is to be tried will have venue over that case.

verdict. The decision rendered by a jury.

vicarious liability. Indirect liability for the actions of others.

W

waive. To voluntarily give up a right or a claim.

warranty. A kind of contract with respect to property. For example, a deed for the sale of land can be a full covenant and warranty deed, or a warranty may be granted when personal property is sold.

will. The legal declaration that governs the disposition of a person's property when that person dies. Also often known as a last will and testament.

work. Text, images, music, or performances.

work for hire. A work that was created by an employee as part of his or her job duties; or a work that was specially ordered or commissioned with an agreement in writing that states the work is a work for hire, and the work falls into nine enumerated categories which are specified in definitional section of the Copyright Act.

About the Authors

Leonard D. DuBoff

Leonard D. DuBoff, founder of the law firm The DuBoff Law Group, PC, graduated magna cum laude from Hofstra University with a degree in engineering and summa cum laude from Brooklyn Law School, where he was the research editor of the *Brooklyn Law Review*. He was a professor of law for almost a quarter of a century, first teaching at Stanford Law School, then at Lewis & Clark Law School in Portland, Oregon. He also taught at The Hastings College of Civil Advocacy and lectured for the AAA of The Hague Academy of International Law. He is the founder and past chairperson of the Art Law Section of the Association of American Law Schools; the founder and past president of the Oregon Volunteer Lawyers for the Arts; the former president of the Tigard, Tualatin, and Sherwood Arts Commission; past member of the board of the Oregon Committee for the Humanities; former special projects coordinator for the National Endowment for the Arts; and a recipient of the governor of Oregon's prestigious Arts Award in 1990. DuBoff has testified in Congress in support of many laws discussed in this text, including the Visual Artist's Rights Act of 1990. In fact, he assisted in drafting that law, as well. He is also responsible for drafting and testifying in support of numerous states' art laws and is a practicing attorney specializing in the field of art law and publishing law. He has also represented numerous prominent writers and publishers. His scholarly articles and books are frequently cited by courts and commentators. DuBoff is a pioneer of the field of art law and remains one of its most important and influential scholars in that field. He is a prolific author of law review articles and other publications and has written numerous books on art law, business law, and other related subjects. For more information about his writing, you can consult Amazon.

Amanda Bryan

Amanda-Ann Bryan graduated from Brigham Young University with a degree in music and received her Master's Degree in Writing with an emphasis on book publishing from Portland State University. She graduated magna cum laude from Lewis & Clark Law School with a certificate in intellectual property law. Amanda was the National Jurist Law Student of the Year for Oregon and was the recipient of numerous academic scholarships and awards. She was the ghostwriter for a book on entertainment law while in law school and edited a case book on copyright law. She is a practicing lawyer representing clients from all over the world, specializing in intellectual property including copyright, trademark, and related subjects. Amanda ran a digital publishing services company for many years; has taught digital publishing, ebook production, and legal publishing at Portland State University; and has presented continuing legal education programs for attorneys.

Index

Books from Allworth Press

The Author's Toolkit (Fourth Edition)
by Mary Embree (5½ × 8¼, 272 pages, paperback, $16.99)

Business and Legal Forms for Authors and Self-Publishers (Fourth Edition)
by Tad Crawford with Stevie Fitzgerald and Michael Gross (8½ × 11, 176 pages, paperback, $24.99)

The Business of Writing
by Jennifer Lyons with Foreword by Oscar Hijuelos (6 × 9, 304 pages, paperback, $19.95)

The Copyright Guide (Fourth Edition)
by Lee Wilson (6 × 9, 288 pages, hardcover, $24.99)

The Fiction Writer's Guide to Dialogue
by John Hough, Jr. (6 × 9, 144 pages, paperback, $14.95)

Internet Book Piracy
by Gini Graham Scott (6 × 9, 322 pages, paperback, $24.99)

The Law (in Plain English)° for Writers (Fifth Edition)
by Leonard D. DuBoff and Sarah J. Tugman (6 × 9, 272 pages, paperback, $19.99)

The Online Writer's Companion
by P.J. Aitken (6 × 9, 344 pages, paperback, $19.99)

The Pocket Small Business Owner's Guide to Building Your Business
by Kevin Devine (5¼ × 8¼, 256 pages, paperback, $14.95)

The Pocket Small Business Owner's Guide to Business Plans
by Brian Hill and Dee Power (5¼ × 8¼, 224 pages, paperback, $14.95)

The Pocket Small Business Owner's Guide to Negotiating
by Richard Weisgrau (5¼ × 8¼, 224 pages, paperback, $14.95)

Promote Your Book
by Patricia Fry (5½ × 8¼, 224 pages, paperback, $19.95)

Propose Your Book
by Patricia Fry (6 × 9, 288 pages, paperback, $19.99)

Publish Your Book
by Patricia Fry (6 × 9, 264 pages, paperback, $19.95)

Starting Your Career as a Freelance Editor
by Mary Embree (6 × 9, 240 pages, paperback, $19.99)

Starting Your Career as a Freelance Writer (Third Edition)
by Moira Allen (6 × 9, 352 pages, paperback, $19.99)

Starting Your Career as a Professional Blogger
by Jacqueline Bodnar (6 × 9, 192 pages, paperback, $19.95)

Talk Up Your Book
by Patricia Fry (6 × 9, 320 pages, paperback, $19.95)

The Trademark Guide (Third Edition)
by Lee Wilson (6 × 9, 272 pages, hardcover, $24.99)

Website Branding for Small Businesses
by Nathalie Nahai (6 × 9, 288 pages, paperback, $19.95)

The Writer's Guide to Queries, Pitches & Proposals (Second Edition)
by Moira Allen (6 × 9, 288 pages, paperback, $19.95)

The Writer's Legal Guide (Fourth Edition)
by Kay Murray and Tad Crawford (6 × 9, 352 pages, paperback, $19.95)

Writing the Great American Romance Novel
by Catherine Lanigan (6 × 9, 224 pages, paperback, $19.99)

Writing What You Know
by Meg Files (6 × 9, 212 pages, paperback, $16.99)

To see our complete catalog or to order online, please visit *www.allworth.com*.